THE COMMON LAW LIBRARY

THE LAW OF EVIDENCE

AUSTRALIA
Law Book Co.
Sydney

CANADA and USA
Carswell
Toronto

HONG KONG
Sweet & Maxwell Asia

NEW ZEALAND
Brookers
Wellington

SINGAPORE and MALAYSIA
Sweet & Maxwell Asia
Singapore and Kuala Lumpur

THE COMMON LAW LIBRARY

PHIPSON ON EVIDENCE

SECOND SUPPLEMENT
TO THE
FIFTEENTH EDITION

Up-to-date until
October 2002

LONDON
SWEET & MAXWELL
2002

First Edition	(1892)	By Sidney L. Phipson
Second Edition	(1898)	"
Third Edition	(1902)	"
Fourth Edition	(1907)	"
Fifth Edition	(1911)	"
Sixth Edition	(1921)	"
Seventh Edition	(1930)	By Roland Burrows
Eighth Edition	(1942)	By Roland Burrows, K.C.
Ninth Edition	(1952)	By Sir Roland Burrows
Second Impression	(1959)	" "
Tenth Edition	(1963)	By Michael V. Argyle, Q.C.
Eleventh Edition	(1970)	By John Buzzard
		Roy Amlot
		Stephen Mitchell
Twelfth Edition	(1976)	By John Buzzard
		Richard May
		M. N. Howard
Thirteenth Edition	(1982)	By John Buzzard
		Richard May
		M. N. Howard
Fourteenth Edition	(1990)	By M. N. Howard, Q.C.
		Peter Crane
		Daniel Hochberg
Fifteenth Edition	(2000)	By M. N. Howard, Q.C.
		and Specialist Editors
First Supplement	(2002)	By M. N. Howard, Q.C.
		and Specialist Editors
Second Supplement	(2002)	By Hodge M. Malek Q.C.
		and Specialist Editors

Published in 2002 by
Sweet & Maxwell Ltd of
100 Avenue Road, Swiss Cottage,
London NW3 3PF
http://www.sweetandmaxwell.co.uk
Typeset by Interactive Sciences Ltd
Printed and bound in Great Britain by Ashford Colour Printers

No natural forests were destroyed to make this product;
only farmed timber was used and replanted.

A CIP catalogue record for this book is available from the British Library.

ISBN 0 421 828005

HOW TO USE THIS SUPPLEMENT

This is the Second Supplement to the Fifteenth Edition of
Phipson on Evidence, and has been compiled according to the
structure of the main volume.

At the beginning of each chapter of this Supplement is a mini table
of contents from the main volume. Where a heading in this table of
contents has been marked by the symbol ■, this indicates that there is
relevant
information in the Supplement to which the reader should refer.

Within each chapter, updating information is referenced to
the relevant paragraph in the main volume.

It should be noted that many of the Practice Directions relating to criminal
proceedings have been recently incorporated into the *Practice Direction
(Criminal Proceedings: Consolidation)* [2002] 1 W.L.R. 2870.

TABLE OF CASES

TABLE OF STATUTES

TABLE OF STATUTES

TABLE OF STATUTORY INSTRUMENTS

TABLE OF CIVIL PROCEDURE RULES

TABLE OF PRACTICE DIRECTIONS

INTRODUCTORY

3.—Inspection, Production, View, Comparison, Search

(4) View, search, physical examination, finger prints, etc.

A visit by a member of the jury, acting on his own initiative, to the scene of **1–17** the crime was found to constitute a serious material irregularity in the course of the trial; *R. v Davis (Michael George)* [2001] Cr.App.R. 115. The circumstances of his visit tended to suggest that he had been focusing on a "mystery" as to timing, which was a central issue in the case. If he had gone back to the jury with his own "solution" then there was no guarantee that the jury reached their verdict on a proper evidential basis. In combination with other irregularities, this was enough to render the conviction unsafe. The Court of Appeal suggested that, in future, the trial judge consider giving a warning to the jury not to visit the scene of the crime unless as part of a court organised visit.

In the slightly unusual case of *R. v Sawoniuk* [2000] 2 Cr.App.R. 220, the judge and the jury travelled to Poland to view the scene of an alleged war crime 58 years after the events had occurred. The purpose of the view was to assess the quality of the evidence of an eyewitness to the massacre who claimed to have seen the appellant carrying out the shooting whilst hidden some distance away in the woods. On the status of a view as real evidence and the need for greater safeguards to obviate the risk of prejudice in such cases as *Sawoniuk*, see Ormerod, "A Prejudicial View" in [2000] Crim.L.R. 452.

NOTE 92. The photographing of suspects is now specifically permitted and **1–19** governed by s.64A of the Police and Criminal Evidence Act 1984, which was inserted by virtue of s.92 of the Anti-Terrorism, Crime and Security Act 2001 with effect from December 14, 2001.

NOTE 95. Section 61 of the Police and Criminal Evidence Act 1984 relating to **1–19** fingerprinting has been amended by s.90 (2) of the Anti-Terrorism, Crime and Security Act 2001 with effect from December 14, 2001. Article 8 of the E.C.H.R. is not infringed by the power to retain samples and fingerprints of a person who has been acquitted: *R (Marper) v Chief Constable of South Yorkshire* [2002] EWCA Civ 1275, *The Times*, October 3, 2002.

4.—LEX FORI

1–20 NOTE 3. See Dicey and Morris, *The Conflict of Laws* (13th ed., 2000), Rule 172; the Contracts (Applicable Law) Act 1990.

5.—FUNCTIONS OF JUDGE AND JURY

(2) Production and effect

1–27   The judge must not abandon his duty to give the jury a summary of the evidence at the end of the trial; *R. v Amado-Taylor* [2000] 2 Cr.App.R. 189. The summing-up must be more than a mere rehearsal of the evidence; the judge must marshal the evidence and arrange it according to the issues in the case. In *R. v Marashi* [2002] 1 Archbold News 3, CA a conviction was overturned where the judge had failed to make detailed reference to the evidence of any witness other than the victim and the defendant, even though there was a number of material witnesses who gave contradictory evidence.

CHAPTER 2

MATTERS OF WHICH EVIDENCE IS UNNECESSARY

1.—FORMAL ADMISSIONS FOR PURPOSES OF TRIAL

(2) Criminal cases

A defendant may withdraw an admission only with the leave of the court. This **2–05** is not likely to be forthcoming where the admission was made with the benefit of advice unless there is clear evidence from the defendant and his advisers that the admission was made as a result of a mistake or misunderstanding: *R. v Kolton* [2000] Crim.L.R. 761.

2.—JUDICIAL NOTICE

(1) Scope of the rule

(a) *Judge or jury as witnesses*

In *R. v Fricker, The Times*, July 13, 1999, the Court of Appeal held that it was **2–08** entirely inappropriate for a member of the jury with specialist knowledge of the tyre industry (which was relevant to an issue in the case) to introduce new evidence into the case of which neither the prosecution nor the defence had prior warning.

(2) Law, procedure, custom

(a) *Law*

In *R. v Okolie, The Times*, June 16, 2000, the appellant's conviction for **2–11** handling stolen goods was quashed. The offence had taken place in Germany and the prosecution had failed to prove by expert witness that the appellant's actions had amounted to a criminal offence under German law. The Court of Appeal said it was not enough to rely on the rebuttable presumption that foreign laws were the same as English law, and that foreign law could not be the subject of judicial notice.

CHAPTER 3

THE DEFINING OF THE ISSUES

2.—VARIANCE AND AMENDMENT

(1) Civil cases

3–06   In *Woods v Chaleff, The Times*, May 28, 1999, the Court of Appeal confirmed that, under the new CPR regime, last minute amendments would not readily be allowed, especially if there was a risk of losing the trial date as a result. For the jurisdiction to allow amendments after judgment has been given but not yet perfected, see *Stewart v Engel* [2000] 1 W.L.R 2268. For the principles on leave to amend after the expiry of the limitation period within CPR, r.17.4(2), see *Goode v Martin* [2001] EWCA Civ 1899; [2002] 1 W.L.R. 1828 CA and *Latreefers Inc v Hobson*, July 25, 2002 (Ch D, unreported) (Morritt V.C.). On the application of CPR, r.17.4(3) to amend where there has been a genuine mistake as to the name of a party, see *Gregson v Channel Four Television Corp* [2000] C.P.Rep.60. In relation to amendments to alter a party's capacity after the limitation period has expired, see CPR, r.17.4(4) and *Haq v Singh* [2001] 1 W.L.R. 1594, CA.

(2) Criminal cases

3–07   On the question of amending the indictment to add a count charging an offence not disclosed in the committal evidence, but disclosed in evidence served after committal, see *R. v Adams and Davy* [2001] 7 Archbold News 2, CA. Section 5 of the Indictments Act 1915 permits the amendment of an indictment to add a person as a defendant who is the subject of a second indictment, having been committed or transferred for trial after the first indictment was served (not necessary to prefer a fresh indictment with such joinder): *R. v Palmer, The Times*, April 18, 2002, CA; *Practice Direction Indictment—Joinder of Counts* (1976) 62 Cr.App.R. 251. For the power to amend a fresh indictment on a retrial see *R v Hemmings* [2000] 1 W.L.R. 661.

(3) Inferior courts

3–08   In *R v Harlow Magistrates' Court, Ex p. O'Farrell* [2000] Crim.L.R. 589, the court was of the opinion that it would be an abuse of process for the magistrates to allow the prosecution to amend the information to prefer a more serious charge after the magistrates had withdrawn to consider their verdict.

CHAPTER 4

BURDEN AND STANDARD OF PROOF

2.—THE BURDEN OF PROOF

(7) The Human Rights Act 1998

The Human Rights Act is now in force and has spawned a number of important **4–09A** decisions on evidential and legal burdens of proof.

The first case was *R. v DPP, Ex p. Kebilene* [2000] 2 A.C. 326, a decision prior to the coming into force of the Human Rights Act. In the Divisional Court, Lord Bingham L.C.J. said that in the context of a serious offence (terrorism) a reverse legal burden of proof provision on a matter central to the wrongdoing alleged against the defendant would breach Article 6(2). On appeal to the House of Lords [2000] 2 A.C. 326, the majority suggested that once the Act was in force, reverse legal burden provisions might have to be interpreted as imposing merely an evidential burden on the defendant. The Terrorism Act 2000 responded to *Kebilene* because by s.118 it provided that the reverse onus of proof is satisfied if the person adduces evidence which is sufficient to raise an issue with respect to the matter unless the prosecution can prove the contrary beyond reasonable doubt.

By the time of *R. v Lambert (Steven)* [2001] UKHL 37; [2001] 3 W.L.R. 206, HL, the Human Rights Act had come into force. Lambert raised two issues. Firstly, the House of Lords held that a defendant who had been convicted before the Human Rights Act came into force could not rely upon Convention rights on appeal ("the retrospectivity point"). Secondly, they held that where a statute might on its natural construction impose a reverse burden of proof on the defendant, such a transfer of the burden of proof might not be consistent with Article 6 of the Convention ("the burden of proof point"). In such cases, the court would construe the section as imposing no more than an evidential burden, so that the legal burden remained with the crown, *Lambert* involved s.28 of the Misuse of Drugs Act 1971. Whilst on its ordinary construction this would impose a legal burden on the defendant, this would be incompatible with Article 6(2) of the Act as a disproportionate reaction to perceived difficulties facing the prosecution in drug cases. Thus the provision was after the coming into force of the Act to be read as imposing an evidential rather than a legal burden.

The retrospectivity point has caused further difficulty. By s.22(4) of the Human Rights Act, where proceedings are brought by or at the instigation of a public authority, the Human Rights Act does have retrospective effect, and where the original proceedings are brought by a public authority, an appeal is part of those proceedings to which s.22(4) applies; see *R. v Benjafield* [2002] UKHL 2; [2002] 2 W.L.R. 235, CA. It became apparent in *R v Kansal (Yash Pal) (No 2)* [2001] UKHL 62; [2001] 3 W.L.R. 1562, HL that their Lordships recognised that in *Lambert* they had given insufficient weight to the relevance of s.22(4) in reaching their decision on the provisions of the Act which did not apply to public authorities. A majority in *Kansal* took the view that the decision in *Lambert* on the retrospectivity point had been erroneous but a different majority further took the view that it was wrong to depart from *Lambert* so soon after it had been decided. Thus *Lambert* still represents the law on the retrospectivity point.

The effect of *Lambert* on the burden of proof point is that it will be difficult in any particular case to determine whether a statute which on its natural construction provides for a reverse burden of proof should now be construed as imposing only an evidential burden on the defendant. As this depends on whether the reverse burden of proof offends Article 6 on grounds that it is a disproportionate response, it is not an exercise which it will be easy for trial judges to carry out. Thus in *R. v Carass (Clive Louden)* [2001] EWCA Crim 2845; [2002] 1 W.L.R. 1714, the court considered the burden of proof for criminal offences of concealing debts in anticipation of a winding-up under s.206 of the Insolvency Act 1986, and held that the provision that it was a defence for the defendant to prove he had no intent to defraud imposed only an evidential burden; if a reverse burden of proof was to be imposed, it must be justified and demonstrated why it was necessary. By contrast, in *SL (A Juvenile) v DPP* [2001] EWHC Admin 882; [2002] 3 W.L.R. 863; [2002] 2 All E.R. 854; [2002] 1 Cr.App.R. 32, the Divisional Court held that where it was a defence to show that a defendant had good reason or lawful authority for carrying a bladed knife, a reverse burden of proof on the balance of probabilities was not inconsistent with Article 6; the defendant would be proving something within his own knowledge.

A financial penalty by way of confiscation order under the Drug Trafficking legislation was not imposed on persons "charged with a criminal offence" and thus the greater protection under s.6(2) of the Convention (which impacts on the burden of proof) was not available: *H.M. Advocate v McIntosh (Robert) (No.1)* [2001] UKPC D1; [2001] 3 W.L.R. 107, PC.

Disciplinary proceedings were not criminal charges for the purpose of Article 6: *R. (on the application of Fleurose) v Securities and Futures Authority Ltd* [2001] EWCA Civ 2015; [2002] I.R.L.R. 297.

4.—STANDARD OF PROOF: CRIMINAL CASES

(2) What is meant by a reasonable doubt?

4-32   See *R. v Bentley* [1999] Crim.L.R. 330, CA.

5.—STANDARD OF PROOF: CIVIL CASES

(2) Serious or criminal allegations

In applications for anti-social behaviour orders, the criminal standard applies   **4–36** to proof that the defendant has acted in an anti-social manner, despite the fact that these are civil cases: *R. (McCann) v Manchester Crown Ct* [2002] UKHL 39; [2002] 3 W.L.R. 1313 at [37].

ESTOPPELS

1.—INTRODUCTORY

5–01   NOTE 7. See now the remarks of Robert Walker L.J. in *Gillett v Holt* [2001] Ch. 210, CA, where he stated (at 232) that "[t]he detriment alleged must be pleaded and proved" (the passage is set out in full *post*, para. 5–28).

NOTE 9. See the recent review of legal professional privilege by the House of Lords in *R. (Morgan Grenfell & Co Ltd) v Special Commissioners of Income Tax* [2002] UKHL 21, [2002] 2 W.L.R. 255.

NOTE 10. See also *National Westminster Bank PLC v Somer International (UK) Ltd* [2001] EWCA Civ 970, [2002] 3 W.L.R. 64.
    The quotation from *Cross and Tapper on Evidence* with which this paragraph concludes does not appear in the current (9th) edition of that work (1999). The entire section in which this quotation appeared has been excised.

2.—LEGAL ESTOPPELS

(1) General

5–03   See also *Yaxley v Gotts* [2000] Ch. 162, CA and *Shah v Shah* [2001] EWCA Civ 527, [2002] Q.B. 35, CA, discussed *post*, paras 5–06 and 5–22. See also *London Borough of Hillingdon v ARC Ltd (No. 2)* [2001] C.P.Rep. 33.

5–04   The subject matter of the paragraph which commences "An estoppel cannot be raised against a public body" must now be read in the light of the decision of the House of Lords in *R. v East Sussex County Council, Ex p. Reprotech (Pebsham) Ltd* [2002] UKHL 8, [2002] 4 All E.R. 58. The House of Lords held (at 66) that "it is unhelpful to introduce private law concepts of estoppel into planning law" (with which the majority of the cases referred to in the footnotes to this paragraph are concerned), referring to the remarks of Lord Scarman in *Newbury D.C. v Secretary of State for the Environment* [1980] A.C. 578 at 616 and of Dyson J. in *R. v Leicester City Council, Ex p. Powergen UK Ltd* [1999] 4 P.L.R. 91 at 100. While their lordships recognised (*ibid.*) "the analogy between a private law estoppel and the public law concept of a legitimate expectation created by a public authority" referred to in this paragraph, "the denial of which may amount to an abuse of power", referring to *R. v North and East Devon Health Authority, Ex p. Coughlan (Secretary of State for Health intervening)* [2001] Q.B. 213, CA, they held that "it is no more than an analogy because remedies against public authorities have to take into account the interests of the general public which the authority exists to promote", including "the hierarchy of individual rights which exists under the Human Rights Act 1998". Their lordships concluded (*ibid.*) that "in this area, public law has already absorbed whatever is useful from the moral values which underlie the private law concept of estoppel and the time has come for it to stand on its own two feet".

It is difficult to see how the decision of the Court of Appeal in *Wells v Minister of Housing and Local Government* [1967] 1 W.L.R. 1000, CA, can have survived this onslaught, although the House did not actually have to decide whether or not it had been correctly decided. There must now also be considerable doubt about the decision of the same court in *Western Fish Products Ltd v Penwith D.C.* [1981] 2 All E.R. 204, CA; the House of Lords described that decision (*ibid.*) as one in which "the Court of Appeal tried its best to reconcile these invocations of estoppel [in the *Wells* case] with the general principle that a public authority cannot be estopped from exercising a statutory discretion or performing a public duty" and stated that "the results did not give universal satisfaction", referring again to the comments of Dyson J. in *R. v Leicester City Council, Ex p. Powergen UK Ltd, ante,* at pp.100–101. The general principle with which this paragraph commences has thus been strengthened and it is doubtful whether the two exceptions to that principle referred to have survived. What is more, although the public law concept of a legitimate expectation has been expressly confirmed, it is now inconceivable that principles of estoppel will remain relevant to its application or development.

(2) Types of legal estoppel

(b) *Estoppels by deed*

An estoppel by deed may now arise even where the document in question has **5–06** failed to comply with the formal requirements for the execution of a deed (which since September 27, 1989 must make clear on its face that it is intended to be a deed, must be signed by the person making it in the presence of a witness who attests his signature, and be delivered as a deed by him or by a person authorised to do so on his behalf—Law of Property (Miscellaneous Provisions) Act 1989, s.1). In *Shah v Shah* [2001] EWCA Civ 527, [2002] Q.B. 35, CA, the deed in question had been improperly witnessed because the purported witness had not been present at the time of signature. The claimants successfully asserted that the defendants were estopped from denying the validity of the deed. Having examined the public policy behind the formal requirements of s.1 of the Law of Property (Miscellaneous Provisions) Act 1989, Pill L.J. concluded that it had not been the statutory intention to exclude the operation of estoppel in all cases of a formal defect. The signatory to the deed, who represented that he had signed the deed in the presence of a witness, could not later deny its validity by asserting that the witness had not in fact been present. This decision appears to confirm the view expressed by the Court of Appeal in *First National Bank plc v Thompson*

[1996] Ch. 231, CA, that the execution of a deed can give rise to an estoppel by representation and the criticism of that view expressed in the text must now be read in the light of that confirmation.

(c) *Estoppels in pais (or by conduct)*

(ii) BY CONVENTION

5–22   The second criticism of the statement of the law in Spencer Bower and Turner to which reference is made in the text may well now be inappropriate in the light of the speech of Lord Goff of Chieveley in *Johnson v Gore Wood & Co* [2002] 2 A.C. 1. He stated (at 40) that "he was reluctant to proceed on the basis of estoppel by convention" in respect of what he categorised as a matter of law, namely whether the plaintiff was abusing the process of the court. He preferred the approach of Lord Millett, who (at 61) regarded the question of abuse of process as turning on the presence or absence of unconscionability rather than on the ground of estoppel by convention. However, Lord Bingham of Cornhill, with whose speech the remaining two members of the House of Lords agreed on this point (at 42 and 50 respectively), upheld (at 33–34) the existence of an estoppel by convention without drawing any distinction between matters of fact, where such an estoppel is clearly feasible, and matters of law, where Lord Goff stated that it was not (the issue was whether the plaintiff was abusing the process of the court by bringing proceedings for professional negligence against the defendant solicitors arising out of the same matters in respect of which a company of which he was the principal shareholder had already brought and settled proceedings against the same defendants). While Lord Goff's remarks clearly reinforce the statement of the law in Spencer Bower and Turner at the expense of this second criticism of that statement referred to in the text, the failure of the majority of the House of Lords to deal with this point means that it is unlikely that the last has yet been heard of this question.

In *Yaxley v Gotts* [2000] Ch. 162, CA, the court disapproved of the notion that there were any "no go areas" for equitable proprietary estoppel (*per* Robert Walker L.J. at 174). The defendant argued that equitable proprietary estoppel could not be used to "outflank" s.2 of the Law of Property (Miscellaneous Provisions) Act 1989, which renders void any agreement for the disposition of an interest in land other than one made in writing signed by both (or all) the parties. The Court of Appeal decided the case on the basis that estoppel interests of this type take effect behind a constructive trust. Consequently, such interests were exempted from the formal requirements of s.2 by subs.2(5), which provides that that section does not affect the creation or operation of resulting, implied and constructive trusts. Although it is difficult to criticise this conclusion as a matter of statutory interpretation, it was not an anticipated consequence of the reforms made in 1989 and produces the curious and somewhat unsatisfactory consequence that someone who has failed to comply with the statutory formalities at all is in a better position than someone who has entered into a valid contract for the disposition of an interest in land which he has failed to protect by the necessary registration—the Court of Appeal held in *Lloyd's Bank plc v Carrick* [1996] 4 All E.R. 630 that the latter was unable to rely on equitable proprietary estoppel at all.

The court went on to comment that the operation of equitable proprietary estoppel could nevertheless be restricted in the face of such statutory enactments; whether it was to be restricted in a particular case depended upon an analysis of the "general social policy" behind the enactment. This was not simply a question of wording but of statutory intent. This approach was followed and endorsed by the Court of Appeal in *Shah v Shah* [2001] EWCA Civ 527, [2002] Q.B. 35, CA, a decision on s.1 of the Law of Property (Miscellaneous Provisions) Act 1989 (already considered *ante*, under para. 5–06). In that case, having examined the public policy behind the formal requirements of s.1, Pill L.J. concluded that it had not been the statutory intention to exclude the operation of estoppel in all cases of a formal defect. Consequently, a signatory to a deed, who represented that he had signed the deed in the presence of a witness, could not later deny the validity of the deed by asserting that the witness had not in fact been present. These authorities are important illustrations of the doctrine that there is no general rule that "there can be no estoppel against a statute". Whether or not an estoppel can avail against formal requirements imposed by a statute depends on the wording and purpose of the particular provision under consideration. See also *London Borough of Hillingdon v ARC Ltd (No. 2)* [2001] C.P.Rep. 33.

NOTE 35. But see *London Borough of Hillingdon v ARC Ltd (No. 2)*, *ante*, (the carrying on of negotiations when both parties were ignorant as to the existence of a limitation period did not constitute a common assumption that a limitation defence would not be relied on).

NOTE 40. See the discussion of *Johnson v Gore Wood & Co* [2002] 2 A.C. 1, *ante*.

(iii) FROM REPRESENTATION

Add: (f) A party may be estopped from relying on a statutory limitation period; **5–23**
see *Cotterrell v Leeds Day (a firm)* [2001] W.T.L.R. 435, where the defendants represented that the claimant's personal representatives would be able to bring a claim against them after her death if she failed to live long enough to avoid a potential inheritance tax liability to which the solicitors, through their negligence, had exposed her.

The position regarding mistaken overpayments is no longer so clear. The Court of Appeal recently reviewed the law on this subject in *National Westminster Bank Plc v Somer International Ltd* [2001] EWCA Civ 970, [2002] 3 W.L.R. 64, CA. The court felt itself unable, on the present state of authority, to conflate the defences of estoppel by representation and change of position in the mistaken overpayment cases. However, noting the anomalies this caused in terms of the amount of the repayment recoverable, the court adopted a broad "equitable" approach which may in future render the distinction one of little practical effect. The court found as follows:

(1) Estoppel by representation was a rule of evidence. Despite academic criticism of this categorisation, it was not open to the court to reclassify this estoppel as a matter of substantive law; see *Avon County Council v Howlett* [1983] 1 W.L.R. 605.

(2) As a result of this classification, a successful plea of estoppel by representation was a complete bar to recovery of a mistaken overpayment.

The estoppel could not operate *pro tanto* so as to bar recovery only in the amount of the detriment suffered in reliance. Where estoppel was raised, it was a matter of "all or nothing" again; see *Avon County Council v Howlett, ante.*

(3) The defence of change of position only operated to prevent recovery of the amount by which the recipient had suffered detriment as a result of his change of position. Any excess overpayment could be recovered; see *Lipkin Gorman v Karpnale Ltd* [1991] 2 A.C. 548.

(4) The existence of a representation in the case of mistaken overpayments was largely fortuitous. It was unattractive that a finding of such a representation would often have the effect of awarding the recipient of the overpayment a windfall over and above the detriment he had suffered. Absent such a representation, the recipient was thrown back on the defence of change of position and would receive no windfall.

(5) However, in the light of the decision of the Court of Appeal in *Avon County Council v Howlett, ante,* the two defences will remain distinct in this area unless or until the House of Lords rules otherwise.

(6) Regardless of whether estoppel by representation is properly to be classified as a creature of law or of equity, it is clear that principles of justice and equity underpin its application.

(7) Therefore, and as was recognised by the court in *Avon County Council v Howlett, ante,* there may be occasions where it would be inequitable or unconscionable to allow the recipient of the overpayment to retain the entire sum even though he is able to raise an estoppel by representation. Such occasions were not restricted to where the detriment was *de minimis* as regards the overpayment. In determining the extent of the restitution that the recipient of the overpayment should make, the court could have regard to, without being bound by, the change of position line of cases.

NOTE 54. The current edition of *Goff and Jones on The Law of Restitution* is the 6th (2002) edition, Chap. 40. See also Hedley and Halliwell (eds.), *The Law of Restitution* (2002), Chap. 21.

5–26 NOTE 79. The current edition of *Bowstead and Reynolds on Agency* is the 17th (2001) edition, art.74.

3.—Equitable Estoppels

5–28   Although the text states that a "full discussion of these estoppels is beyond the scope of this work" and that "no attempt is made to cite all the authorities", attention must be drawn to an important statement of principle as to when a person will be regarded as having acted in reliance on a position formerly adopted by another and as to how his actions must be proved. In *Gillett v Holt* [2001] Ch. 210, CA, Robert Walker L.J., with whose judgment the other two members of the Court of Appeal agreed, stated (at 232):

"The overwhelming weight of authority shows that detriment is required. But the authorities also show that it is not a narrow or technical concept. The detriment need not consist of the expenditure of money or other quantifiable financial detriment, so long as it is something substantial. The requirement must be approached as part of a broad enquiry as to whether repudiation of an assurance is or is not unconscionable in all the circumstances."

" . . . . There must be sufficient causal link between the assurance relied on and the detriment asserted. The issue of detriment must be judged at the moment when the person who has given the assurance seeks to go back on it. Whether the detriment is sufficiently substantial is to be tested by whether it would be unjust or inequitable to allow the assurance to be disregarded—that is, again, the essential test of unconscionability. The detriment alleged must be pleaded and proved."

This test was applied in *Gillett v Holt* to find detriment on the part of a plaintiff who had worked for the defendant, a gentleman farmer, for almost 40 years and had effectively provided the defendant with a surrogate family on the basis of assurances that the bulk of the farming business would be left to the plaintiff in the defendant's will. He was held to have incurred sufficient detriment to be able to rely on the assurances during the defendant's lifetime once the defendant began to transfer all his assets to a third party. The test was also cited with approval and applied by the Court of Appeal in *Lloyd v Dugdale* [2001] EWCA Civ 1754, [2002] 2 P.&C.R. 13, CA, to the majority shareholder and managing director of a company who had acted in reliance on an assurance that he would be granted a long sub-lease of premises of which the company was licensee and in respect of which the company had incurred expenditure; he, as distinct from the company, was held to have suffered detriment by virtue of the fact that, but for the assurance, he would have bought alternative premises and would thus have acquired a property of his own with all the contemplated advantages of ownership—the expenditure on the property by the company meant that he was "effectively locked in".

Gillett v Holt also re-emphasises the statement in the text that "the effect of recognising one of the estoppels discussed in this section is . . . a matter for the discretion of the court". The plaintiff was awarded one of the defendant's farms outright and financial compensation for the loss of the others. In cases of this type, the court will consider the whole of the circumstances down to the time of the action (this was held in *Sledmore v Dalby* (1996) 72 P.&C.R. 196, CA). The position now seems to be as follows.

(1) Where the assurances and the claimant's reliance on them have a consensual character, both his expectations and his detriment will have been defined with reasonable clarity; such a case was *Yaxley v Gotts* [2000] Ch. 162, CA (already considered *ante*, under para. 5–22) where a claimant who had been promised the ground floor of a building in exchange for renovating and managing the whole building was awarded a lease of it for 99 years rent-free.

(2) Where the claimant's expectations are uncertain or are at a level which is not fairly derived from the assurances which he received, the court "may still take the expectations (or the upper level of any range of expectations) as a starting point but . . . as no more than a starting point" (*Jennings v Rice* [2002] EWCA Civ 159, [2002] W.T.L.R. 367 *per* Robert Walker L.J. at 383). But "[t]he essence of the doctrine of proprietary estoppel is to do

what is necessary to avoid an unconscionable result, and a disproportionate remedy cannot be the right way of going about that" (*ibid.* at
386).

(3) At the other extreme, the claimant must receive the minimum which is
necessary in order to give effect to his equity. This "does not require the
court to be constitutionally parsimonious, but it does implicitly recognise
that the court must also do justice to the defendant" (*ibid.* at 384). This
may mean that the claimant receives nothing at all in the event that his
minimum equity is held to have expired. In *Sledmore v Dalby, ante,* this
conclusion was reached in respect of a person who had expected to be
allowed to stay rent-free in a house for the rest of his life because he had
lived there rent-free for over 18 years, his use of the property was minimal
and he was in employment and capable of paying for this own accommodation whereas the owner of the property was in financial difficulties
and had an urgent need for the property herself.

(4) The combined effect of the principles set out in (2) and (3) above in
Jennings v Rice, ante, was that a former employee who had provided a
substantial amount of care for an elderly lady with no immediate family
to care for her in reliance on assurances that her house and furniture "one
day will be yours" was, following her death intestate, awarded not the
house and furniture (worth about £435,000) but the sum of £200,000,
more or less what a live-in carer would have cost for the relevant period,
although it was emphasised that this was no more than "a useful cross-
check in the exercise of the court's discretion" and that in cases of this
type "it would rarely if ever be appropriate to go into detailed enquiries
as to hours and hourly rates" (*ibid.* at 385).

These authorities emphasise that in this field equity is both inventive and
flexible.

Lloyd v Dugdale also confirms that equitable proprietary estoppels can bind
third parties, as had previously been stated by Morritt L.J. in *Lloyds Bank plc v
Carrick* [1996] 4 All E.R. 830 (this is also specifically provided by s.116 of the
Land Registration Act 2002, which is not yet in force). However, in *Lloyd v
Dugdale* the Court of Appeal actually held that such interests will not bind a third
party purchaser for value who has taken free of them under the provisions of the
Land Registration Act 1925 (this will also be the position under the Land
Registration Act 2002) unless a constructive trust is imposed on the purchaser on
the grounds of unconscionability in that, for example, he paid a lower purchase
price because of the existence of the proprietary estoppel interest.

NOTE 93. There are some further authorities in the Second Cumulative Supplement to *Chitty on Contracts* (28th ed., 1999).

NOTE 96. See also M Pawlowski, *The Doctrine of Proprietary Estoppel* (1996),
pp. 73–102 and M. Spence, *Protecting Reliance, the Emergent Doctrine of
Equitable Estoppel* (1999), pp.66–77.

CHAPTER 6

RELEVANCE, ADMISSIBILITY AND WEIGHT; PREVIOUS AND SUBSEQUENT EXISTENCE OF FACTS; THE BEST EVIDENCE RULE

4.—RELEVANCE AND ADMISSIBILITY

In *R. v Byrne* [2002] EWCA Crim 632, [2002] 2 Cr.App.R. 21, CA, the Court of Appeal reiterated that all evidence "that is irrelevant or is not sufficiently relevant to the case as put should, generally speaking, be excluded." Further, "[t]he second part of this principle must be particularly observed where the admission of irrelevant evidence (which, by definition, is not probative of the alleged offence) is likely to be prejudicial to the defendant" (*per* Aikens J. at [31]). **6–05**

(3) Relevance: tests and scope

In *R. v Nethercott* [2002] EWCA Crim 3535, [2002] 2 Cr.App.R. 7, the Court of Appeal cited the definition of relevance in Article 1 of Stephen's *Digest* with approval, and held that evidence that the appellant had subsequently been stabbed by his co-defendant was relevant to whether the appellant had been in fear of the co-defendant at the time of the alleged offence. **6–08**

(6) Illustrations of relevance

(a) *Relevance of possession of cash in drugs cases*

R. v Wahab and Cromer [2002] EWCA Crim 1570; *The Times*, July 22, 2002, CA suggested a further way in which evidence of access to large amounts of cash may be relevant in a drugs case: it could explain how a person who was apparently short of money could afford to become involved in a substantial conspiracy. **6–13**

7.—The Best Evidence Rule

6–22   In *Kajala v Noble* (1982) 75 Cr.App.R. 159, CA, Ackner L.J. stated: "The old rule, that a party must produce the best evidence that the nature of the case will allow, and that any less good evidence is to be excluded, has gone by the board long ago. The only remaining instance of it is that, if an original document is available in one's hands, one must produce it." But in *Masquerade Music Ltd v Springsteen* [2001] EWCA Civ 563, [2001] C.P.L.R. 369; [2001] E.M.L.R. 25, Jonathan Parker L.J., with whom the other members of the court agreed, stated at para. [80],

> "For my part, I would not even recognise the continuing existence of that "remaining instance" of the application of "the old rule". In my judgment, the "obligation" of a party who has a document to produce the original in evidence is founded not on any rule of law but is simply a reflection of the fact that a party to whom a document is available will by reason of that very fact be unable to account to the satisfaction of the court for his non-production of it when inviting the court to admit secondary evidence of its contents, with the practical consequence that the court will attach no weight to the secondary evidence."

He continued, at [85]:

> "In my judgment, the time has now come when it can be said with confidence that the best evidence rule, long on its deathbed, has finally expired. In every case where a party seeks to adduce secondary evidence of the contents of a document, it is a matter for the court to decide, in the light of all the circumstances of the case, what (if any) weight to attach to that evidence. Where the party seeking to adduce the secondary evidence could readily produce the document, it may be expected that (absent some special circumstances) the court will decline to admit the secondary evidence on the ground that it is worthless. At the other extreme, where the party seeking to adduce the secondary evidence genuinely cannot produce the document, it may be expected that (absent some special circumstances) the court will admit the secondary evidence and attach such weight to it as it considers appropriate in all the circumstances. In cases falling between those two extremes, it is for the court to make a judgment as to whether in all the circumstances any weight should be attached to the secondary evidence. Thus, the "admissibility" of secondary evidence of the contents of documents is, in my judgment, entirely dependent upon whether or not any weight is to be attached to that evidence. And whether or not any weight is to be attached to such secondary evidence is a matter for the court to decide, taking into account all the circumstances of the particular case."

Thus, it would appear that the best evidence rule has, in civil cases at least, been consigned to the history books. Indeed there is little basis for thinking that the rule survives in criminal cases beyond the fact that the hearsay rule has persisted in that area. When the matter is raised in criminal courts they often rely on the statement of Beldam L.J. in *R v Wayte* (1982) 76 Cr.App.R. 110, that, "The best evidence rule has now been so emaciated and attenuated that it hardly exists. Lord Denning made this clear in [*Garton v Hunter* [1969] 2 Q.B. 37, 44], when he said compendiously that 'nowadays we do not confine ourselves to the best evidence.'"

10.—ACTS AND DOCUMENTS SHOWING OWNERSHIP

(2) Scope of rule

The decision of the House of Lords in *J. A. Pye (Oxford) Ltd v Graham* [2002] **6–36** UKHL 30, [2002] 3 W.L.R. 221, is relevant to the point made in the second sentence of this paragraph. In this case the House of Lords confirmed that in English law there can be no possession without the requisite intention to possess and, at [42], approved the formulation of Slade J. in *Powell v McFarlane* (1977) 38 P.&C.R. 452 that the requisite intention is an "intention, in one's own name and on one's own behalf, to exclude the world at large, including the owner with the paper title if he be not himself the possessor, so far as is reasonably practicable and so far as the process of the law will allow." Lord Hutton, at [77], cited a further passage from *Powell v McFarlane*, which corresponds to the point made in the second sentence of this paragraph:

> "In my judgement it is consistent with principle as well as authority that a person who originally entered another's land as a trespasser, but later seeks to show that he has dispossessed the owner, should be required to adduce compelling evidence that he had the requisite *animus possidendi* in any case where his use of the land was equivocal, in the sense that it did not necessarily, by itself, betoken an intention on his part to claim the land as his own and exclude the true owner" (*per* Slade J., (1977) 38 P.&C.R. 452, 476).

Lord Hutton explained, at [76], however, that the use of the land would *not* be equivocal "if the actions of the occupier make it clear that he is using the land in the way in which a full owner would and in such a way that the owner is excluded." Similarly, Lord Hope held, at [72], "if the evidence shows that the person was using the land in the way one would expect him to use it if he were the true owner, that is enough." Lord Browne-Wilkinson, who gave the main speech with which all the other Lords agreed, applied a similar approach (see [61]).

Lord Browne-Wilkinson also discussed *Leigh v Jack* (1879) 5 Ex.D. 264, CA, (cited in footnote 35) and held that the part of Bramwell L.J.'s judgment which considered the relevance of the true owner's intentions for the land was "heretical and wrong" (at [45]). Lord Browne-Wilkinson stated, at [45], that the correct proposition was that:

> "if the squatter is aware of a special purpose for which the paper owner uses or intends to use the land and the use made by the squatter does not conflict with that use, that may provide some support for a finding as a question of fact that the squatter had no intention to possess the land in the ordinary sense but only an intention to occupy it until needed by the paper owner. For myself I think there will be few occasions in which such inference could be properly drawn in cases where the true owner has been physically excluded from the land. But it remains a possible, if improbable, inference in some cases."

11.—TREATMENT

(4) Its present scope: best evidence not generally necessary

See para. 6–22, above.   **6–41**

CHAPTER 7

ATTENDANCE OF WITNESSES

2.—ATTENDANCE OF WITNESSES IN CIVIL CASES

(2) When may a witness summons be issued?

7–03   One factor which the court may take into account in deciding whether a witness summons or an application for non-party disclosure under CPR, r.31.17 is more appropriate is that in the latter case the non party's costs may be recoverable generally rather than the limited costs available in respect of witness summonses: see *Re Howglen Ltd* [2001] 1 All E.R. 376, Ch D.

(5) The interaction between witness summonses and non-party disclosure

7–08   See *Re Howglen Ltd* [2001] 1 All E.R. 376 at 384 referred to under para. 7–03 above.

(7) Who can apply to set aside and on what grounds?

7–11   As to taking into account the interests of the witness in determining whether a witness summons should be set aside, see *Omar v Omar*, unreported, October 11, 1996, CA, *Harrison v Bloom Camillin*, unreported, May 15, 1999, *per* Neuberger J. and *cf. Anselm v Anselm*, unreported, December 15, 1999, *per* Neuberger J.

6.—EVIDENCE IN THE JURISDICTION FOR FOREIGN PROCEEDINGS

(2) Powers of English court: civil proceedings

7–19   As to use of the procedure in aid of foreign arbitration, see *Commerce and Industry Insurance Co of Canada v Certain Underwriters at Lloyd's of London* [2002] 1 W.L.R. 1323, Com. Ct (Moore-Bick J.).

(4) Principles applied by the English court on application

NOTE 69. Add *Securities and Exchange Commission v Credit Bancorp Ltd*   **7–22**
unreported, February 20, 2001, *per* Wright J.

7.—EVIDENCE FROM WITNESSES, ETC. OUT OF THE JURISDICTION OR FOR PROCEEDINGS ABROAD: CRIMINAL CASES

BOC v Instrument Technology Ltd [2002] Q.B. 537, CA; *Abacha v Secretary*   **7–26**
of State for the Home Department [2001] EWHC Admin 787, Admin. Ct.

CHAPTER 8

COMPETENCE AND COMPELLABILITY, OATH AND AFFIRMATION

1.—COMPETENCE

(4) Defective intellect

8–10   The Court of Appeal in *R. v D* [2002] EWCA Crim 990; *The Times*, May 21, 2002, a case principally concerned with the Criminal Justice Act 1988, ss.23 and 26, upheld the decision of the judge at a pre-trial preliminary hearing that a witness with long-standing delusional problems in the early stages of Alzheimer's disease was a competent witness for the purposes of the Youth Justice and Criminal Evidence Act 1999, s.53 (at the time not yet in force), such that her video testimony was admissible in the defendant's trial.

2.—COMPELLABILITY

Exceptional cases

8–16   In *R. v Budai* (1999) 180 D.L.R. (4th) 565, the issue was a juror's relationship with one of the accused during the trial. The British Columbia Court of Appeal, following *R. v Valentine*, unreported, March 29, 1996, CA, held by a majority that the juror was a competent but not compellable witness.

3.—COMPETENCE AND COMPELLABILITY IN CRIMINAL PROCEEDINGS OF DEFENDANTS AND THEIR SPOUSES

(2) The wife or husband of the defendant

(c) *Compellability of the wife or husband of the defendant for the prosecution*

8–24   The Court of Appeal in *R. v Pearce* [2001] EWCA Crim 2834; [2002] 1 W.L.R. 1553 rejected the appellant's submissions: (i) that the word "wife" in the

Police and Criminal Evidence Act 1984, s.80(3) was capable of being expanded so as to embrace a person in the *position* of a wife; and (ii) that the Police and Criminal Evidence Act 1984, s.80(3) infringed Article 8 of the European Convention for the Protection of Human Rights and Fundamental Freedoms.

In *R. v Registrar General for Births, Deaths and Marriages Ex. p. CPS*, CA November 7, 2002, the court held that neither the Registrar General, nor a prison director had the power to prevent a proposed marriage taking place until after the criminal trial of a man on remand, where the proposed wife was to be called to give evidence at that trial, but would cease to be a compellable witness following marriage to the prisoner by reason of s.80 of the Police and Criminal Evidence Act 1984 (summary at Lawtel document number: C9600545).

NOTE 26. For a recent decision on the competence and compellability of spouses   **8–24** against each other, see *Graham v Chief Constable of the Bedfordshire Constabulary* [2002] I.R.L.R. 239, EAT.

(d) *Compellability of the wife or husband of the defendant for a co-defendant*

NOTE 35. See also *R. v TC*, unreported, January 14, 2000, CA (98/1431/Y3).   **8–25**

4.—OATH AND AFFIRMATION

(3) Forms of oath, or affirmation

(e) *Other non-Christian forms*

In *R. v Mehrban* [2002] EWCA Crim 2627; [2002] 1 Cr.App.R. 561, CA, the   **8–34** Court of Appeal held that the defendants' convictions were not unsafe in circumstances where the trial judge had allowed questioning on their reasons for choosing to affirm rather than take the oath on the Koran.

CHAPTER 9

EVIDENCE TAKEN OR SERVED BEFORE TRIAL; DUTY TO DISCLOSE EVIDENCE

1.—CIVIL CASES

(2) Disclosure of evidence before trial

9–08   NOTE 33. Add *Aquarius Financial Enterprises Inc v Certain Underwriters at Lloyd's* (2001) 151 New L.J. 694 (importance of statement being in own words of witness).

2.—CRIMINAL CASES

(2) Evidence taken or served before trial

(a) *Magistrates courts*

9–13   Article 6 and the Criminal Procedure and Investigations Act 1996 do not require advance disclosure of prosecution witness statements to the defence in summary proceedings, but disclosure ought to be given if requested by the defence in all but the most exceptional cases: *R. v Stratford Justices, Ex p. Imbert* [1999] 2 Cr.App.R. 276. Without first having seen prosecution witness statements, the defence is in no position to serve a defence case statement on the prosecution and, under the terms of the Criminal Procedure and Investigations Act 1996, thereby obtain secondary prosecution disclosure (see below, para. 9–48). The Attorney-General's Guidelines on Disclosure of Information in Criminal Proceedings (at: *www.lslo.gov.uk/pdf/guidelinespr*) issued late in 2000 provide:

> "The prosecutor should, in addition to complying with the obligations under the CPIA, provide to the defence all evidence upon which the Crown proposes to rely in a summary trial. Such provision should allow the accused or their legal advisers sufficient time properly to consider the evidence before it is called. Exceptionally, statements may be withheld for the protection of witnesses or to avoid interference with the course of justice" (para. 42).

It could be that a failure to disclose material in summary proceedings where disclosure has been requested is a breach of Article 6(1) (see, para. 9–47, below).

On this issue, see B. Emmerson & A. Ashworth, *Human Rights and Criminal Justice* (London, 2001), paras 14–107 et seq.

(d) *Written statements and documents admissible in committal proceedings*

A written statement for the purposes of s.5A(3)(a) of the Magistrates' Courts **9–16** Act 1980 has to be the statement of the witness himself and not an interpreter's translation of what he said: *R. v Raynor* (2000) 165 J.P. 149, CA.

(w) *Tape-recorded evidence*

The Divisional Court said in *R. v X Justices, Ex p. J* [2001] 1 All E.R. 183 that **9–34A** there is a strong presumption that the defence will be provided in good time before trial with copies of copiable exhibits such as tape-recordings on which the prosecution proposes to rely, particularly where the exhibits are an important part of the prosecution case and the defence will want to examine them closely in the preparation of its case for trial. In the instant case, the prosecution refused to make copies of audio and video surveillance tapes available to the defence to protect the identity of an undercover police officer with a distinctive voice. Auld L.J. said that if copies of exhibits are withheld and only restricted inspection of the originals offered (as in this case), the trial judge would have to consider whether a fair trial within the meaning of Article 6 was possible. The matters to be considered include:

"(1) the issues or likely issues in the case to which the evidence in question goes;

(2) the importance of what is at stake to both sides if controlled inspection, not provision of copies, is to take place;

(3) the extent, if at all, to which any prejudice to the defence otherwise resulting from non-provision can be overcome by the specific arrangements for inspection proposed"

and whether the defendants had an ulterior motive for seeking free access to copies of the exhibits (p.190).

(3) Video-recorded evidence

(a) *The Pigot report*

For a critical analysis and a helpful flow diagram of the revised statutory **9–35** framework for admitting video-recorded interviews contained in the Youth Justice and Criminal Evidence Act 1999, see L. Hoyano, "Variations on a Theme by Pigot: Special Measures Directions for Child Witnesses" in [2000] Crim.L.R. 250. The Act makes provision for video-recorded evidence-in-chief, cross-examination and re-examination by vulnerable adults (ss.27 and 28) as well as children.

(f) *Principles relating to leave*

9–40   In *R. v Redbridge Youth Court, Ex p. DPP* [2001] Crim.L.R. 473, the Divisional Court said that s.32A of the Criminal Justice Act 1988 created a statutory presumption in favour of admitting a video recording of an interview with a child in lieu of evidence-in-chief but leave to adduce a video recording could be refused if the defence (as in the instant case) satisfied the court that there was no real risk that the quality of the child's evidence would be impaired by the child testifying in the courtroom. The legislative purpose of s.32A was to provide conditions in which the child was able to give as full an account of events as possible it was not to protect the child from embarrassment. For a trenchant criticism of this decision and its possible implications for the Youth Justice and Criminal Evidence Act 1999, see Professor Birch's commentary in [2001] Crim.L.R. 475–478.

(4) The duty to disclose evidence

(d) *Common law rules on disclosure*

9–44   At common law, failure by the prosecution to disclose information to the defence may justify the staying of proceedings as an abuse of process: *R. v Birmingham* [1992] Crim.L.R. 117.

(e) *Disclosure in other situations*

9–45   The Criminal Procedure and Investigations Act 1996 does not address disclosure during the period between arrest and committal. The following guidance was offered by the Divisional Court in *R. v DPP, Ex p. Lee* [1999] 1 W.L.R. 1950:

> "Generally the prosecution need not make any disclosure before committal has taken place. A responsible prosecutor should ask himself what, if any, immediate disclosure justice and fairness requires. Situations in which pre-committal disclosure might be necessary include:
>
> 1. previous convictions of complainant or a deceased if that information could reasonably be expected to assist the accused's bail application;
> 2. information that might support a pre-committal application to stay criminal proceedings as an abuse of process;
> 3. anything that might affect the outcome of the committal or the charges on which the accused is committed to the Crown Court;
> 4. material the defence needs to prepare for trial which would be significantly less effective if disclosed after committal."

Pre-committal disclosure should not normally exceed primary disclosure required under s.3 of the 1996 Act (see para. 9–47, below). If, however, the defendant supplies the prosecution with the defence statement before committal, justice may require the prosecution to give secondary disclosure before committal also (see para. 9–48). In *Wildman v DPP, The Times*, February 8, 2001, the

Divisional Court recognised that some pre-committal disclosure might be necessary to enable the defence to oppose a Crown application for an extension of custody time limits.

Also see *DPP v Ara* [2001] EWHC Admin 492; [2002] 1 Cr.App.R. 16 (whether police have a duty to disclose copy of taped interview with defendant so that solicitor could advise him as to whether he should accept a caution).

(g) *Primary disclosure under the 1996 Act*

Article 6(1) of the European Convention on Human Rights provides that **9–47** everyone is entitled to a fair trial. Article 6(3)(b) provides that everyone charged with a criminal offence has the right to have adequate time and facilities for the preparation of his defence. These rights include a right to "equality of arms" with the prosecution: *Foucher v France* (1998) 35 E.H.R.R. 234, para. 34; *R. v Smith*, unreported, November 5, 2000, CA. The judgment of the European Court of Human Rights in *Rowe and Davis v UK* (2000) 30 E.H.R.R. 1 (where the prosecution of its own volition withheld evidence from the defence without notifying or involving a judge) raises doubts about whether the disclosure regime set up under the Criminal Procedure and Investigations Act 1996 complies with Article 6 in its entirety. The following points were made by the Strasbourg Court:

1. Article 6(1) requires the prosecuting authorities to disclose to the defence all material evidence in their possession for and against the accused (para. 60);

2. the duty of disclosure is not absolute—the defendant's right to disclosure may have to yield to competing interests, such as national security or protection of witnesses at risk of reprisals or maintaining the secrecy of police methods of investigation (para. 61);

3. only such restrictions on disclosure as are strictly necessary are permissible (para. 61);

4. a prosecution decision to withhold relevant evidence from the defence without reference to a judge does not comply with Article 6(1) (paras 63 and 66);

5. difficulties caused to the defence by restricted prosecution disclosure must be sufficiently counterbalanced by judicial safeguards at first instance (paras 61, 62, and 65) and

6. decision-making procedures must, as far as possible, comply with the requirements to provide adversarial proceedings and equality of arms, and incorporate adequate safeguards to protect the interests of the defendant.

Points 1 and 2 are consistent with the common law test of materiality laid down in *R. v Keane* [1998] 1 Cr.App.R. 43 but not necessarily with the more restrictive duties of primary and secondary disclosure imposed on the prosecution in the 1996 Act. If, for example, the prosecution were to withhold evidence at the secondary disclosure stage because it was not pertinent to "the accused's defence as disclosed by the defence statement" (s.7) Article 6 is arguably violated. The High Court of Justiciary held in *Re Maan* [2001] S.C.C.R. 172 that Article 6 gives the defence a prima facie entitlement before trial to be provided not only with information which bears directly on the guilt or innocence of the accused but also information that has a more limited bearing, such as information which would tend to undermine the credibility of a Crown witness. For further discussion of where the new regime complies with the Convention, see B. Emmerson, "Prosecution disclosure in Criminal Cases: The European Convention on Human Rights and the Human Rights Act 1998" in [2000] Med. Science Law 125 B. Emmerson & A. Ashworth, *Human Rights and Criminal Justice* (London, 2001), paras 14–96 et seq.

(i) *"Prosecution material"*

9–49   On the question of whether the prosecution is obliged by Article 6 to disclose a prison psychiatric report relating to a co-accused who might be prejudiced by the disclosure see *Hardiman v UK* [1996] E.H.R.L.R. 425, *R. v Reid* [2002] 1 Cr.App.R. 234, CA and B. Emmerson & A. Ashworth, *Human Rights and Criminal Justice* (London, 2001), paras 14–94 and 15–142.

(k) *Public interest immunity*

9–51   On the necessity for the prosecution to provide the judge with "scrupulously accurate" and complete information on an application (*ex parte* or otherwise) for public interest immunity see *R. v Jackson* [2000] Crim.L.R. 377.

(l) *Ex parte applications*

9–52   In *Fitt v UK* (2000) 30 E.H.R.R. 480 and *Jasper v UK* (2000) 30 E.H.R.R. 441, the European Court of Human Rights (by a 98 majority) found no violation of Article 6(1) where the procedures laid down by the Court of Appeal in *R. v Rowe and Davis* [1993] 1 W.L.R. 613 for handling an *ex parte* prosecution application to conceal information from the defence were followed in relation to trials on indictment. In both cases, the defence was given advance notification of the prosecution application but only in *Fitt* was the defence informed of the category of material which the prosecution wanted withheld. The majority judgments of the Strasbourg Court make the following points:

1. the independent counsel scheme proposed by the applicant was not necessary to ensure compliance with Article 6(1);
2. the defence was kept informed and permitted to make submissions and participate in the decision-making process as far as was possible without revealing to the defence the material which the prosecution sought to keep secret on public interest grounds;

3. the trial judge was well versed in all the evidence and issues and was under a continuing duty to monitor the fairness or otherwise of the evidence being withheld;

4. in weighing the public interest in concealment against the interest of the accused in disclosure, the trial judge attached great weight to the interests of justice and

5. the information that was not disclosed formed no part of the prosecution case.

There is no indication of whether in "highly exceptional" circumstances the defence may be kept in ignorance of an *ex parte* prosecution application, a possibility suggested by the Court of Appeal in *R. v Rowe and Davis* [1993] 1 W.L.R. 613. In *R v Botmeh* [2001] EWCA Crim 226, [2002] 1 W.L.R. 531 the Court of Appeal held that a without notice hearing of an application for public interest immunity (in this instance in the Court of Appeal) did not infringe the accused's right to a fair trial under Article 6. However in *Altan v United Kingdom* (2002) 34 E.H.R.R. 33, E.Ct.H.R. it was held that Article 6 had been breached where there had been a non-disclosure of PII evidence to the trial judge and this breach was not remedied by the without notice procedure before the Court of Appeal. In *R. (DPP) v Acton Youth Court*, [2001] EWHC Admin 402, [2001] 1 W.L.R. 1828, DC, Lord Woolf said that the Davies and Rowe procedures should be applied, in so far as this is practicable, to public interest immunity applications in a Magistrates' Court and that it is generally desirable to have the same district judge or bench of lay justices deal with both the application and the subsequent trial because the court had a continuing duty to protect the interests of the defendant. See also *R. v Stipendiary Magistrate for Norfolk, Ex p. Taylor* (1997) 161 J.P. 773, DC. It is noteworthy that s.14 of the Criminal Investigation Procedure Act 1996 (unlike s.15(3) which applies to the Crown Court) does not impose any obligation to review non-disclosure on public interest immunity grounds in summary proceedings. Arguably, the Divisional Court was right to read in such a requirement for summary proceedings to ensure compliance with Article 6. For a discussion of the compatibility of the *ex parte* procedure with Article 6, see B. Emmerson & A. Ashworth, *Human Rights and Criminal Justice* (London, 2001), paras 14–114 et seq.

In *R v Farrell* [2002] EWCA Crim 1223, the Court of Appeal accepted that the existence of an informant does not always have to be disclosed to the defence but the judge must be told so that the appropriate balancing exercise can be undertaken (see *Phipson*, para. 24–24). In *R. v Smith (Joe)* [2001] 1 W.L.R. 1031, CA the judge at a criminal trial was entitled to rely upon PII material not disclosed to the defence in ruling whether there had been reasonable grounds for suspicion. In *R. v Doubtfire* [2001] 2 Cr.App.R. 209, CA an appeal against conviction was allowed on the basis of PII evidence not disclosed to the defendant without the court giving detailed reasons or referring to the contents of such evidence.

CHAPTER 10

RULES OF EVIDENCE RELATING TO THE COURSE
OF A TRIAL: GENERAL

1.—CIVIL

(7) The right and obligation to call witnesses

10–09   Where a party declines to call a witness in respect of whom he has served a witness statement, the court cannot compel the party to call him as a witness: *Jaffray v Society of Lloyd's* [2002] EWCA Civ 1101 at [567–8]. The court may draw an adverse inference against a party in failing to call a witness to deal with certain evidence [at 406–7], applying the principles in *Wisniewski v Central Manchester Health Authority* [1998] P.I.Q.R. 324.

(10) Power of court to control evidence

10–12   See *Burnstein v Times Newspapers* [2001] 1 W.L.R. 579, CA.

(12) Calling of witnesses by the judge

10–14   In *Kesse v Secretary of State for the Home Department* [2001] EWCA Civ 177; [2001] Imm. A.R. 366, the Court of Appeal held that an Immigration Appeal Tribunal has the power to summon a witness against the wishes of the parties under rule 27(1) of the Immigration Appeals (Procedure) Rules. The court left open the question of whether a judge in a civil case has the power to summon a witness against the wishes of both parties in the light of the CPR. In *Jaffray v Society of Lloyds* [2002] EWCA Civ 1101, the Court of Appeal did not dissent from the trial judges view that he had no power to compel a party to call a witness in respect of whom the party had served a witness statement but decided not to rely on it and did not call him [at 567–8]. In *Tarajan Overseas Ltd v Kaye, The Times*, January 22, 2002, CA, it was held that the court does have the power to order a party to attend a hearing using the general power under CPR, r.3.1(2)(c).

(14) Submission of no case to answer

10–16   NOTE 40. For the practice under the CPR of putting a defendant to his election, see *Boyce v Wyatt Engineering, The Times*, June 14, 2001; *Bentley v John Harris and Co* [2001] EWCA Civ 1724; *Miller v Cawley, The Times*, September 6, 2002, CA.; *Karia v. I.C.S. (Management) Services Ltd* [2001] EWCA Civ 1025.

2.—CRIMINAL

(3) Hearing cases in camera or in chambers

At common law it is not permitted to hold a hearing in camera to preserve   **10-19**
privacy (*Scott v Scott* [1913] A.C. 417), it has to be shown that justice would
directly or indirectly be denied by a public hearing (see para. 10–19, below).
Since the coming into force of the Human Rights Act 1998, witness and party
privacy is a relevant consideration because of Article 8(1) (respect for private
life), but there are also two countervailing Convention rights: Article 6(1) (right
to a public hearing) and, when the media want to report the case, Article 10(1)
(freedom of expression). The relevance of Article 10(1) lies in the fact that it may
confer a right of access to judicial proceedings (*cf. Richmond Newspapers v
Virginia* (1980) 448 U.S. 555). Had the public not been excluded in *Z v Finland*
(1998) 25 E.H.R.R. 371 at 408 when doctors gave evidence of the applicant's
HIV status in criminal proceedings against the applicant's husband, the European
Court of Human Rights indicated that it would have found a violation of the
applicant's right to respect for private life. The husband did not apparently object
to this evidence being given in camera. Had he done so, the court would have had
to balance the wife's Article 8(1) right against the defendant's right to a public
hearing. Article 6(1) contains qualifications to the right to a public hearing,
namely the interests of public order, morals, national security, juveniles,
protecting the private life of "the parties" and avoiding prejudice to the interests
of justice. None of these would have been relevant because the wife was not a
co-accused and the administration of justice was not put at risk by a public
hearing (as it might be if there was danger to the safety of a witness: *X v UK*
(1977) 2 Digest 452). For a discussion of the privacy rights of witnesses in
criminal trials under the Convention see B. Emmerson & A. Ashworth, *Human
Rights and Criminal Justice* (London, 2001), paras 14–141 et seq., 18–62 et
seq.

The public conduct of the proceedings against the child-defendants, Thompson
and Venables, who were tried for the murder of a toddler, was one of the reasons
that the European Court of Human Rights found that they had been denied a fair
trial: *T v UK* (2000) 7 B.H.R.C. 659, paras 80–89. This judgment has been put
into effect in domestic English law by the Practice Direction (Crown Court:
Young Defendants) [2001] 1 W.L.R. 659 (*www.courtservice.gov.uk/pds/crown/
yngperpd*). For an analysis of *T v UK*, above, see B. Emmerson & A. Ashworth,
Human Rights and Criminal Justice (London, 2001), paras 14–151 et seq.

The way a judge should handle an application for witness anonymity is set out
in *R. v Bedfordshire Coroner, Ex p. Local Sunday Newspapers Ltd*, unreported,
October 29, 1999, DC:

1. The applicant must establish an objective need for anonymity.

2. If the applicant succeeds, the court should conduct a balancing exercise
   taking into account *inter alia* the fact that anonymity involves less of a
   departure from open justice than clearing a courtroom of spectators, the
   nature of the hearing and the reasons advanced for the order.

For the Convention implications of witness anonymity, see *Doorson v
Netherlands* (1996) 22 E.H.R.R. 330, *Van Mechelen v Netherlands* (1998) 25

E.H.R.R. 647 and discussion by B. Emmerson & A. Ashworth, Human Rights and Criminal Justice (London, 2001), paras 14–124 et seq.

For ECHR Article 6(1) see *Stefanelli v San Marino* (2001) 33 E.H.R.R. 16 and *Tierce & Ors. v San Marino* (2002) 34 E.H.R.R. 25.

For anonymity of witnesses in care proceedings, see *Re W (Children), The Times*, November 1, 2002.

(9) Reporting restrictions

10–25   Reporting restrictions may have to be imposed to protect a witness's Convention right to respect for private life: see, *e.g. Z v Finland* (1988) 25 E.H.R.R. 371 *cf.* B. Emmerson & A. Ashworth, *Human Rights and Criminal Justice* (London, 2001), para. 18–63. In *Clibbery v Allan* [2001] 2 F.L.R. 819, (2001) 151 N.L.J. 969, Munby J. said that a balance must be struck between the private and public interest in preserving an individual's privacy and the private and public interest in enabling a party who wishes to do so to publicise the proceedings. A balance must also be struck between the public interest in maintaining the privacy of proceedings in order to enable justice to be done and the public interest in the publicity of proceedings to ensure public confidence in the administration of justice:

> "Those balances could very well be required to be struck in such a way as would justify... the restraint of the publication of certain types of personal information of a genuinely confidential or sensitive nature notwithstanding that such material had been deployed in the course of judicial proceedings. Equally those balances could well require to be struck in such a way as to justify restraining in the same way the publication of materials disclosed under judicial compulsion" (*ibid.* at 970).

The decision was affirmed by the Court of Appeal, which stressed that the principle of open justice applied to all courts [2002] EWCA Civ 45, [2002] 2 W.L.R. 1151.

Under normal circumstances, the media is entitled to identify witnesses who did not give evidence anonymously even if not permitted to report what they say: *X v Dempster* [1999] 1 F.L.R. 894.

10–25   NOTE 69. Add *Briffett and Bradshaw v DPP*, 166 J.P. 66, DC.

(10) Proceedings in English; interpretation

10–26   Articles 6.1 and 6.3(e) of the ECHR may be infringed where a defendant does not have the benefit of an interpreter. It is the trial judge's duty to reassure himself that the absence of an interpreter did not prejudice the accused's full involvement in a matter of crucial importance to him, see *Cuscani v United Kingdom, The Times*, October 11, 2002, ECHR.

(14) Screens

10–30   NOTE 90a. Sections 16–27 and 30–33 of the Youth Justice and Criminal Evidence Act 1999 were brought into force on the July 24, 2002 (The Youth Justice and Criminal Evidence Act 1999) Commencement No. 7 Ord. 202, SI 2002/1739. Associated rules for the Crown Court and the Magistrates Court came into effect on the same day, see the Crown Court (Special Measures and Directions and

Directions Prohibiting Cross-examination) Rules 2002, SI 2002/168; the Magistrates' Courts (Special Measures Directions) (Rules 2002, SI 2002/1687). See generally, D. Wurtzel, "Special Measures Directions" [2002] 8 Archbold News 5.

(15) Evidence through television links

NOTE 92a. The Youth Justice and Criminal Evidence Act 1999 makes provision   **10–31** for vulnerable adults as well as child witnesses to give evidence through a live television link (s.24). It also introduces, or places on a statutory basis, other special measures: screens (s.23), removal of wigs and gowns (s.26), pre-recorded cross-examination and re-examination (s.28) and, for young or disabled witnesses, communication aids (s.30) and evidence through an intermediary (s.29). The special measures provisions are depicted in a helpful flow-chart format by L. Hoyano, "Variations on a Theme by Pigot: Special Measures Directions for Child Witnesses" in [2000] Crim.L.R. 250 at 257–259. See also, J. McEwan, "In defence of vulnerable witnesses: The Youth Justice and Criminal Evidence Act 1999", in (2000) 4 E. & P. 1; B. Emmerson & A. Ashworth, *Human Rights and Criminal Justice* (London, 2001), paras 14–138 et seq. (screens) 18–59 et seq. (general). See also *Rowland v Bock* [2002] 4 All E.R. 370 (video link evidence in a civil case).

(17) Television link evidence by a child

Section 32 of the Criminal Justice Act 1988 contains no presumption as to how   **10–33** a child should give evidence. The prosecution must establish some good reason that is in accordance with the purpose of s.32 before a court makes an order allowing a child witness to give evidence by television link. The purpose of s.32 of the Criminal Justice Act 1988 is:

> "to provide . . . conditions which are most conducive to ensuring that a child is able to give as full an account as possible of the events in question. The procedures are intended to provide a mechanism whereby a child witness who might otherwise be upset, intimidated or traumatized by appearing in court is not as a result inhibited from giving a full and proper account of the events of which he or she was a witness", *per* Latham L.J. in *R. v Redbridge Youth Court, Ex p. DPP* (2001) Crim.L.R. 473, DC.

Accordingly, a court should allow a child to give evidence by a television link where there is a real risk that the child might otherwise refuse to give evidence or that the quality of the evidence given might be affected by the stress of appearing in court but not because a television link would make it easier to get the child to court: a witness summons could achieve that. There is no question of Article 6 of the European Convention on Human Rights being infringed by the television link procedure. The European Court of Human Rights recognised in *Doorson v The Netherlands* (1996) 22 E.H.R.R. 330 that it is appropriate to provide protection for certain classes of witnesses this class must include children. Fairness to the defendant, according to the Divisional Court, is achieved by enabling the defendant to see the child give evidence by the television link and to test that evidence by cross-examination.

NOTE 96. The offence of attempted child abduction is an offence "which involves an assault on, or injury or threat of injury to a person": *R. v McAndrew-Bingham*

[1999] 1 W.L.R. 1897. Without deciding the issue, the court, at 1903, expressed a preference for the view that s.32(2) refers to the nature of the offence charged in the indictment and does not require the court to have regard to the evidence supporting the charge in the particular case. The court also said, obiter, that the "person" injured or threatened with injury, need not be the child witness.

(19) Absence of the defendant

10–35   In *R. v Hayward* [2001] EWCA Crim 168, [2001] QB 862, the Court of Appeal, after reviewing the common law and European Convention authorities, held that a judge has a discretion to continue a trial in the absence of a defendant or his legal representatives, or both, without the defendant's express consent. Factors relevant to the exercise of this discretion are listed. *R. v Hayward* was upheld in the House of Lords sub nom *R. v Anthony William Jones* [2002] UKHL 5, [2002] 2 W.L.R. 524 where it was reiterated that the discretion should be exercised with great caution and with close regard to the overall fairness of the proceedings:

> "If the judge decides that a trial should take place or continue in the absence of an unrepresented defendant, he must ensure that the trial is as fair as the circumstances permit. He must, in particular, take reasonable steps, both during the giving of evidence and in the summing up, to expose weaknesses in the prosecution case and to make such points on behalf of the defendant as the evidence permits. In summing up he must warn the jury that absence is not an admission of guilt and adds nothing to the prosecution case", *per* Rose L.J. in [2001] EWCA Crim 168, para. 22.

For a discussion of the relevant European Convention law see B. Emmerson & A. Ashworth, *Human Rights and Criminal Justice* (London, 2001), paras 14–145 et seq.

NOTE 11. This should read *ibid* s.11, not *ibid.*, s.12. If a defendant facing a criminal charge in Magistrates' Court wishes to defend the charge and is shown by medical evidence to be unfit to attend court, it is rarely, if ever, right for a court to proceed with the trial in the defendant's absence. The court is not obliged to accept a medical certificate but is not entitled, without further investigation, to discount a medical excuse: *R. v Barnet Justices, Ex p. Haines*, unreported, March 12, 2001, DC. See also *Popely v Scott (Kent County Council)*, unreported, December 21, 2000, DC.

(22) Evidence from the witness box, use of handcuffs in court

10–38   In *R. v Mullen*, unreported, May 5, 2000, CA, the defendant was handcuffed to a prison officer throughout his trial, including when he gave evidence. Mantell L.J. said that:

> "the principle in general must be that unless there is danger of escape or violence the defendant ought not to be handcuffed or otherwise restrained in the dock or . . . in the witness box. (See *R. v Vratsides* (1998) C.L.R. 251, HCA). Usually there are other means of protecting the public and preventing escape which involve less risk of prejudice . . . "

If handcuffs are used the jury must be warned not to draw adverse inferences. The decision whether to handcuff the accused is one for the court, not for the police or the prison authorities: *R. v Cambridgeshire Justices, Ex p. Peacock* (1992) 152 J.P. 895, DC. Handcuffing of a defendant is not necessarily incompatible with Convention rights: *Kaj Raninen v Finland* (1998) 26 E.H.R.R. 563. See further, B. Emmerson & A. Ashworth, *Human Rights and Criminal Justice* (London, 2001), para. 14–156.

(30) Prosecution obligation to call evidence before the close of its case

The decision whether to allow the prosecution case to be re-opened is **10–46** essentially a question of admissibility and therefore for the judge when a judge hears a case with justices. An application to recall a witness to remedy a technical omission may properly be allowed where there is no absence of good faith on the part of the prosecution and no possible material prejudice to the defendant: *R. v DPP, Ex p. Cook*, unreported, December 19, 2000, DC. The principles to be applied in summary trials were fully reviewed in *Jolly v DPP* [2000] Crim.L.R. 471 where Kennedy L.J. said:

> "[I]t is now beyond argument that there is a general discretion to permit the calling of evidence at a later stage, which extends in a Magistrates Court up to the time when the Bench retires. Before exercising that discretion, the Court will look carefully at:
>
> (1) the interests of justice overall, and in particular
> (2) the risk of any prejudice whatsoever to the defendant.
>
> The result will be that the discretion will be sparingly exercised, but I venture to doubt whether it assists any longer to speak in terms of exceptional circumstances."

In some circumstances late introduction of evidence by the prosecution violated the accused's Article 6 right to a fair trial. The relevant Strasbourg cases are discussed by B. Emmerson & A. Ashworth, *Human Rights and Criminal Justice* (London, 2001), para. 14–160. The Supreme Court of Canada will only permit the prosecution to re-open its case once the prosecution has begun to call evidence in the narrowest circumstances: *P(MB)* [1994] 1 S.C.R. 555.

R. v Hinchcliffe & Others [2002] 4 Archbold News 1, CA (22/03/2002) where **10–46** it was stated that the discretion could be exercised more generally with regard to the interests of justice and the risk of unfair prejudice to the accused. See also *R. v Johnson* [2002] 1 Archbold News 1, CA, where the prosecution were permitted to call evidence of identification, having been misled into thinking that identification was not in issue by a defence case statement alleging a defence of duress.

(31) Calling of witness by the judge

The judge's refusal to call a witness who had made a statement partially **10–47** damaging to the defence and who was regarded as unreliable by the prosecution was approved in *R. v Clarke*, unreported, February 15, 1999, CA.

(38) The effect of an erroneous overruling of a submission

The Court of Appeal has made it clear, in *R. v Smith and Others* (1999) 2 **10–54** Cr.App.R. 238, that if a submission of no case to answer is wrongly rejected by the Trial Judge an appeal must be allowed even where the defendant has subsequently admitted his guilt under cross-examination. Such a conviction is unsafe since the defendant is entitled to an acquittal after the evidence against him has been heard and to allow a trial to continue beyond the end of the prosecution case would be an abuse of process and fundamentally unfair.

(39) Inviting the jury to stop the case

10–54   NOTE 26. See also *Attorney General's Reference* (No. 2 of 2000) [2002] 1 Cr.App.R. 503.

(40) Power of the judge to withdraw case from the jury at the end of the evidence.

10–56   NOTE 17. See also *R. v Brown* [2001] EWCA Crim 961.

NOTE 27. The power should be exercised sparingly see *R. v Brown (Davina)* also reported at [2001] Crim.L.R.675, [2002] 1 Cr.App.R. 5.

(43) Failure by the defendant to give evidence

10–59   NOTE 46. A direction under s.35 is inappropriate where there is no dispute on the central facts, the issue being whether those facts amount to the offence charged, *R. v McManus and Cross* [2002] 1 Archbold News 2, CA.

(45) Failure by the defendant to call evidence

10–61   The authorities on whether a judge may comment on the failure of the defence to call a witness are not entirely consistent. In *R. v Hickey*, unreported, July 30, 1997, CA, Roch L.J. ruled that:

> "there can be no objection to the judge commenting adversely upon the failure of the defence to call a particular witness providing:
>
> (i) it is appropriate so to do;
> (ii) the comment is fair and is expressed in terms appropriate to the circumstances;
> (iii) the impression is not thereby created either that the burden of proof has (or may have) moved onto the defence or that there was some obligation upon the defence to call the witness and
> (iv) great care is taken to avoid the possibility that injustice may be done by leaving the jury with the impression that the failure to call a particular witness is something of importance when in fact there may have been a good and valid reason why a witness should not be called which would not bear on a jury's decision."

The court approved of a direction to the jury that they could take into account the accused's failure to call a witness to support his alibi. Later decisions indicate that extreme caution is required when the judge contemplates commenting about the failure of the defence to call a potential defence and disapprove of the directions that the judge in fact gave. It is recognised that an appellate court cannot provide a blueprint as to when comment is appropriate or not, and when it is, what to say. In *R. v Wright* [1999] All E.R. (D.) 1485, the Court of Appeal said that a judge should not comment without first discussing the matter with counsel at the end of the evidence in the absence of the jury. In *R. v Khan* [2001] All E.R. (D.) 48, Pill L.J. said at para. 17 of the judgment:

> "In the absence of guidance, juries will inevitably speculate... There will be situations in which the jury are entitled to ask themselves why the defence have not called a witness... A universal requirement to direct the jury that they must not speculate as to why a witness has not been called might, as between prosecution and defence, work unfairness... On the other hand, to give no direction may be to invite speculation and thereby to work injustice. To comment adversely may work injustice to the defence because there may be a good reason, but one which in some circumstances it would be unfair to disclose to the jury, such as previous convictions which may damage the defendant by association, why the witness has not been called. Moreover, there may be an issue between prosecution and defence as to whether a witness is available. The judge cannot be expected to try an issue as to availability... There is no simple answer... [T]he dangers of making adverse comment and of failing to warn the jury not to speculate will usually be the paramount consideration. On the other hand, now that a defendant's failure to give an explanation in interview or his failure to disclose his case in advance may be the subject of comment, the case for permitting comment on failure to call an available and obviously relevant witness may be stronger. The absence of power to comment would be an encouragement of dishonest evidence naming persons alleged to know of relevant events... "

NOTE 51. *R. v Pearce* [2002] EWCA Crim 2834, [2002] 1 W.L.R. 1553 **10–61** cohabitees, as distinct from husbands and wives, are competent and compellable and the interference with the cohabitees' rights under ECHR Article 8(1) was in accordance with the law and necessary in a democratic society for the prevention of crime and fell within Article 8(2).

(47) No evidence after jury retirement

Although no additional evidence should be placed before the jury after their **10–63** retirement, it is perfectly permissible for the jury to have a repeat of evidence that has already been given: *R. v Davis* (1975) 62 Cr.App.R. 194. If the jury request to re-view evidence of police surveillance it is better for this to be done in open court to ensure that nothing untoward takes place, *e.g.* the tape is played backwards or holding pictures: *R. v Imran* [1997] Crim.L.R. 754.

(49) Provision of tape recordings for the jury

NOTE 71. Permitting the jury to retire with a video recording does not necessarily **10–65** create an automatic irregularity once they have been clearly directed as to how they are to approach it *R. v Briggs* [2002] EWCA Crim 612, [2002] 4 Archbold News 3, CA, where the jury were directed not to use it for identification purposes.

(50) Communications between judge and jury

NOTE 76. The approach taken in *R. v Gorman* (1987) 85 Cr.App.R. 121 at 126 **10–66** was endorsed by the majority opinion of the Privy Council in *Ramstead v R.* [1999] 2 A.C. 92. See also *R. v Tantram* [2001] EWCA Crim 1364.

CHAPTER 11

RULES RELATING TO THE COURSE OF A TRIAL: EXAMINATION OF WITNESSES

1.—CIVIL

(2) Examination in chief

11–02   In *Mander v Evans*, *The Times*, June 25, 2001, the judge refused to permit a party to amplify a statement to remedy deficiencies.

2.—CRIMINAL

(4) Witness's name and address

11–10   On the compatibility of witness anonymity with Article 6 of the ECHR: see *Doorson v Netherlands* (1996) 22 E.H.R.R. 330 and B. Emmerson & A. Ashworth, *Human Rights and Criminal Justice* (London, 2001), para. 18–54. The ECHR said in *Doorson* that case that victims' and witnesses' rights are protected by the Convention: "principles of fair trial . . . require that in appropriate cases the interests of the defence are balanced against those of witnesses or victims called upon to testify" (transcript p. 24).

11–10   NOTE 8. See also *R. (Al Fawwaz) v Governor of Brixton Prison* [2001] UKHL 69; [2002] 1 A.C. 556.

(12) Leading questions in cross-examination

11–18   NOTE 44. See also *Mooney v James* [1949] V.L.R. 22 at 28–29 which suggests that there is no absolute right to put leading questions to a witness who shows clear partisanship towards the cross-examining party.

(15) Oppressive cross-examination

11–21   NOTE 47a. The powers contained in ss.36 and 37 of the Youth Justice and Criminal Evidence Act 1999 came into force on July 24, 2002.

11–21   NOTE 48. The Bar's rule was endorsed in *R. v Gurney*, *The Times*, March 9, 1998, CA.

The Youth and Criminal Justice Act 1999, s.34 prevents a defendant charged with a sexual offence from cross-examining the complainant in person in connection with the sexual offence or any other offence for which the accused is standing trial at the time. The court is empowered to appoint a legal representative to carry out the cross-examination (s.38(4)). "Where on a trial on indictment an accused is prevented from cross-examining a witness in person . . . the judge must give the jury such warning (if any) as the judge may consider necessary to ensure that the accused is not prejudiced" (s.39). For restrictions on cross-examination of the victims of sexual offences about their sexual history, see para. 19–30 below.

NOTES 48 and 49. See now, *Code of Conduct of the Bar* (7th ed., 2000), para. 610;   **11–21**
Medcalf v Mardell [2002] UKHL 27; [2002] 3 W.L.R. 172, HL.

(28) Examination by judge

It is not only permissible, but the judge's duty, to ask questions which clarify   **11–34**
ambiguities in answers given by a witness or which identify the nature of the defence, if this is unclear and such questions, particularly in a very long case, are most likely to help the jury if they are asked close to the time when the ambiguity is first apparent: *R. v Tuegel* [2000] 2 All E.R. 872 at 888–889.

In *R. v Cameron, The Times*, May 3, 2001, CA, the rape complainant, who was 14 years old and gave evidence by video link, refused to allow defence counsel to continue with his cross-examination after 15 minutes. The judge took over the questioning of the witness, putting to her material supplied by defence counsel but omitting questions that he regarded as mere comment or that would unproductively inflame the witness. The prosecution was directed by the judge in the interests of fairness to forego re-examination. This solution was approved on appeal. Potter L.J. expressed certain qualifications:

1. the judge must be satisfied the procedure is fair and once the procedure is followed must take it into account when making subsequent rulings;

2. the jury must be directed "of the unusual and less satisfactory nature of the procedure as a substitute for the traditional right of the defendant or his advocate to cross-examine prosecution witnesses";

3. the solution "would not ordinarily be appropriate to the situation of an adult witness who, without good excuse, refuses to answer questions put in cross-examination, though we do not necessarily, for example, exclude such a procedure in the case of a witness who is labouring under a mental handicap or a frightened or traumatized witness in the case of a sexual complaint".

NOTE 7. *R. v Wiggan, The Times*, March 22, 1999, CA.   **11–34**

(31) No contradiction on collateral matters: the principle

R. v Fahy [2002] Crim.L.R. 596; where the judge stops cross-examination on   **11–37**
the erroneous basis that it goes only to collateral matters, a conviction is liable to be quashed where the effect of the further but unobtained evidence on the view of the jury cannot be ascertained.

NOTE 41. See also *R. v Willshire*, unreported, December 13, 1999, CA.   **11–37**

11–37   NOTE 43. In *R. v Somers* [1999] Crim.L.R. 744, CA, Henry L.J. said that a flexible approach to the rule of finality or collateral matters is required "so that a general rule designed to serve the interests of justice should not be used to defeat justice by an over-pedantic approach". The issue of relevance is one for the trial judge and will rarely be questioned by the Court of Appeal.

(34) Exception (2): previous conviction

11–40   In *R. v Lawler*, unreported, May 6, 1999, the Court of Appeal rejected the argument that the 1974 Practice Direction issued by Lord Widgery C.J. in (1975) 61 Cr.App.R. 260 is *ultra vires* and should be disregarded.

(35) Exception (3): evidence of reputation for untruthfulness

11–41   NOTE 64. *R. v Colwill* [2002] EWCA Crim 1320, [2002] 6 Archbold News 2, CA; evidence of an allegation unrelated to the charge before the jury (previous false reports of crime) that was proposed to be used to undermine the credibility of a witness was not evidence that the witness had a general reputation for untruthfulness. It was therefore not an exception to the principle preventing contradiction on matters of credit or collateral matters. Consequently, evidence from those against whom the previous allegations had been made was inadmissible.

(36) Exception (4): Medical evidence affecting reliability of a witness's evidence

11–42   The Privy Council held polygraph evidence to support the credibility of a defendant was inadmissible in *Bernal v R.*, unreported, April 28, 1997. The Judicial Committee referred to the summary of reasons for inadmissibility in *R. v Beland* (1987) 43 DLR (4th) 641, SCC, Article 6 of the Convention confers no right on the defence to insist on the introduction of polygraph evidence: *Application No. 9696/82* (1983, unpublished) 2 Dig. Supp. 6.1.1.4.4.5 at 6 cited in B. Emmerson & A. Ashworth, *Human Rights and Criminal Justice* (London, 2001), para. 15–144.

11–42   NOTE 75. See also *R. v Robinson* [1994] 3 All E.R. 346; *G v DPP* [1997] 2 All E.R. 755. In both these cases the rejected evidence was from a psychologist. The cases are discussed by D. Birch, "A Better Deal for Vulnerable Witnesses?" in [2000] Crim.L.R. 223 at 235 and M. Redmayne, *Expert Evidence and Criminal Justice* (OUP, Oxford, 2001), pp.164 et seq.

(40) Material that may be used to refresh memory

11–46   NOTE 2. In *R. v Bailey* [2001] EWCA Crim 733, the Court of Appeal said that there was no reason why a witness should only refresh his memory by reading from a piece of a paper. If modern technology provided for a better or different means of refreshing memory this should be allowed.

(50) Hostile witnesses at common law

11–56   In *R. v Honeyghon* [1999] Crim.L.R. 221 and in *R. v Dat* [1998] Crim.L.R. 488, the Court of Appeal rejected submissions that the Crown should not call a witness who has retracted all evidence favourable to the Crown before the trial. The Crown is entitled to explore the possibility that the witness will return to his original statement.

(52) Whether a witness is adverse

A witness who retracts evidence supportive of the Crown's case or purports to have no recollection but does not change sides in the sense of giving evidence that is actually damaging to the Crown's case may be treated as hostile: *R. v Dat* [1998] Crim.L.R. 488; *R. v Honeyghon* [1999] Crim.L.R. 221.

11–58

NOTE 59. See also *R. v Honeyghon* [1999] Crim.L.R. 221.

11–59

(55) Status of statement and evidential value of evidence of hostile witness

In *R. v Ugorji* [1999] All E.R. (D.) 603, the Court of Appeal said that it was inappropriate to give the standard hostile witness direction if a hostile witness gives evidence that is consistent with his earlier statement but something needs to be said if the witness would not have given that evidence had he not been treated as a hostile witness. The case also illustrates that a prior inconsistent statement is not necessary for a witness to be treated as hostile. In this case, the witness failed to turn up to give evidence and had to be arrested.

11–61

(57) Previous consistent statements: the common law

But see *R. v Evans and Caffrey* [2001] 6 Archbold News 2, CA (22/03/2001), where it was said that there may be circumstances where, although it is not possible to say that a prosecution witness is "adverse" to one defendant, fairness will demand that that defendant should be entitled to bring out a previous consistent statement in order to enhance the evidence of that witness for the benefit of that defendant, even though the effect of such statement was to incriminate a co-defendant. This decision is best seen as one depending on its own facts, including the court's view that the evidence could have been elicited by putting questions differently without infringing any rule.

11–63

(59) Exception (1): complaints in sexual cases

The jury must be directed about the significance of a recent complaint: *R. v Islam* [1999] 1 Cr.App.R. 22. In *R. v NK* [1999] Crim.L.R. 980, the Court of Appeal approved the Judicial Studies Board standard direction, viz. the evidence " ... may possibly help you to decide whether she had told you the truth. It cannot be independent confirmation of *X*'s evidence since it does not come from a source independent of her". This was said to convey "the peculiar nature of evidence of a complaint: that it has more significance than merely as evidence of the fact of the complaint having been made, whilst at the same time emphasizing that it is not evidence of the facts complained of. We add that on occasions judges may also think it appropriate to remind the jury that a person fabricating an allegation may support it by an equally false complaint", *per* Gage J. In *R. v Croad* [2001] EWCA Crim 644, the Court of Appeal said that where there was a previous account by a complainant before the jury which did not itself

11–65

constitute evidence but to which the jury might have regard in reaching a verdict, the jury had to be directed that recent complaints are not evidence of what happened whether or not the Crown relied upon the complaint.

In *R. v Milner*, unreported, August 9, 2000, the Court of Appeal recognised that in cases of sex abuse involving children "the opportunity to make complaint often follows some time after the conduct in question", *per* Newman J. In that particular case the alleged abuse occurred between 1983 and 1987 and the complaint was made in 1988 after the defendant had left the family home. In Milner, the complainant had written a letter to Childline alleging "sexual abuse" but had not sent it. The Court of Appeal held that it was unnecessary for a written complaint to make particularised allegations of sexual abuse or to have been communicated to anyone provided that it was composed as a complaint and not pure narrative and that it was consistent with the complainant's account of conduct by the defendant that was in issue. The fact that the complaint was not sent is relevant to its weight, as is any explanation of this fact.

CHAPTER 12

EVIDENCE TAKEN AFTER TRIAL

1.—CIVIL CASES

(1) Further evidence on appeal

Appeals to the Court of Appeal are now governed by Pt 52 of the Civil **12–01**
Procedure Rules ("CPR"). Rule 52.11(2) sets out the provisions regarding the
receipt of fresh evidence: "Unless it orders otherwise, the appeal court will not
receive—(a) oral evidence or (b) evidence which was not before the lower
court." The stipulation under the previous rules that fresh evidence should not be
received save on special grounds has been removed. However, this change in
wording does not appear to have precipitated a change in attitude by the courts.
The Court of Appeal has confirmed in several recent cases, that the principles
established in *Ladd v Marshall* [1954] 1 W.L.R. 1489 still govern the exercise of
the court's discretion to receive fresh evidence; see *Hertfordshire Investments v
Bubb* [2000] 1 W.L.R 2318, *Townsend v Achilleas* [2000] C.P.L.R. 490, *Banks v
Cox*, unreported, July 17, 2000; *Hamilton v Al Fayed (No.2)* [2001] E.M.L.R.
394; *Gillingham v Gillingham* [2001] EWCA Civ 906, CA; *Prentice v Hereward
Housing Association* [2001] 2 All E.R. (Comm) 900; *Shaker v Al-Bedrawi* [2002]
EWCA Civ 1452, CA.

In *Hamilton v Al Fayed (No.2)* [2001] E.M.L.R. 394 the Master of the Rolls
said that the principles established by other pre-CPR authorities do not have to
be slavishly followed (see also *Yukong Line Ltd v Rendsburg Investments Corp*
[2001] 2 Lloyd's Rep 113 para. 53). However, they "remain powerful persuasive
authority, for they illustrate the attempts of the courts to strike a fair balance
between the need for concluded litigation to be determinative of disputes and the
desirability that the judicial process should achieve the right result" (para. 11).
That task is one which accords with the overriding objective. The *Ladd v
Marshall* [1954] 1 WLR 1489, 1491 requirements do not conflict with the
overriding objective and, in particular, "it will not normally be in the interests of
justice to reopen a concluded trial in order to introduce fresh evidence unless that
evidence will probably influence the result" (para. 13).

(c) *Credibility*

Two recent cases have concerned the discretion of the trial judge to receive **12–07**
new evidence after judgment has been given but before an order has been drawn
up. In *Charlesworth v Relay Roads Ltd* [2000] 1 W.L.R. 230, Neuberger J. held

that the trial judge had the necessary jurisdiction to allow a party to amend his pleadings and to call new evidence in such circumstances. Whilst his lordship held that the *Ladd v Marshall* principles should be in the forefront of the court's mind, he also expressed the view that a trial judge is entitled to be more flexible than the Court of Appeal when considering such an application to admit new evidence. There may be exceptional cases where the application should be granted even though all three *Ladd v Marshall* requirements were not fulfilled. The trial judge, having heard the case, would be in a better position to receive fresh evidence than the Court of Appeal, who would be faced with the choice of attempting to decide what effect the new evidence would have had on the trial judge or ordering a retrial.

The Court of Appeal in *Townsend v Achilleas* [2000] C.P.L.R. 490, confirmed that the *Ladd v Marshall* principles apply to the exercise of the court's discretion to allow new evidence to be called after judgment but before the drawing up of the order. The court expressed support (obiter) for the application of a slightly more flexible approach for the reasons given by Neuberger J. in *Charlesworth v Relay Roads Ltd*, above.

It should be noted that in both of the above cases, the *Ladd v Marshall* principles were not seen as the only relevant considerations. They are of central importance. However, the court is entitled to take into account other factors in deciding whether to receive fresh evidence. The court, in exercising its discretion, must seek to give effect to the overriding objective as set out in CPR, r.1.1. One of the matters the court now has to consider is the finite nature of court time and resources and the need to allocate these fairly between all litigants, not just those in the case in which the application is made.

In the county court, the exercise of the court's discretion to order a rehearing, pursuant to CCR, Ord. 37, r.1 (as preserved in Sch. 2 to the CPR), is also to be exercised on *Ladd v Marshall: Hertfordshire Investments Ltd v Bubb* [2000] 1 W.L.R. 2318, CA. The more lenient approach of the district judge in that case, who allowed the application even though he found that the evidence could have been produced with reasonable diligence at trial, was rejected. It was held to be desirable under the CPR that whatever route was taken by a litigant to reopen a case after final judgment in order to admit fresh evidence, the same principles should apply.

2.—CRIMINAL CASES

(2) Evidence on appeal to the Court of Appeal (Criminal Division)

12–11   In *R. v Criminal Cases Review Commission, Ex p. Pearson* [1999] 3 All E.R. 498 at 517, DC, Lord Bingham C.J. said on the subject of whether fresh evidence would be admitted by the Court of Appeal following a conscious decision not to call available evidence at the trial:

> "Wisely and correctly, the courts have recognized that the statutory discretion conferred by section 23 cannot be constrained by inflexible, mechanistic rules. But the cases do identify certain features which are likely to weigh more or less heavily against the reception of fresh evidence: for example, a deliberate decision by a defendant whose

decision-making faculties are unimpaired not to advance before the trial jury a defence known to be available evidence of mental abnormality or substantial impairment given years after the offence and contradicted by evidence available at the time of the offence expert evidence based on factual premises which are unsubstantiated, unreliable or false, or which is for any other reason unpersuasive. But even features such as these need not be conclusive objections in every case. The overriding discretion conferred on the court enables it to ensure that, in the last resort, defendants are sentenced for the crimes they have committed and not for psychological failings to which they may be subject."

NOTE 54. See also R. Pattenden, *English Criminal Appeals 1844–1994* (Oxford University Press, Oxford, 1996), pp.130–140, P. Taylor (ed.), *Taylor on Criminal Appeals* (Sweet & Maxwell, London, 2000), pp.270–289.

It is possible for the Court of Appeal to receive evidence when all four matters **12–12** mentioned in s.23(2) are not satisfied, provided the court has regard to them. Thus "credible admissible evidence affecting the safety of a conviction may, in an appropriate case, be admitted even though no reasonable explanation is provided for the failure to adduce it at trial", *per* Rose L.J. in *R. v Sales* [2000] 2 Cr.App.R. 431, CA. See also on this point *R. v Cairns* [2000] Crim.L.R. 473, CA. At some future date, Rose L.J. said in *R. v Sales*, the court may have to consider "whether the *Melville* and *Richardson* approach still precludes the admissibility in this court of evidence on an issue not raised at trial". In *R. v B* [2000] Crim.L.R. 50, the Court of Appeal relied upon a report of a social service interview that was not admissible evidence, to hold the conviction unsafe. It would appear, therefore, that the interpretation of s.23(2)(c) advocated in the text is not correct.

In *Sales*, above, the court noted that the wording of s.23 of the 1968 Act has changed since *Melville* as a result of the 1995 amendment, s.23(2) now speaks of the court having regard to the four matters under that subsection rather than setting them out as preconditions to the reception of fresh evidence. The court held (obiter) that, under the new wording, it was possible for the Court of Appeal to receive fresh evidence even though one of the matters set out in s.23(2)(a) to (d) was not satisfied. In the case before the court, the appellant had pleaded guilty to manslaughter at trial and so had admitted that he stabbed the victim. On appeal, he sought to have fresh evidence admitted which suggested that another person had stabbed the victim to death. Thus the evidence which it was sought to admit went to an issue which had not been raised at the trial the identity of the assailant had not been an issue, only provocation had. However, the court decided the matter on another ground it refused to admit the fresh evidence because it was incapable of belief.

A witness who could give evidence through a live television link at the trial may be allowed to give evidence by these means to the Court of Appeal also: Criminal Justice Act 1988, s.32(1A).

In *R. v Cairns* [2000] Crim.L.R. 473 (transcript: New Law Online, case **12–13** 300119602), the Court of Appeal decided to receive fresh evidence from two experts who had been instructed prior to trial. The court held that there was no reasonable explanation for the failure to adduce the evidence at trial: there was no reason to think that, had they been asked, the experts would not have said at trial what they were now saying before the Court of Appeal. However, the court went on to hold that this conclusion regarding s.23(2)(c) was not decisive: it was only one of the matters to which the court was to have regard. The overall consideration was whether it was expedient in the interests of justice to receive the evidence. In the case before the court, the other considerations to which it was to have regard under s.23(2) were all met. The court received the evidence.

Once admitted under s.23(1) the fresh evidence becomes evidence for all purposes *R. v Ali and Ali* [1999] Crim.L.R. 663, CA. A husband and wife were jointly convicted of murder. Both had run cut-throat defences. Both appealed. Counsel for the husband sought to have fresh evidence admitted which indicated that the wife was the murderer. The Court of Appeal admitted the evidence and held that it became evidence not just in the husband's appeal but also (and obviously to her detriment) in the wife's appeal also. Professor Sir John Smith makes a cogent point in his commentary to this case in the Criminal Law Review. The case proceeds on the assumption that fresh evidence can only be tendered by an appellant if the appeal had been by the wife alone, and the prosecution rather than another appellant had sought to have the fresh evidence admitted this would not have been allowed. However, s.23(1) contains no such restriction on which party may tender the fresh evidence. The section allows fresh evidence to be received if the court thinks it "necessary or expedient in the interests of justice". The interests of justice could well require that, on an appeal, the prosecution be allowed to tender fresh evidence confirming the appellant's guilt.

Where the defence adduces fresh evidence that calls into question the fairness of the trial and the safety of the conviction, the Court of Appeal may admit fresh evidence for the Crown that was not previously available and consider the jury's verdict in the light of all the fresh evidence that is available to it. Consideration of all the available evidence secures the rights of the defence for the purposes of Article 6 of the ECHR: *R. v Craven, The Times*, February 2, 2001, CA. On the admissibility of fresh evidence for the prosecution in support of a conviction, see also *R. v Ali and Ali* [1999] Crim.L.R. 663.

In *R. v Hanratty* [2002] EWCA Crim 1141; [2002] 2 Cr.App.R. 30 the Court of Appeal held that the prosecution may tender fresh evidence on appeal that is not relevant to a specific ground of appeal but to the question whether the appellant committed the crime of which he was convicted. The court, however, said that where the issue was not whether the appellant committed the crime but the procedural quality of the trial, evidence relating to guilt would not be admissible unless it helped place the defect complained about in context.

(a) *Existing evidence*

12–14 In *R. v Weekes* [1999] 2 Cr.App.R. 520, the Court of Appeal admitted fresh evidence of the appellant's mental illness even though the appellant had refused to allow it to be called at trial. Schiemann L.J. noted the approach of the Court of Appeal in *R. v Straw* [1995] 1 All E.R. 187, of which he was a member, where the question of fitness to plead had been determinative. The appellant had been fit to plead, had made a decision not to allow the psychiatric evidence to be called, and was not to be allowed to resile from that decision. Whilst the court in *R. v Weekes* did not doubt that this strict approach to fitness to plead would often be appropriate, it declined to apply it in the present case. Although it was not claimed that he had been unfit to plead, the court had before it undisputed evidence that the appellant's mental condition had seriously affected his judgment at the time of the trial. The court followed the approach in *R. v Borthwick* [1998] Crim.L.R. 274 and allowed the psychiatric evidence to be admitted.

In *R. v Botmeh* [2001] EWCA Crim 226, [2002] 1 WLR 531 the Court of Appeal decided that it could consider an *ex parte* application by the Crown to withhold relevant evidence on the ground of public interest immunity where that evidence had not been the subject of a public interest immunity application to the trial judge. Rose L.J. said that if the "Court examines undisclosed material which was not, but should have been, shown to the trial judge and concludes that disclosure in an edited form would have been ordered by the trial judge, the test then to be applied by this Court is whether a reasonable jury, had edited disclosure been made, could have come to a different conclusion." *R. v Botmeh* was followed in *R. v Farrell* [2002] EWCA Crim 1223 in which the prosecution had failed to disclose to the trial judge the active involvement of an informer in the offence. The Court of Appeal held that despite non-disclosure the conviction was not unsafe because the judge had directed the jury to treat the as an informer. On the question whether the Court of Appeal can dismiss an appeal by finding that the trial judge, had he been given the opportunity, would not have ordered disclosure see *Atlan v UK* (2002) 34 E.H.R.R. 33, E.Ct.H.R. It is suggested in *R. v Farrell supra* that a conviction can be upheld if the Court of Appeal is satisfied that no properly informed judge would have ordered disclosure. For the effect of inadequate disclosure at a public interest immunity hearing coupled with dishonest prosecution evidence see *R. v Early* [2002] EWCA Crim 1904. See also para. 9–52 above.

NOTE 77. See also *R. v Ullah (Naveed)* [2000] 1 Cr.App.R. 351, and *R. v Nangle*   **12–14** [2001] Crim.L.R. 506 in which the Court of Appeal raised a doubt as to whether the test of flagrant incompetence was still appropriate in the light of the right to a fair trial under Article 6 of the ECHR.

NOTE 79. See *R. v King* [2000] 2 Cr.App.R. 91; [2000] Crim.L.R. 835 where the   **12–14** fresh evidence related to a significant advance in the assessment of a vulnerable person's "suggestibility" in the 15 years since the trial.

NOTE 80. But see *R. v Horsman* [2001] EWCA Crim 3040 where a psychological   **12–14** reason was not accepted as a reason for a litigant in person failing to adduce non-psychiatric evidence.

(c) *Evidence of matters occurring after the hearing*

NOTE 93. See also *R. v Twitchell* [2000] 1 Cr.App.R. 373 (following *Edwards*)   **12–16** and *R. v Martin*, July 12, 2000, New Law Online, case 300075801, CA.

When fresh evidence involves retraction by a witness of an earlier statement,   **12–16** the court must be supplied with affidavit evidence from all those involved in the taking of the new statement because the circumstances in which it came into existence is highly relevant to its credibility: *R. v Gogana* [1999] All E.R. (D.) 608, CA; *R. v James* [2000] Crim.L.R. 571.

In *R. v McLoughlin*, unreported, November 30, 1999, the Court of Appeal said that it was the court's duty to receive written evidence by reference to matters set out in s.23(2) without hearing an overall version of the evidence. This was criticised as contrary to practice and the wording of the subsection in *R. v Sales*, above. Fresh evidence in written form is likely to be (1) plainly capable of belief or (2) plainly incapable of belief or (3) possibly capable of belief. "In relation to evidence in the third category, it may be necessary for [the] Court to hear the witness *de bene esse* in order to determine whether the evidence is capable of belief." Further, the court may need to hear evidence in category (1) in order to determine whether to allow the appeal. "This may be so where fresh expert evidence is proffered (see, *e.g. R. v Jones* [1997] 1 Cr.App.R. 86) but it may also be necessary in relation to lay evidence, particularly conflicting lay evidence (see, *e.g. R. v Callaghan* (1989) 88 Cr.App.R. 40)", *per* Rose L.J.

In order to comply with Article 6, it is not necessary to order a re-trial in a fresh evidence case: *Callaghan v UK* (1989) 60 D.R. 296.

(d) *Post-trial change in the rules of Evidence*

12–17   Article 7 of the Convention does not prevent the Court of Appeal from relying on a post-trial change in the law of evidence to uphold the conviction: *X v UK* (1976) 3 D.R. 95.

CHAPTER 13

CORROBORATION AND SUPPORTING EVIDENCE

2.—SITUATIONS WHERE SUPPORTING EVIDENCE IS REQUIRED BY STATUTE

(1) Treason Act 1795, s.1

Treason Act 1795, s.1 repealed on September 30, 1998 by art.2(1)(g) of **13–02** statutory instrument 1998/2327, made under the Crime and Disorder Act 1998, s.36(3). Treason Act 1842, s.1 repealed by Treason Act 1945, s.2, Schedule. As respects Northern Ireland, Treason Act 1842, s.2 repealed in part by Treatment of Offenders (Northern Ireland) Act 1968, ss. 22, 35(3), Sch. 5, Pt II. Words omitted in Treason Felony Act 1848, s.3 repealed by Statute Law Revision Acts 1891 and 1892.

3.—SITUATIONS WHERE A WARNING MAY BE NECESSARY

(1) Types of witness

(a) *Accomplices and Sexual Complainants*

In *R. v Gilbert* [2002] UKPC 17; [2002] 2 W.L.R. 1498, the Privy Council, **13–06** allowing the appeal, held that the question whether to give a corroboration warning in sexual cases was a matter for the discretion of the trial judge, save in clear and exceptional cases in which interference on appeal was justified. The Court of Appeal in *R. v H* [2001] EWCA Crim 1922, dismissing the appellant's appeal against his conviction for four sexual offences, accepted nevertheless that there may be cases in which material is known to the trial judge but not to the jury, such that a full corroboration warning should be given.

For a recent example in a sexual case of the requirement in Scots law for the proof of a criminal charge by corroborated evidence, see *H.M. Advocate v Beggs (No.3)* 2002 S.L.T. 153. See also *R. v Bromfield* [2002] EWCA Crim 195, a rape case, for a brief discussion on corroboration.

(b) *Co-defendants*

13–08   NOTE 37. See also *R. v Francom* [2001] 1 Cr.App.R. 237 (cut-throat defences) in which support is given for this approach. In another cut-throat defences case, the Court of Appeal highlighted the need for the judge to avoid an accusation that he has failed to allow the jury to approach the evidence with open minds when directing the jury to approach the evidence with caution; *R. v Burrows* [2001] Crim.L.R. 48.

4.—WHAT CONSTITUTES SUPPORTING EVIDENCE?

13–14   In *R. v B* [2000] Crim.L.R. 181, the Court of Appeal held that, once a judge has decided to give a modified corroboration warning, following *Makanjuola*, he must proceed to identify what supporting evidence there is in the case; if there is no supporting evidence, the judge must say so. There is a wide discretion as to whether to give a warning. However, having decided to give a warning, the duty to identify supporting evidence is strict.

CHAPTER 14

IDENTIFICATION

2.—VISUAL IDENTIFICATION

(3) Photographs and video-films

In *R. v Loveridge* [2001] 2 Cr.App.R. 591 the Court of Appeal held that the **14–05** fact that the photographs given to experts to compare with C.C.T.V. film had been obtained in violation of both Criminal Justice Act 1925, s.41 and Article 8 of the European Convention on Human Rights did not interfere with the fairness of the hearing at which the experts gave evidence of identification. Thus the judge had not fallen into error in refusing to exclude the evidence. See also *Attorney General's Reference (No. 2 of 2002)*, *The Times*, October 17, 2002 on admissibility of film identification evidence.

(4) Protection against weak and unfair identification evidence

(b) *Excluding identification evidence under the Police and Criminal Evidence Act 1984, s.78*

The Police and Criminal Evidence Act 1984 (Codes of Practice) (Temporary **14–08** Modifications to Code D) Order 2002 (SI 2002/615) came into force on April 1, 2002 and has made significant changes to Code of Practice D, the code of practice dealing with identification procedures. Alongside the changes of substance, which are discussed below, the new Order has also altered the numbering of familiar provisions. Below we indicate the new numbers of the provisions which correspond to the provisions cited in the footnotes in the 15th edition.

In *R. v Perry*, *The Times*, April 28, 2000, the Court of Appeal criticised extensive reference to the European Convention on Human Rights and the Human Rights Act 1998 in a case where the breaches of Code D could "properly and readily be dealt with" using the principles relevant to s.78 of the Police and Criminal Evidence Act 1984. In *R. v Forbes* [2001] 1 A.C. 473, the House of Lords considered the relationship between breaches of the Codes governing identification procedures and Article 6 of the European Convention on Human Rights. Lord Bingham drew attention to the fact that the Privy Council had decided in *Brown v Stott* [2001] 2 W.L.R. 817, PC, that the subsidiary rights comprised within Article 6 are not absolute and "it is always necessary to consider all the facts and the whole history of the proceedings in a particular case to judge whether a defendant's right to a fair trial has been infringed or not" (*per* Lord Bingham at [24]). On the facts in *Forbes* the House of Lords agreed with the Court of Appeal that the defendant's right to a fair trial had not been infringed despite the Recorder having wrongly concluded that there had been no breach of Code D, consequently not having considered whether to exclude the identification evidence, and not having given a direction about the significance of the breach.

(c) *Important elements of fair identification procedure*

(i) DESCRIPTIONS

14–09   In *R. v Nolan* [2002] EWCA Crim 464 the Court of Appeal considered how much detail about the witness's description of the person seen should be disclosed to the suspect before formal identification procedures. Longmore L.J. stated, at para. [36],

> "we do not consider that it is a necessary part of a potential witness's first description that the witness's opportunity to see the suspect should be included. It cannot be required that the description should include, for example, the angle at which the witness saw the suspect's face or the distance from which the witness saw the suspect or the fact that the witness is a short-sighted witness, even if the witness in his first statement has mentioned these things."

Applying this, the Court of Appeal found that there had been no breach of Code D in not informing the suspect that the witness had initially claimed to have seen only the back of the perpetrator.

14–09   NOTE 71. Code D 2.2, 2.26(a).

14–09   NOTE 74. Code D 2.2.

(iii) IDENTIFICATION PARADES

14–11   The modifications made to Code D by the Police and Criminal Evidence Act 1984 (Codes of Practice) (Temporary Modifications to Code D) Order 2002 (SI 2002/615) make clear that identification parades should no longer be considered "the normal method of identification". Instead parades become one of the two normal procedures, the other normal procedure being video identification. The modified Code D 2.16 permits the officer in charge of the case to "choose freely" between a video identification and an identification parade (unless a group identification would be more suitable than either of these, Code D 2.18). The Code suggests that a video identification might be more practical than a parade if there were difficulties involving the witnesses "number, state of health, availability and travelling requirements" and might be more suitable than a parade if it "could be arranged and completed sooner". It is open to a suspect to refuse the procedure offered and make representations as to why another procedure should be used. Although the language of Code D 2.17 is somewhat opaque it seems that the identification officer should then offer an alternative procedure unless that alternative is not suitable and practicable.

The last sentence of para. 14–11 should be deleted and replaced with: The correctness of the decision in *R. v Popat* was re-asserted by the Court of Appeal in *R. v Popat (No. 2)* [2000] 1 Cr.App.R. 387, CA. Subsequently, however, and consistently with the view expressed in the text, the House of Lords in *R. v Forbes* [2001] 1 A.C. 473 upheld the Court of Appeal decision in that case. Lord Bingham held, at [20], that the language of Code D did not support the distinction drawn in *R. v Popat*, between a suspect being produced by the police to a witness rather than by a witness to the police, and that Code D 2.3 (1995 version) required an identification parade to be held even after an "actual and complete", "unequivocal" informal identification. (Under the modified Code D the comparable duty is found in 2.14 and is a duty to hold an identification *procedure* rather than specifically an identification parade.) The House of Lords also confirmed the lines of authority supporting the propositions that evidence obtained in breach of Code D will not inevitably be excluded by reason of that breach alone ([2001] 1 A.C. 473 at [23]. See above, para. 14–08) and that where evidence is admitted despite a breach of Code D the judge should direct the jury on that breach and its possible effect ([2001] 1 A.C. 473 at [27]. See below, para. 14–30).

In *R. v Chen and others* [2001] EWCA Crim 885, decided after *R. v Forbes* [2001] 1 A.C. 473, HL, the Court of Appeal held that Code D did not require an identification parade to be held in a case where the accused persons admitted being present at the scene of the crime but disputed the roles that the witnesses alleged that they had played. Longmore L.J. stated, at [40], "a dispute about roles or about the commission of particular acts in the context of criminal activity sustained up to the moment of arrest is not, in our view, a dispute about identification, since the suspects are disputing not identification but criminal participation." An identification parade would clearly have been a most ineffective way of confirming whether the witnesses were correct in attributing particular roles to particular individuals. In such a case, however, a warning about the risks of mistake and confusion by eyewitnesses might still be necessary, see para. 14–23.

The modified Code D expressly authorises the use of plasters and hats in order to increase similarity between a suspect with a distinctive feature and the other members of an identification parade (Code D, Annex B, para. 10). In *R. v Marrin* [2002] EWCA Crim 251, the Court of Appeal held that similar steps did not breach the previous version of Code D provided that they were bona fide, sensible and reasonable. The Court also suggested, however, that identification officers should seek to avoid resort to hats or caps if possible because "it makes identification by the witness that much more difficult" (*per* Keene L.J. at [17]).

NOTE 78. Code D, 2.6, 2.7, Annex B.   **14–11**

NOTE 80. The definitions of "known" and "available" are now in Code D   **14–11**
2.12.

NOTE 80a. The wording of the provisions which define when an identification   **14–11**
procedure must be held has changed. The relevant provisions are Code D 2.14,
2.15. The proposition for which *R. v Nicholson* [2001] 1 Cr.App.R. 182, CA, is
cited, is still correct.

14–11 NOTES 81–83 The modified Code D structures the choice of identification procedure differently. See update above, para. 14–11.

14–11 NOTE 84. The modified Code D 2.13 allows identification parades to be arranged by "approved persons" as well as by identification officers.

14–11 NOTE 85. Code D, Annex B, para. 23.

14–11 NOTE 87. Code D, 2.26.

14–11 NOTE 91a. *R. v Popat (No. 2)* is now reported: see [2000] 1 Cr.App.R. 387, CA. It was followed in *R. v Ryan, The Times,* October 13, 1999, CA, but has been overtaken by the decision of the House of Lords in *R. v Forbes* [2001] 1 A.C. 473, HL, discussed above, para. 14–11.

(iv) SHOWING PHOTOGRAPHS BEFORE PARADES

14–12 NOTE 92. Code D, Annex E.

14–12 NOTE 93. The final sentence should now read: The showing of photographs is not a permitted method of identification after a suspect is "known" (Code D 2.27) but video identification in accordance with Code D, Annex A will often be a permitted method.

14–12 NOTE 94. Code D, Annex E, para. 6.

(v) GROUP IDENTIFICATIONS

14–13 NOTE 98. Code D 2.8, 2.9, Annex C

14–13 NOTE 99. The statement corresponding to this footnote is no longer correct. Code D 2.18, 2.19.

14–13 NOTE 1. Code D 2.19.

14–13 NOTE 3. Code D, Annex C, paras 23, 28 and 29.

14–13 NOTE 4. Code D, Annex C, para. 37.

(vi) VIDEO FILM IDENTIFICATIONS

14–14 One of the primary purposes of the 2002 Order was to increase the use of video identification. This was principally achieved by permitting identification officers a choice between a video identification and an identification parade as the primary identification procedure. Video identification was also made more practicable, however, by minor changes to the relevant annex governing the procedure (now Code D, Annex A). These changes made allowance for the difficulties in obtaining pictures taken under identical circumstances, particularly if the suspect is unwilling to co-operate (Code D, Annex A, para. 3).

14–14 NOTE 7. Code D 2.4, 2.5, Annex A.

NOTE 8. The statement corresponding to this footnote is no longer correct. Code   **14–14**
D 2.16.

NOTE 9. Code D 2.19, 2.25   **14–14**

(vii) CONFRONTATIONS

The reference in this paragraph should now be to Code D, Annex D. Code D,   **14–15**
Annex D, para. 3 states that "[f]orce may not be used to make the face of the
suspect visible to the witness". This change does not go as far as *R. v Jones &
Nelson, The Times*, April 21, 1999, CA, which held that it was a breach of Code
D to use, or threaten to use, force on the suspect in order to secure a con-
frontation.

NOTE 10. Code D 2.10, 2.11, 2.20, Annex D.   **14–15**

NOTE 11. Code D 2.10, 2.20.   **14–15**

NOTE 13. Moreover, where a confrontation is arranged, neither force nor the   **14–15**
threat of force should be used: *R. v Jones & Nelson, The Times*, April 21, 1999,
CA.

(viii) INFORMAL IDENTIFICATIONS

NOTE 15. Code D 2.26   **14–16**

(xi) CIRCUMSTANTIAL EVIDENCE OF IDENTITY

In *R. v George* [2002] EWCA Crim 1923; *The Times*, August 30, 2002, the   **14–18A**
Court of Appeal held that witnesses could testify as to the appearance and
behaviour of an offender and to events at an identification parade even if they had
failed to pick out the accused as the offender at the identification parade. Before
admitting the evidence it was necessary for the trial judge to consider whether it
was more prejudicial than probative. But where several witnesses provided
consistent descriptions of an offender it might be of significant probative
force.

Similar issues were considered by the High Court of Australia in *Festa v R.*
[2001] H.CA 72; (2001) 185 A.L.R. 394. In that case one eyewitness had picked
three photographs from a photoboard, including one of the accused, saying that
they had similar skin and hair types, and three other eyewitnesses had identified
the accused outside a courtroom (where she may have been the only woman
present) with such equivocal statements as "looks familiar" and "75 percent
sure". A majority of the High Court of Australia thought that the trial judge had
been correct to admit this evidence, but that a direction to the jury should have
stressed the weaknesses of identification in courtroom settings. McHugh J.
discussed how in certain cases identification might be established by a combination of witnesses, each of whom could only testify to one feature of the offender,
such as age, race, stature, colour, voice, distinctive mark or gait. Indeed McHugh
J. suggested, at paras [56]–[57], that an identification based on such a circumstantial case might be more reliable than one based on a purported recognition of
the offender. Kirby J., however, expressly rejected this suggestion, at [166].

3.—OTHER MEANS OF IDENTIFICATION

(1) Fingerprints or footmarks and similar bodily impressions

14-31   In *R. v Dallagher* [2002] EWCA Crim 1903, [2002] Crim.L.R. 821; *The Times*, August 21, 2002, CA, the Court of Appeal considered the admissibility of expert evidence that an ear-print on a window at a crime-scene matched ear-prints provided by the accused. The court held that such evidence is admissible, but allowed the appeal because the jury had not heard live testimony from defence experts and consequently had not been properly equipped to evaluate the probative value of the evidence. It appears to be the case that ear shapes are highly variable but, because ears are flexible and can print at different angles, comparison of ear-prints is subjective. Further, some experts believe that there has been insufficient research on the frequency of particular ear shapes in the population.

(3) Voice recognition

14-33   It should be noted that there is academic evidence which concludes that accurate voice recognition is more difficult than visual identification by a witness: see *R. v Roberts* [2000] Crim.L.R. 183, CA; D. Ormerod, "Sounds Familiar?—Voice Identification Evidence" [2001] Crim.L.R. 595.

CHAPTER 15

PHYSICAL CONDITIONS, STATES OF MIND AND EMOTIONS

3.—PROOF OF STATES OF MIND AND BODY

(1) Knowledge and notice

The fivefold categorisation of knowledge (from *Baden*) presented in this **15–04** paragraph has fallen out of favour in several areas of the law. In *Royal Brunei Airlines Sdn. Bhd. v Tan* [1995] 2 A.C. 378, PC, it was held that in claims against a person for dishonestly procuring or assisting in a breach of trust or fiduciary obligation the essential question was whether the person was acting *dishonestly*, and that "'knowigly' is better avoided as a defining ingredient of the principle, and in the context of this principle the *Baden* scale of knowledge is best forgotten" (at 392, *per* Lord Nicholls); see also *Twinsectra Ltd v Yardley* [2002] UKHL 12; [2002] 2 A.C. 164. In *Bank of Credit and Commerce International (Overseas) Ltd v Akindele* [2001] Ch. 437, CA, it was held that even in a claim against a person for knowing receipt of funds following a breach of trust, a type of claim which does not depend on proof of dishonesty, no useful purpose was served by the categorisation of knowledge. Instead the court held that there was a single test of knowledge in knowing receipt claims, which asked if the recipients state of knowledge was "such as to make it unconscionable for him to retain the benefit of the receipt" (at 455, *per* Nourse L.J.). It was suggested that such a unified test would avoid the difficulties of definition and allocation flowing from the fivefold categorisation, and would better enable courts to give "commonsense decisions" in commercial contexts.

In *Manifest Shipping Co Ltd v Uni-Polaris Shipping Co Ltd* [2001] U.K.H.L. 1, [2001] 2 W.L.R. 170, the House of Lords considered what had to be proved in order to establish an assured's "blind-eye knowledge" of the unseaworthiness of a ship. Their Lordships concluded that such knowledge requires proof of three elements: (i) "at least a suspicion of a truth about which you do not want to know" (*per* Lord Clyde, at [3]. See also [25] (Lord Hobhouse) and [115] (Lord Scott)); (ii) "a deliberate decision not to enquire" (*per* Lord Scott, at [115]. See also [26] (Lord Hobhouse).); and, (iii) the reason for not inquiring "was because he did not want to know for certain" (*per* Lord Hobhouse, at [25]. See also [3] (Lord Clyde) and [115] (Lord Scott).). Lord Scott went deeper into the definition of "suspicion" in stage (i) of the test than the other Lords. He explained, at [116], that, "[s]uspicion is a word that can be used to describe a state-of-mind that may, at one extreme, be no more than a vague feeling of unease and, at the other extreme, reflect a firm belief in the existence of the relevant facts. In my opinion, in order for there to be blind-eye knowledge, the suspicion must be firmly grounded and targeted on specific facts." Lord Hobhouse offered a helpful list of reasons for not inquiring which would not satisfy state (iii) of the test. He stated, at [25], that "blind-eye knowledge" would not have been proved if the assured "did not inquire because he was too lazy or he was grossly negligent or believed there was nothing wrong".

(2) Consciousness of guilt: flight, lies and false alibis

15–07   In *R. v Middleton* [2001] Crim.L.R. 251, CA, the Court of Appeal expressed concern about the number of appeals raising issues relating to directions about lies and recommended that when deciding whether a warning was necessary "it will usually be more useful to analyse the question in the context of the individual case by examining the principles rather than by laboriously trawling through hosts of reported and unreported cases and learned commentaries" (*per* Judge L.J. at [23]).

There are grounds to doubt some of the specific guidance offered in some of the recent cases. In *Middleton*, at [22], Judge L.J. suggested that "it is inherently unlikely that such a direction will be appropriate in relation to lies which the jury conclude that the defendant must have told them in his evidence" and in *R. v Quang Van Bui* [2001] EWCA Crim 1, CA, at [27], Laws L.J. suggested that a direction would not be appropriate if the lies were integral to the accused's defence rather than about a collateral matter. But both of the statements seem too bold because the situation where an accused has misguidedly relied on a false alibi to bolster an apparently weak defence is one where a warning is obviously necessary, even if the lie is central and is repeated in court. It is better to state that where the jury will not be able to find that the accused lied about a matter without *also* concluding that he committed the crime a warning will be unnecessary and inappropriate: See, *R. v Harron* (1996) 2 Cr.App.R. 457, CA. See also *R. v Barnett* [2002] EWCA Crim 454, CA, where the jury could not plausibly have found that the accused's story about how the stolen painting came to be under his bed was untrue without *also* concluding that he knew that he was handling stolen goods.

Of course, situations where a lie was about a collateral matter and the prosecution introduced evidence specifically to prove it was a lie and where a lie was told at a previous stage and has now been confessed will be situations where it will be easy for the jury to find that the accused lied without *inevitably* concluding that he committed the crime. But these are not the only situations where a lie will not inevitably establish guilt.

For a more detailed discussion of recent cases concerning lies see below, update relating to para. 31–35.

A direction about how lies should be treated may be combined with a direction under s.34 of the Criminal Justice and Public Order Act 1994 regarding the accused's failure to mention a relevant matter when questioned by police: *R. v O(A)* [2000] Crim.L.R. 617, CA. See further below, update relating to para. 32–07.

(3) Intention

(a) *When in issue, or relevant*

R. v Woollin [1999] 1 A.C. 82, HL was applied in *Re A (Children) (Conjoined*   **15–08**
Twins: Surgical Separation) [2001] Fam. 147, CA.

(4) Motive and relationship

More recently, the limit to background evidence and the caution with which it   **15–10**
should be admitted have been recognised by the Court of Appeal in *R. v Butler*
(Diana) [2000] Crim.L.R. 835, CA. Where an issue as to the use of background
evidence arises, the parties should try to agree an account of the background so
not to distract the jury's attention from central events. Failing an agreement, of
which the judge approves, a full analysis of the situation will be carried out in the
absence of a jury.

NOTE 75. *R. v M(T); R. v M(PA)* [2000] 1 W.L.R. 421, CA; *R. v Sawoniuk* [2000]   **15–10**
Crim.L.R. 506.
For discussion of the subsequent cases dealing with background evidence see
updates to para. 17–52.

(6) Fraud and dishonesty

(a) *Dishonesty*

In *Twinsectra Ltd v Yardley* [2002] UKHL 12, [2002] 2 A.C. 164, the House   **15–13**
of Lords considered whether "dishonesty" in the context of a claim against a
solicitor for dishonestly assisting in breach of trust required proof that the
solicitor knew that what he was doing would be regarded as dishonest by honest
people. A majority of the House of Lords concluded that this subjective element
was a necessary part of proof of dishonesty in the context. Lord Millett dissented,
arguing that the relevant question should be whether an honest person, having the
same knowledge, experience and attributes as the defendant, would have
appreciated that what he was doing would be regarded as wrong or improper.

4.—PERMISSIBLE INFERENCES FROM STATES OF MIND AND BODY

(1) Inferences from knowledge

Evidence of a confession made to witnesses, from a different suspect, are   **15–19**
inadmissible under *R. v Blastland* (the correctness of whose reasoning is doubted
in the text): *R. v Parsons*, unreported, LTL, December 17, 1999, CA.
In *R. v Garvey* [2001] EWCA Crim 1365, at [77], the Court of Appeal treated
it as obvious that a co-accused could not elicit evidence that a witness *believed*
a particular fact to be true in order to establish that the fact was true when that

belief was based on hearsay. Any other decision would have made it easy to circumvent the rule against hearsay.

(4) Inferences from motive

15–22   NOTE 31. The subsequent appeal to the House of Lords in *R. v Acott* [1997] 1 All E.R. 706, HL, did not affect the correctness of the ruling referred to in the text.

CHAPTER 16

CHARACTER: GENERAL AND INTRODUCTORY

3.—DIRECT ISSUE CASES

(1) Civil cases

NOTE 9. In *Burstein v Times Newspapers Ltd* [2001] 1 W.L.R. 579, CA, it was **16–04**
held that evidence of particular acts and facts might properly be adduced where
directly relevant to the background context.

CHAPTER 17

CHARACTER OF THE ACCUSED (OTHER THAN UNDER CROSS-EXAMINATION)

1.—GOOD CHARACTER OF THE ACCUSED

(6) "Good character" for the purposes of the direction

(a) *The convicted accused*

17–17   It was stated in *R. v Martin* [2000] 2 Cr.App.R. 42 at 45, CA, that the case of *R. v MacDonald*, unreported, March 25, 1999, CA, is authority for the proposition that a spent conviction does not deprive the accused of "the right to a full character direction". It is not clear if this poses a challenge to the view, expressed in the text, that, in such cases, the matter is one for the informed discretion of the trial judge.

(b) *The unconvicted accused*

17–19   It has been held that the judge enjoys this residual discretion where the previous criminal conduct led to a police caution: see *R. v Martin* [2000] 2 Cr.App.R. 42, CA. No reference at all had been made, during the course of the evidence, to the accused's two cautions. The judge gave him the benefit of a first limb, but not a second limb, direction. The Court of Appeal thought the judge's decision sound, saying that, having chosen not to make a clean breast of his past conduct, the accused could not properly expect to be given the advantage of an absurd, indeed, misleading, propensity direction. There is now Privy Council authority favouring the discretionary approach. In *Shaw v R.* [2002] 1 Cr.App.R. 77, at the accused's trial for murder, evidence for the defence had shown him to be a dealer in cocaine on a substantial scale, as well as to have been part of an armed group that had set out to obtain reparation from the victim. The trial judge's decision to give the jury neither limb of the direction was ruled to be absolutely correct by the Judicial Committee.

2.—BAD CHARACTER OF THE ACCUSED

(5) Proof and prejudice

(a) *Probative value*

(i) COGENCY

NOTE 47. The potential interaction of *H* and *Z* [2000] 2 A.C. 483, HL, is   **17–30**
considered below, paras 17–56A to 17–56E.

(6) The scope of the rule

(c) *Previous relationship cases*

The doctrine announced in *R. v Pettnam*, unreported, May 2, 1985, CA,   **17–52 &**
continues to bear fruit, and it must now be accepted that it is a much wider one   **17–53**
than that which would flow from Lord Atkinson's well-known remarks in *Ball*
[1911] A.C. 47 at 68, HL. It seems that the key phrase in the dictum in *Pettnam*
is, "evidence of part of a continual background of history relevant to the offence
charged". So, we must now no longer regard this part of the law as concerned
only with evidence of the previous relationship between the accused and some
other person. This is put beyond doubt by *R. v Sawoniuk* [2000] 2 Cr.App.R. 220,
CA, though one might now regard *R. v Sidhu* (1992) 98 Cr.App.R. 59, CA, as
standing for the same proposition. In *R. v Sawoniuk*, the two charges of which the
accused had been convicted related to events that had allegedly taken place in
1942 in what is now Belarus. They concerned the murders of two unknown
Jewish women during the course of the Nazi occupation of that country. The
prosecution had relied on the evidence of one eye-witness in relation to each
murder. It alleged that the two women had been killed in the course of a "search
and kill" operation to eliminate Jewish survivors of an earlier massacre and that
the accused had been one of a group of locally-recruited police officers involved
in the operation. The evidence to which objection had been taken at trial was that
of two people who said that they had seen the accused herding Jewish persons
towards a location or locations that was or were used for executions, and that
they had never again seen the relevant persons. In one case, it was said, a Jewish
woman had been seriously assaulted by the accused. The Court of Appeal ruled
the evidence in question admissible for one of two alternative purposes, neither
of which, in its view, was such as to render it evidence of the accused's
propensity. First, it demonstrated, contrary to his own sworn testimony, that he
had been a member of the relevant "search and kill" squad. (For comment upon
this ground of admissibility, see below, para. 17–56.) Secondly, it was admissible
on the broader ground that it was necessary, in order for the jury to be able to
make a rational assessment of the direct eye-witness evidence, to describe for
them, in some detail, the context and circumstances in which the offences were
said to have been committed. In this respect, reliance was placed upon
Pettnam.

Two comments about this second ground may be apposite. First, there was,
quite plainly, no question of the evidence demonstrating the nature of a previous

relationship. Secondly, it is submitted that the decision is rather hard to support on the facts. The court was clearly troubled by the prospect that a jury so remote in time and place from the events might find hard to accept the notion that such gruesome acts as those testified to by the eye-witnesses could really have been carried out. However, there was a great deal of prosecution evidence both of the general Nazi policy towards the Jews and of the use by the Nazis of locally recruited police forces to carry out that policy. The defence was that the accused himself had not been a party to any such activity. Surely, the evidence of the accused herding persons to their deaths went beyond what was necessary to render the prosecution's account complete and comprehensible. The eye-witness evidence was quite capable of standing or falling on its own, against the background of the general evidence, not pointing at the accused in particular, about local conditions. There was no function left for the extrinsic evidence to perform, except to demonstrate his propensity, yet the ordinary rule of law, balancing probative value against prejudicial effect, was misapplied.

In *R. v M (T)* [2000] 1 W.L.R. 421, the charge against the accused was that he had, when aged 16, raped his sister, then aged 10. She gave evidence, but the trial judge also permitted the prosecution to call evidence from other siblings that the accused had been present when they had been raped and buggered by their father and, indeed, that he himself had been made to take part. The case was one of alleged serial child abuse, carrying down from generation to generation, the effect of the siblings' evidence being that the accused had been "groomed" into the family web of abuse, and so was more likely to have raped his sister as alleged. According to the Court of Appeal, their testimony was evidence of "a continuous family history relevant to the offences charged" (at 427). This is hard to fathom. It was certainly the case that evidence that the accused had witnessed abuse by his father had probative value, since it showed that he would realise that there would be nobody for his sister to turn to for complaint were he to abuse her himself. However, the evidence went beyond that, in showing that he had previously had sexual intercourse with her, albeit apparently under duress, and so might be thought propensity evidence. Kennedy L.J. referred to the discretion, under s.78 of the Police and Criminal Evidence Act 1984, to exclude evidence that would put the fairness of the proceedings in jeopardy. He concluded that it would not be prejudicial because the earlier abuse had been coerced, so that the jury would not blame the accused for it. Yet, he was able to offer nothing to show its probative value, beyond the mysterious cloak of a "continuing family history". Once again, this was, it is submitted, clearly a case where the ordinary rule of law should have been applied.

One useful suggestion to emerge recently is that it may be possible to avoid or limit both prejudice to the accused and distraction of the jury from the central issue by encouraging opposing counsel to agree a statement of the relevant facts: see *R. v Butler* [1999] Crim.L.R. 835, CA.

(d)   *"Forbidden" mode of reasoning not relied upon*

17–56 The fragility of the idea that whether or not the rule of exclusion must be satisfied turns upon the use to which the prosecution claims to put the evidence of bad character is demonstrated by *R. v Sawoniuk* [2000] 2 Cr.App.R. 220, dealt with in detail above, paras 17–52 to 17–53. As an alternative to the background evidence ground of admissibility, the Court of Appeal accepted counsel's submission that the evidence was admissible to prove that the accused was a policeman involved in the "search and kill" operation. By identifying him as a member of the group to which the killer belonged, it rendered him one of the possible killers. Thus, the evidence in question was not called to prove his propensity. This clearly smacks of the now-discredited Makin-type approach, but, in any event, it might be thought rather difficult for a jury to distinguish use of membership of the squad merely to place the accused in the group of possible murderers from use of it as evidence of his propensity to search for and kill Jews.

Though the decision of the House of Lords in *R. v Z* [2000] 2 A.C. 483 is most   **17–56A** fundamentally concerned with whether or not an acquittal may be challenged in later criminal proceedings not themselves directly concerned with the correctness of that verdict itself, it also has very real significance for the general rule preventing the prosecution from adducing evidence of the bad character of the accused. In short, the case decides that evidence of the commission of an offence by the accused is not rendered inadmissible merely because he has already been acquitted of that offence. As long as the ordinary requirement that, in order for such evidence to be admissible, probative value must exceed prejudicial effect is satisfied, the fact of acquittal is of no account. The facts of *Z* demonstrate the point very clearly; at his present trial for rape, details underlying his three earlier acquittals of that offence were no less admissible than those underlying his one conviction therefor. In effect, a jury is now quite entitled to find that the accused was wrongly acquitted before then using that conclusion, along with all the other evidence in the case, in convicting him of the present offence.

This is not the place to discuss the merits of *Z*: the reader is referred to the   **17–56B** academic literature, some in support and some against: see Roberts [2000] Crim.L.R. 952; Birch [2000] Crim.L.R. 293 and [2001] Crim.L.R. 222; Tapper (2001) 117 L.Q.R. 1; Mirfield (2001) 117 L.Q.R. 194; Munday [2000] Camb.L.J. 468. However, there are several difficult consequential issues that arise from it, some of which are dealt with here, but others at subsequent points in the text at which they naturally arise. First, it may be recalled that the House's decision in *R. v H* [1995] 2 A.C. 596—paras 17–30 to 17–36 of the text—tells us that, where the defence challenges the cogency of bad character evidence, whether because collusion or some other kind of contamination is alleged, that evidence is, as a general rule, to be treated as true, for the purpose of assessing its probative value under the test for admissibility. In *H* itself, the bad character evidence in question was also direct evidence on another count on the indictment, but the principle announced seems to be no less applicable to uncharged allegations. Therefore, it is conceivable that an accused acquitted of a given offence may face the argument, not only that the evidence relating to that offence should be called against him again, on a similar fact basis, at a later trial for a different offence, but also that it should be deemed true for purposes of applying the probative value/prejudicial effect test. Logic seems to dictate that such an argument would have to succeed, though it has been pointed out that there might be thought to be an incompatibility between such a conclusion and the guarantee of the presumption of innocence afforded by Article 6(2) of the European Convention on Human Rights: see Tapper (2001) 117 L.Q.R. 1 at 3.

17–56C   Secondly, there must be an obvious temptation for jurors persuaded that the accused's earlier acquittal was wrongful to balance that injustice by convicting on a less than sufficient basis on the present occasion. Dr Munday has provided an example of a tribunal of fact apparently giving way to just such a temptation: see [2000] C.L.J. 468 at 471. It might be supposed that the courts would seek to obviate or attenuate that risk by developing a rule requiring juries to be instructed appropriately, while magistrates might be invited to self-instruct themselves. Whatever one might think about the likely efficacy of any such instruction or self-instruction, it seems improbable that judges will accept that the potential for prejudice is such that explicit account ought to be taken of it, in the balancing exercise.

17–56D   Thirdly, it is to be noted that, in Z, the earlier rape charges which had led to acquittals presumably all involved decisions by juries left free to reach their own conclusions. Therefore, one argument available in that case was that all that could be known about those decisions was that the juries had not been persuaded beyond reasonable doubt of guilt. Just such an argument was specifically relied upon by Lord Salmon in *DPP v Humphrys* [1977] A.C. 1 at 43–44, as one of the reasons for rejecting the doctrine of issue estoppel in criminal cases. In effect, it is impossible to divine whether or not an acquitting jury positively found the accused to be innocent. Even though counsel for the prosecution relied upon that argument in Z—see at 485E–F—it may be significant that it was left unendorsed by the House itself. All that appears is one brief allusion to the technical basis for acquittal in the speech of Lord Hobhouse of Woodborough—see at 508G. The importance of all of this becomes apparent when one reflects upon the other ways in which an acquittal may come about.

Under s.17 of the Criminal Justice Act 1967, the judge may order a verdict of not guilty without the accused having been put in the jury's charge. This allows for cases where the prosecution elects to offer no evidence. Once in charge of the jury, the accused may be acquitted by them on the direction of the judge. Typically, he will take that step where he finds there to be no case to answer or that the evidence is not such that a reasonable jury could convict. In each of these cases, the verdict would seem more obviously indicative of "true" innocence than a verdict following substantive jury deliberation, though it should be noted that s.17 gives the judge's order "the same effect as if the defendant had been tried and acquitted on the verdict of a jury". It remains to be seen whether or not what might be termed the "inconclusivity argument" will re-emerge as a reason for treatment of orders under s.17, or verdicts on the basis that there is no case to answer, differently from jury verdicts preceded by substantive deliberation. A final situation in which the accused ends up having been acquitted is when a successful appeal has been made. This case might seem to pose even more difficult questions, given that an appeal may be allowed for a variety of reasons, some entirely consistent with the notion that the accused is actually guilty, others wholly inconsistent therewith. It will be interesting to find out how the courts come to solve these various problems.

17–56E   Finally, the House in Z was at pains to emphasise the importance of the judicial discretion to exclude evidence, under s.78 of the Police and Criminal Evidence Act 1984. Indeed, the answer to the certified question refers in terms to the discretion to exclude evidence after weighing its prejudicial effect against its probative force or under s.78. It is not at all clear how this is intended to fit in with the trial judge's (necessary) prior conclusion that the test of admissibility in law, also in terms of the balance between probative value and prejudicial effect, has been satisfied. One can make sense of sequential applications of the rule and the discretion only if some element is added at the discretionary stage. Lord Hobhouse alone provided assistance with regard to that additional element, saying (see [2000] 2 A.C. 483 at 510):

> "Any prejudice to the defendant arising from having to deal a second time with evidence proving facts which were in issue at an earlier trial is simply another factor to be put in the balance."

This clearly does not refer to a fear, referred to earlier, that the jury might match one perceived injustice by perpetrating another. Rather, it seems to advert to the notion that the accused has a case for not being *bis vexatus*.

CHAPTER 18

CROSS-EXAMINATION OF THE ACCUSED AS TO HIS CHARACTER

1—INTRODUCTION

18–01   The relevant changes were brought into effect by The Youth Justice and Criminal Evidence Act 1999 (Commencement No. 7) Order 2002, July 8, 2002, as from July 24, 2002.

2.—THE STRUCTURE OF THE CROSS-EXAMINATION RULES

(3) The accused who does not testify

18–06   It is otherwise where the accused has given some evidence, but following the judge's ruling that he has lost his shield and may be cross-examined about his character, he has either refused to return to the witness-box or, once back in it, has simply refused to answer questions about his character. Here, a refusal will be taken to be equivalent to a denial that he has a bad character, which denial may be rebutted by the prosecution in the ordinary way: see *R. v Forbes* [1999] 2 Cr.App.R. 501, CA.

3.—THE GENERAL PROHIBITION

(1) The overriding significance of relevance

18–10   *Maxwell v DPP* [1935] A.C. 309, HL, must be re-evaluated in the light of *R. v Z* [2000] 2 A.C. 483, HL. Though *Maxwell* was not referred to in *Z*, it must surely be the case that evidence tending to show the accused to be guilty of an offence of which he has been acquitted, is, at a later trial for a different offence, equally available to the prosecution for purposes of cross-examination, as it is in-chief. In other words, as long as it would have been permissible to use it to cross-examine him as to the issue had he been convicted, it is no less permissible so to use it where he was acquitted. Thus, it is no longer correct to say, as does the text, that "someone acquitted of manslaughter could not legitimately be regarded as therefore more likely to have committed that offence on the present occasion" (see at 420–421). It does not follow that the decision in *Maxwell* has been overruled. That case was concerned with cross-examination under the first part of what was then s.1(f)(ii). As explained in the text, the permissible purposes of cross-examination thereunder are limited to attacking the accused's credibility and to correcting a misleading picture of his character ("character correction"): see paras 18–38 to 18–41, below. Though it is conceivable that a court might regard a previous acquittal as relevant to credibility, presumably on the basis that the more often one stands accused, the less creditworthy one becomes, no such conclusion is required by Z. In this respect, it is to be noted that the element of similarity between sets of alleged facts, whether they resulted in conviction or acquittal, disappears from the picture. It seems no less problematic to argue that a jury would be misled if unaware that a person claiming to be of good character in some respect had earlier been accused of an offence or offences. If acquittals, very unusual circumstances apart, do remain irrelevant under the first part of what is now s.1(3)(ii), the same should go for the second part of s.1(3)(ii) and for s.1(3)(iii).

4.—THE EXCEPTION UNDER SECTION 1(3)(I)

(1) Scope of the exception

(a) *Charges and bad character*

18–24 *R. v Z* [2000] 2 A.C. 483, HL, has significance for the effect of the omission of the word "charged" from s.1(3)(i). The case clearly admits of the jury reasoning that the accused did commit an offence of which he was acquitted and of it going on to use that conclusion as relevant to show that he committed the offence now charged. It must follow that, at the cross-examination stage, the prosecution, in a case like Z, would be relying upon the word "committed" in s.1(3)(i). Thus, in such circumstances, the problem thrown up by *R. v Cokar* [1960] 2 Q.B. 207, CCA, would disappear (*cf. R. v Pommell (No. 2)* [1999] Crim.L.R. 476, CA, cited in the text at note 66). Ironically, *R. v Cokar* itself would seem still to be correctly decided, for there the prosecution was not inviting the jury to reason that Cokar had actually committed the offence of which he had been acquitted. Rather, it wanted the jury to learn that Cokar would have got to know, during the course of the earlier trial, that entry of premises in order to sleep constituted no offence.

5.—THE EXCEPTION UNDER THE FIRST PART OF SECTION 1(3)(II)

(1) When is the shield lost?

(f) *General*

18–36   The position taken in the text is supported by *R. v Robinson* [2001] Crim.L.R. 478. There, the accused, at a particular point or points in his testimony, had taken from his pocket a bible and clutched it to himself. At times, he had waved it around at shoulder height. The trial judge's view that he had, thereby, impliedly claimed that he was religious, and so, unlikely to be lying, thus putting his character in issue, was rejected by the Court of Appeal.

(2) The permissible purposes of cross-examination

(b) *Issue relevance*

18–39 NOTE 1. Viscount Sankey L.C.'s dictum was cited with approval in *R. v Barratt* [2000] Crim.L.R. 847, CA, it being said that the trial judge should, in exercising his discretion, have borne it in mind.

6.—THE EXCEPTION UNDER THE SECOND PART OF SECTION 1(3)(II)

(2) The permissible purpose(s) of cross-examination

(b) *Issue relevance?*

18–56 NOTE 62. See *R. v Barratt* [2000] Crim.L.R. 847, CA.

(3) Discretion and warnings

(a) *Discretion*

18–61   In *R. v Dempster* [2001] Crim.L.R. 567, the Court of Appeal rejected the argument that the trial judge was under a duty, if requested by the defence, to say whether or not he would exercise his discretion in favour of the accused, were his testimony to be to the same effect as indicated by his statements to the police. The court was clearly concerned that any such ruling might provide the accused with too much latitude in testifying. One might add that there could also be great difficulty in determining whether or not the accused had gone beyond his case, as it appeared on the documents.

    Dempster was applied to the discretion under the first part of s.1(3)(ii) in *R. v Mauricia* [2002] EWCA Crim 676; [2002] 2 Cr.App.R. 27.

9.—Spent Convictions

R. v Nye is supported, on the point relating to prosecution cross-examination   **18–80**
of an accused under s.1(3), by *R. v Barratt* [2000] Crim.L.R. 847, CA, though the
court did not refer to *Nye*. In addition, there is now authority on cross-
examination of an accused by a co-accused about the former's spent convictions
under s.1(3)(iii). Here, consistently with *Murdoch v Taylor* [1965] A.C. 574, HL
(on which, see para. 18–71 of the main text), the court has no choice but to allow
the cross-examination—see *R. v Corelli* [2001] Crim.L.R. 913, CA.

CHARACTER OF PERSONS OTHER THAN THE ACCUSED

2.—EVIDENCE OF BAD CHARACTER AS RELEVANT TO THE ISSUE

(2) Criminal cases

19–08   NOTE 33. Further confirmation of the rejection of the reverse similar fact argument, as regards evidence given by police officers, is provided by *R. v Twitchell* [2000] 1 Cr.App.R. 373, CA and *R. v Malik* [2000] 2 Cr.App.R. 8, CA.

3.—EVIDENCE OF BAD CHARACTER AS RELEVANT TO CREDIBILITY

(2) Opponent's witness

(a) *Discreditable acts*

19–24   *R. v Twitchell* [2000] 1 Cr.App.R. 373, CA confirms that findings made by a criminal court, on appeal, and, indeed, by a civil court, are to be treated, in principle, in the same way as jury findings.

19–25   NOTE 92. Several appeal cases since *R. v Whelan* [1997] Crim.L.R. 353, CA, confirm that it is provision to the trier of fact of a fair, balanced picture of the officer's evidence, even in cases where the allegations against him remain unresolved, that is crucial: see, *e.g. R. v Zomparelli (No. 2)*, unreported, March 23, 1999, CA; *Kumar v The State*, unreported, June 14, 2000, PC; *R. v Martin*, unreported, July 12, 2000, CA. See also Dein [2000] Crim.L.R. 801.

4.—SPECIAL PROTECTION FROM BAD CHARACTER EVIDENCE (RAPE AND ALLIED OFFENCES)

(2) The position under statute

19–31   The law laid down by s.41, which is now in force, needs to be completely reconsidered in the light of *R. v A (No. 2)* [2001] UKHL 25; [2002] 1 A.C. 45,

HL. It follows that everything stated in the text about the provisions of that section at paras 19–32 et seq. must be re-evaluated. We shall proceed here by discussing the decision itself under the present paragraph, then by adverting to its possible effects upon the individual elements of the law relating to the admissibility of evidence of the previous sexual behaviour of the complainant at the appropriate points in the text that follows.

In *A (No. 2)*, a man accused of raping a woman on a river towpath alleged that   **19–31A** she had consented to intercourse or, if not, that he believed that she had. At a preparatory hearing, the trial judge ruled that, on the issue of consent, the accused could not cross-examine the complainant about an alleged consensual sexual relationship between the two of them which, he said, had begun about three weeks before the events at issue. The House of Lords found itself unable to decide, given the paucity of information about the alleged previous instances of intercourse, whether or not the judge's ruling was correct, but left him to reconsider his ruling in the light of their own interpretation of s.41(3)(c) of the 1999 Act.

The key problem for the House was how the apparently very restrictive regime   **19–31B** of admissibility provided for by s.41 was to be reconciled with the accused's right to a fair trial under Article 6(1) of the European Convention on Human Rights, as now made part of English domestic law by virtue of the Human Rights Act 1998. The particular way in which the fair trial right impinges upon other statutory provisions is through the special interpretative obligation laid upon the courts by s.3(1) of the 1998 Act. It states:

"So far as it is possible to do so, primary legislation and subordinate legislation must be read and given effect in a way which is compatible with the Convention Rights."

All of their Lordships found themselves able to endorse Lord Steyn's formulation of the answer to the key problem, at least in relation to s.41(3)(c) of the 1999 Act, as follows (see [2002] 1 A.C. 45 at 69 (para. 46)):

"The effect of the decision today is that under section 41(3)(c) of the 1999 Act, construed where necessary by applying the interpretative obligation under section 3 of the Human Rights Act 1998, and due regard being paid to the importance of seeking to protect the complainant from indignity and from humiliating questions, the test of admissibility is whether the evidence (and questioning in relation to it) is nevertheless so relevant to the issue of consent that to exclude it would endanger the fairness of the trial under Article 6 of the Convention."

Notwithstanding this element of agreement, it is not at all clear that their Lordships really were at one about the vital question of the relationship between the various provisions at issue. Still, with the exception of Lord Hope of Craighead, who did not think it necessary, on the particular facts, to get to the point, their Lordships did agree that the meaning properly to be given to s.41(3)(c) by reference to the ordinary canons of statutory interpretation was not the correct legal meaning thereof. Rather, the special canon set out in s.3(1) of the 1998 Act broadened significantly the scope of admissibility of a complainant's sexual behaviour.

A concrete and illuminating example of this broadening effect was given by   **19–31C** Lord Hutton. In his words (*ibid.* at 104 (para. 159)):

"A defendant wishes to give evidence that for a number of months prior to the date of the alleged offence he had had a close and affectionate relationship with the complainant and that he had had frequent consensual intercourse with her during that period. Before intercourse he would kiss her and she would return his kisses. At the time of the alleged offence, before having intercourse, affectionate behaviour took place between them as it had done on the early [sic] occasions. Is this evidence admissible under section 41(3)(c)?"

That subsection states that, to be admissible, the extraneous sexual behaviour must be, in some respect, so similar to the presently alleged such behaviour that the similarity cannot reasonably be explained as a coincidence. Lord Hutton's clear (and compelling) answer to the question he posed was that, without reference to s.3, that evidence would be inadmissible since the (alleged) earlier incidents would not be so similar as not to be reasonably explicable as coincidental. Yet, because it was possible to interpret s.41(3)(c) as rendering such evidence admissible, and because the accused would be deprived of his fair trial right were it not, recourse to s.3 resulted in it being admissible. If this is correct, and there is nothing in the speeches of Lords Slynn, Steyn and Clyde to suggest that it is not, the effect of s.3 is startling. Within the context of a continuing intimate relationship (and, no doubt, in other contexts), it may reasonably be supposed that the exchange of kisses is an ordinary (the ordinary?) preliminary to and concomitant of intercourse. Though this is not the place for a discussion of the extensive literature on the meaning of s.3(1) and, in particular, the word "possible"—see Clayton and Tomlinson, *The Law of Human Rights* (2000), para. 4.06, note 11—not everyone will agree that such a surprising interpretation of s.41(3)(c) really is a possible one. However, the House of Lords has spoken, such that, more generally the effect of its reasoning may turn out to be that the apparently highly structured and restrictive regime of admissibility laid down by s.41 will be transformed into one essentially little different from the discretionary regime, based upon the need to be fair to the accused, that was embraced by s.2 of the 1976 Act.

19–31D   What seems clearly to underpin the views of their Lordships is that previous sexual behaviour of the complainant with the accused is crucially different from such behaviour with a third party. In short, the former evidence will often be relevant and sometimes cogent, whilst the latter will rarely be relevant and even more rarely cogent. Therefore, it seems likely that, as to sexual behaviour with a third party, the courts will not regard their duty under s.3(1) as requiring them to open wider the gateways to admissibility provided by s.41 than an ordinary interpretation would indicate. More than one of their Lordships took pains to stress that, while it is a myth to suppose that a woman who is prepared to consent to intercourse with one man is therefore more likely to consent to it with another, it is not at all a myth to reason that a woman in a continuing relationship with one man will be disposed to consent to him. Of course, this is not to say that such facts would establish or mean that she did consent to him on the present occasion—*cf.* the remarks of the Government spokesman (Lord Williams of Mostyn) during the debates on what became s.41 (see H.L. Deb., Vol. 598, col. 1218, March 23, 1999)—for the point is one about relevance, not certainty—see [2002] 1 A.C. 45 at 101–102 (para. 151), *per* Lord Hutton, and see Galvin (1986) 70 Minn. L. Rev. 763 at 807. Notwithstanding the importance of this distinction, it remains entirely conceivable that an unusual case may arise in which sexual behaviour with a third party, despite carrying high probative value, will fail to get through an unwidened gateway. Therefore, resort to s.3(1) certainly cannot be ruled out for third party cases.

There is another element of uncertainty about the speeches in *A (No. 2)* that **19–31E** may be expected to create problems in future cases. Does s.3(1) merely require the interpreting court to give effect to what it regards as Parliament's "true" intention as to the statutory provision at issue, or does it require that court, if necessary, to fly in the face of that intention? Thus, one can conceive of a court radically rebuilding a provision wholly inadequately designed to respect Convention rights, in a way that would be unjustifiable by reference to ordinary notions of the function of the judicial branch in interpreting statutes, yet without that court having reason to believe that Parliament would have wished it left alone. That is certainly the kind of exercise that Lord Hope believed to be permissible— see *ibid.* at 86–87 (para. 108). On the other hand, both Lord Steyn and Lord Hutton seemed to accept that loyalty to Parliament's intention when it enacted s.3(1) might properly compel a court to effect even more radical rebuilding work, notwithstanding a belief in the court that Parliament would not, when it enacted the present legislation, have wanted that work to be undertaken—see *ibid.* at 65 (para. 36) and at 67–68 (paras 43–44), *per* Lord Steyn and at 104 (para. 159) and at 106 (para. 162), *per* Lord Hutton. It is unclear from the speeches of Lord Slynn and Lord Clyde what, if any, view they took on this particular point.

For comment on *A (No.2)* see Spencer [2001] Camb. L.J. 452; McEwan (2001) 5 E&P 257; Mirfield (2002) 118 L.Q.R. 20; Birch [2002] Crim.L.R. 531.

(a) *Preliminary points*

Add at p. 489, line 21: That a distinction must, in fact, be drawn between sexual **19–32** behaviour of the complainant with the accused and with third parties is made clear by *R. v A (No. 2)* [2002] 1 A.C. 45, on which see para. 19–31D of this Supplement.

What is stated in the text about the meaning of "sexual behaviour" requires **19–32** consideration in the light of two Court of Appeal cases decided in July 2001. In *R. v T, H* [2001] EWCA Crim 1877; [2002] 1 W.L.R. 632, the accused T stood charged with the rape and indecent assault of his niece. The defence had sought leave to question her about two occasions subsequent to the alleged offences when the police had asked her whether she had been sexually abused by anyone. On each occasion, she had made sexual allegations against another or others, but had made no mention of anything allegedly done to her by T. The accused H was alleged to have indecently assaulted his step-daughter. Leave was sought to question her about two occasions on which she had complained of being raped by third parties, it being the defence case that these complaints, just like the present one against H, were untrue. In each case, the trial judge had, at a preparatory hearing, ruled that the questions would be "about any sexual behaviour" of the complainant, and had gone on to rule them inadmissible under s.41.

Both appeals were allowed on the basis that the questions were permissible. But, this was not because the court thought them admissible despite s.41; rather, that section did not apply at all. Putting it aside, the questions were relevant in each case, to the credibility of the complainant, and so were admissible under ordinary common law principles.

Somewhat surprisingly, the court reached the conclusion, even without reference to the special interpretative canon contained in s.3(1) of the 1998 Act, that the questions at issue would not be "about any sexual behaviour" of the relevant complainant. In Keene L.J.'s words (at 639 (para. 33)):

> "It seems to this court that normally questions or evidence about false statements in the past by a complainant about sexual assaults or such questions or evidence about a failure to complain about the alleged assault which is the subject matter of the charge, while complaining about other sexual assaults, are not ones "about" any sexual behaviour of the complainant. They relate not to her sexual behaviour but to her statements in the past or her failure to complain."

More surprisingly, the court found inferential support, in *R. v Cox* (1986) 84 Cr.App.R. 132, CA (see main text, para. 19–48), for its conclusion. In fact, it was there held that a question about the complainant's, allegedly untrue, earlier complaint of rape by a third party *was* one "about" her "sexual experience", though application of the fairness criterion under s.2 of the 1976 Act dictated that the accused should be permitted to ask it.

Of course, had the court decided otherwise, it would, as it itself recognised, have faced a head-on collision with s.41(4) of the 1999 Act, which appears to rule out altogether questions about the complainant's sexual behaviour designed to attack her credibility. Had it been necessary, the court would have been willing, relying on *A (No. 2)*, to employ s.3(1) of the 1998 Act to "read down" s.41(4), thus rendering these entirely relevant questions admissible. Yet, the court's interpretation of "about any sexual behaviour" surely needs that subsection's special canon in order to be even moderately persuasive. There is no difficulty about the decision in *H*, which is supportable on the basis that the defence's case was that the allegations against others were untrue, and so is in line with *R. v S* [1992] Crim.L.R. 307, CA, decided under the 1976 Act—see main text, footnote 32. However, it was part-and-parcel of the questions sought to be put in *T* that the complainant had alleged sexual offences by others, yet certainly not that those allegations were untrue. To avoid application of s.41(4), the defence was quite at liberty simply to ask her why she had not made the complaint against T until long after the alleged events, but that would have been far less damaging to her credibility than was evidence that she had made specific allegations against others at a time when she could equally have made them against T.

This is not at all to say that the result in *T* is wrong; there is all the difference in the world between the very precise point about the complainant's credibility sought to be made by the defence there, on the one hand, and an attempt to blacken the complainant's character by reference to the mere fact of her sexual proclivities, in order to encourage the jury to suppose her likely to lie, on the other. But, bad legislation is just that, and, if courts are to engage in unlikely interpretative actions, it may be better for them to rely upon s.3(1), which at least has the merit of having been laid down by Parliament itself.

A final point about *T, H* is that the court noted that the defence might seek to suggest the untruthfulness of earlier allegations without having any evidential basis for such a suggestion. In its view, the questions would not, then, be designed to show that the complainant had lied, with the result that they *would* tend to show acts amounting to "sexual behaviour".

The second case, *R. v Mokrecovas* [2002] EWCA Crim 1644; [2002] 1 Cr.App.R. 226, was not directly concerned with the meaning of "sexual behaviour", but it is not without interest that the trial judge regarded questions about the complainant's alleged desire to spend the night with the accused's brother and the alleged fact that they had slept in the same bed as not being caught by that phrase. It is not obvious why this should be so, especially having regard to *R. v Viola* [1982] 1 W.L.R. 1138, CA (see this paragraph in main text).

One possible effect of the Court of Appeal having taken a narrow view, in *T, H* [2002] 1 W.L.R. 632, of "sexual behaviour", may be to breathe new life into the common law rules of inadmissibility. Certainly, it would be surprising if counsel were to be permitted to mount a general attack on the sexual character of the complainant simply because it did not reveal her "sexual behaviour". Furthermore, the court did point out that the complainant's interest in not being exposed to such an attack is bolstered by the right to a private life guaranteed by Article 8 of the Human Rights Convention—see at 640 (para. 38). **19–33**

(c) *The grounds for leave*

(i) THE TEST FOR LEAVE

As indicated in the text, according to s.41(2)(b), even evidence that gets through a s.41(3) or (5) gateway is not to be admitted unless the court is satisfied that to exclude it might have the result of rendering unsafe the conclusion of a jury on some relevant issue. No authority has yet emerged on the relationship, if any, between the s.41(2)(b) test and that under s.2(1)(a) of the Criminal Appeal Act 1968 (as amended). However, there is now a lot of authority on the s.2(1)(a) test itself, as well as on its connection with the accused's fair trial right under Article 6(1) of the Convention. What has emerged is a disagreement about the proper relationship between the test and the right. In *R. v Davis, Rowe and Johnson* [2001] 1 Cr.App.R, 115, decided before the Human Rights Act 1998 came into force, the Court of Appeal stressed that the two questions should be kept separate and apart, though the one would obviously and properly impinge upon the other. By contrast, in *R. v Togher, Doran and Parsons* [2001] 1 Cr.App.R. 457, CA, decided after that Act came into force, Lord Woolf C.J. expressed the view that, "if a defendant has been denied a fair trial, it will almost be inevitable that the conviction will be regarded as unsafe" (see *ibid.* at 468). That view was endorsed in a *dictum* of Lord Bingham, delivering the opinion of the House of Lords in *R. v Forbes* [2001] UKHL 40; [2001] 1 A.C. 473, at 487. For other authority, see *R. v Francom* [2001] 1 Cr.App.R. 237; *R. v Craven* [2001] 2 Cr.App.R. 181; *R. v Doubtfire* [2001] 2 Cr.App.R. 209; and *R. v Botmeh* [2002] 1 W.L.R. 531 (all CA). **19–37**

It seems entirely conceivable that it will be argued that, if the liberty to ask a question of a complainant about her sexual behaviour, or to adduce evidence about it, is demanded by the accused's Article 6(1) fair trial right, then, by analogy with Lord Woolf C.J.'s statement in *Togher et al.*, a refusal of the trial judge to allow the question to be asked, or evidence to be adduced, would inevitably render unsafe a jury conclusion on the matter at issue. The potential for s.41(2)(b) to be rendered nugatory by such an argument will be obvious.

(iii) Grounds under Section 2

19–40   In any event, it has recently been held that the matter is one for the trial judge, whose determination should be overturned on appeal only if "the decision to exclude the proffered evidence as being insufficiently relevant was either wrong in principle or plainly wrong as being outside [the] wide ambit" allowed to the judge: see *R. v Somers* [1999] Crim.L.R. 744, CA (transcript through LEXIS).

19–40   NOTE 54. However, an approach similar to the *R. v Nagrecha* one was taken in *R. v Willshire*, unreported, December 13, 1999, CA.

(iv) Grounds under Section 41

19–46   *Add at p. 498, line 31*: All of their Lordships in *R. v A (No. 2)* [2002] 1 A.C. 45 shared the view that it was not possible to use the special power of interpretation given to the courts by s.3(1) of the 1998 Act in order to extend the con-temporaneity requirement laid down by s.41(3)(b), i.e. "at or about the same time", to days, weeks or months. It is noteworthy that, during third reading debates in the House of Lords, a Government spokesman (Lord Williams of Mostyn) was quite willing to conceive of the requirement contemplating events that took place as much as 24 hours, or a little more, before or after the alleged offence: see H.L. Deb., Vol. 598, col. 1217, March 23, 1999.

Add at p. 498, line 34: The reader should bear in mind, at this point, the discussion of *A (No. 2)* [2002] 1 A.C. 45, HL, in this Supplement, particularly at paras 19–31B and 19–31C.

19–48   *Add at p. 499, line 38*: The statement in the preceding sentence in the text may well turn out to be wrong: see para. 19–46, above.

Add at p. 500, line 20: Since no issue about the prohibition in s.41(4) upon questions designed adversely to affect the complainant's credibility arose in *A (No. 2)* [2002] 1 A.C. 45, it is not surprising that their Lordships said little about it. Lord Hope of Craighead expressed the view that the subsection was unlikely to create problems, but that was essentially because he had in mind only inferences about her credibility arising for the mere fact that she had engaged in sexual behaviour on other occasions—see *ibid.* at 83 (para. 95). Lord Clyde was less sanguine, saying that the subsection would need to be "carefully handled in order to . . . secure the availability of evidence of sexual behaviour which is properly admissible as bearing on the issue of consent"—see *ibid.* at 98 (para. 138).
    Reflection upon the facts of *R. v T, H* [2002] 1 W.L.R. 632, considered at para. 19–32 of this Supplement, suggests that Lord Clyde was right to be cautious. In principle, it seems entirely conceivable that evidence of the complainant's sexual behaviour might be highly probative of a lack of specific credibility on her part, yet apparently fall foul of s.41(4). Of course, the narrow view of "sexual behaviour" taken in that case attenuates the risk of a collision between that subsection and Article 6(1), but, as we have seen already, the Court of Appeal declared itself willing to "read down" the subsection, were the need to arise. Though it is speculation, it may be that the answer will be to treat it as governing only questions about sexual behaviour in reality going to the complainant's

general credibility. If so, questions going to specific credibility, like those in *T, H* itself could be regarded as falling within s.41(3)(a), because the issue to which they would go would not be one of consent. This might be to exchange one problem for another, since, as is noted more than once in the main text—see, especially, paras 19–39 and 19–40—the distinction between evidence tending to show, directly, that the complainant consented and evidence tending to show her to be lying in saying that she did not consent has not met with universal judicial approval.

Furthermore, in *R. v Mokrecovas* [2002] 1 Cr.App.R. 226, the Court of Appeal adverted to the danger that defence counsel might seek to use s.41(3)(a) to "ride a coach and horses through the desirable policy reflected in s.41(4)"—see at 232. There, counsel had argued that questions sought to be asked of the complainant about her alleged sexual intercourse with the appellant's brother went, not to support the appellant's defence of consent to the rape charge, but to demonstrate that she had a motive for lying to her parents in accusing him of raping her. In principle, while this argument might have removed the case from the very restrictive régime of s.41(3)(b) and (c), it ought to have delivered it into the wholly negative régime of s.41(4), unless the court were prepared to have recourse to the argument, adumbrated above, that would distinguish specific from general credibility. In fact, the court decided that, given the other questions that could be put to the complainant, in order to establish a motive for lying, the allegations concerning the brother did not even meet the threshold requirement of relevance. Therefore, the court did not reach the issue of the proper ambit of s.41(4).

Add at p. 500, line 37: No detailed consideration was given to s.41(5) in A (No. **19–49** 2) [2002] 1 A.C. 45, yet it seems conceivable that, if the evidence in *R. v Redguard* [1991] Crim.L.R. 213, CA, were to be held inadmissible according to an ordinary interpretation of that subsection, s.3(1) of the 1998 Act might be prayed in aid, perhaps to extend the phrase "sexual behaviour" to include sexual attitudes, or even non-behaviour. However, after *R. v T, H* [2002] 1 W.L.R. 633, CA, considered in detail at para. 19–32 of this Supplement, it is hard to see how such an argument could succeed, unless the magnificent tool forged by Parliament can widen the meaning of the phrase where necessary for the accused's fair trial, just as it can narrow it, to the same end.

CHAPTER 20

PRIVILEGE

1.—THE NATURE OF THE PRIVILEGE

(3) Litigation privilege

20–06   Some Canadian courts have rejected the existence of distinctions between legal advice privilege and litigation privilege: *Lamey v Rice* (2000) 190 D.L.R. (4th) 486, New Brunswick CA; *Morrissey v Morrissey* 196 D.L.R. (4th) 94, Newfoundland CA.

(4) Privilege belongs to the client

20–07   NOTE 26. See now *Professional Conduct of Solicitors* (7th ed., 1999), para. 16.03, note 12.

(5) To what proceedings does privilege apply?

20–08   In *R (on the application of Morgan Grenfell) v Special Commissioners* [2002] UKHL 21, [2002] 2 W.L.R. 1299 the House of Lords held that the Human Rights Act required a different approach to be taken to the issue as to whether statutes abrogated legal professional privilege for the purpose of requiring information for regulatory and similar purposes. A statute should not be taken as abrogating such an important right as the right to claim legal professional privilege from production of documents unless the statute used express words or necessary implication. The House of Lords overruled *Price Waterhouse v BCCI* [1992] B.C.L.C. 583. Footnote 30 and the cases referred to in footnote 34 of the text should be read in the light of the *Morgan Grenfell* decision.

(6) The requirement of confidentiality

20–09   NOTE 35. See now *Professional Conduct of Solicitors* (7th ed., 1999), para. 16.01.

(9) Privilege and Human Rights

See also *Linstead v East Sussex Brighton & Hove Health Authority* [2001]   **20–12**
P.I.Q.R. 25 (a party's Article 6 rights did not have the effect of overriding legal
professional privilege)

(10) Who is a lawyer for this purpose

Also see *Gower v Tolko Manitoba Inc* (2001) 196 D.L.R. (4th) 716, Manitoba   **20–13**
CA upheld decision reported at (2000) 181 D.L.R. (4th) 353.

2.—FACETS OF LEGAL ADVICE PRIVILEGE

(1) What communications are covered

(c) *Lawyers' feenotes*

In *Alcoota v CLC* [2001] N.T.S.C. 30 the Supreme Court of the Northern   **20–20**
Territory held that bills of costs were not privileged *per se*, but could be to the
extent that they contained or referred to confidential matters that disclosed the
subject of the communications.

(d) *Matters within the knowledge of the solicitor about the client*

In *China National Petroleum Corp v Fenwick Elliott*, unreported, January 31,   **20–21**
2002 Morritt V.C. held that where a witness statement was taken in confidence,
the solicitor might be precluded by privilege from revealing the identity of the
person whose statement had been taken

In *Brown v Bennett* (2002) 99(8) L.S.G. 35, The Times December 17, 2001,
Neuberger J held that it would not infringe privilege for counsel to be asked
whether they had seen or knew of certain documents. The documents were not
privileged in themselves. The purpose was to find out whether counsel had seen
the documents, not to find out what was in the brief. The purpose was in aid of
a wasted costs application.

On use of the privilege to protect a client's identity see *Miley v Flood* [2001]
I.E.H.C. 9 (Irish High Court); and *CIBC Mellon Trust Co v Stolzenberg*,
unreported 15 November 2000, Ch D., affirmed [2001] EWCA Civ 1222.

(e) *Facts not being part of the continuum*

See *C v C (privilege: criminal communications)* [2002] Fam. 42; [2001] 3   **20–22**
W.L.R. 446 (conversation with solicitor about quote for conveyancing work not
privileged).

3.—FACETS OF LITIGATION PRIVILEGE

(1) The dominant purpose test

20–26   Also see *Bailey v Beagle Management Pty Ltd* [2001] 182 A.L.R. 264.

(8) Litigants in person

20–36   NOTE 27. In *S County Council v B* [2000] Fam. 76, Charles J. said that although communications with experts in non-adversarial proceedings such as proceedings involving children were not privileged because there was no litigation privilege, that did not mean that the court overrode privilege which had come into existence in other proceedings, namely the father's criminal proceedings.

4.—WHO CAN CLAIM PRIVILEGE: PRINCIPAL AND AGENT

20–37   In *Surface Technology v Young* [2002] F.S.R. 387 Pumfrey J. held that a successor in title to identified property might assert the privilege of his vendor regarding documents prepared for the purpose of legal advice relating to the property transfer and advice given. Where the vendor, which was a subsidiary of another company, sought legal advice with its parent, the successor could claim joint privilege against the third party for such communications.

8.—COPIES

(2) Copy of non-privileged document created for privileged purpose

20–51   In *Sumitomo v Credit Lyonnais Rouse* [2001] EWCA Civ 1152; [2002] 1 W.L.R. 479, the Court of Appeal held that no privilege attached to translations of documents in the possession of a party which were unprivileged in their original form, even though the translations were made (and the translated documents brought into existence) for the purpose of litigation.

(4) The *Lyell v Kennedy* exception

20–53   The *Lyell v Kennedy* exception suffered another blow in *Sumitomo v Credit Lyonnais Rouse* [2001] EWCA Civ 1152; [2002] 1 W.L.R. 479. There the Court of Appeal disapproved *Dubai Bank v Galadari (No. 7)* and held that the *Lyell v Kennedy* exception could not apply to selections of documents which were in the control of the party making the selection (as opposed to selections of third party documents).

CHAPTER 21

PRIVILEGE: OTHER FORMS OF PRIVILEGE

1.—JOINT PRIVILEGE

As to joint privilege claimed by a successor in title see 20–37 supra.   **21–01**

A company may claim litigation privilege in a dispute with its shareholders but   **21–01**
otherwise the company's communications with lawyers are not privileged against
shareholders as the shareholder is a *cestui que trust* and is in principle entitled to
see an opinion as to his property: *CAS (Nominees) Ltd v Nottingham Forest plc*
[2001] 1 All E.R. 954; *Re Hydrosan* [1991] B.C.L.C. 418.

See the recent extraordinary case of *TSB v Robert Irving and Burns* [1999]   **21–01**
Lloyds Rep. I.R. 528 (the Court of Appeal decision is also reported at [2000] 2
All E.R. 826) as to the problems as to conflicts of interest and privilege when the
same lawyers represent insurer and insured.

NOTE 4. A company may claim litigation privilege in a dispute with its   **21–01**
shareholders but otherwise the company's communications with lawyers are not
privileged against shareholders as the shareholder is a *cestui que trust* and is in
principle entitled to see an opinion as to his property: *CAS (Nominees) Ltd v
Nottingham Forest plc* [2001] 1 All E.R. 954, *Re Hydrosan* [1991] B.C.L.C.
418.

2.—COMMON INTEREST PRIVILEGE

(3) What sort of interest will suffice?

Also see *Anderson v John Zivanovic Holdings Ltd* (2000) 195 D.L.R. (4th)   **21–05**
713, Ontario Superior Court of Justice (no common interest between bankrupt
and trustee, but privilege upheld on grounds of public policy); *R. v Trutch*,
unreported Court of Appeal, July 25, 2001 (no common interest privilege in
affidavit sent by one party to another as part of settlement between them).

3.—WITHOUT PREJUDICE PRIVILEGE

(1) The "without prejudice rule"

21–10   As to the rule generally see D. McGrath, "Without prejudice privilege" (2001) 5 E & P 213.

(2) When is correspondence treated as within the without prejudice rule

21–11   The decision of Laddie J. in *Unilever v Procter & Gamble* is reported on appeal at [2000] 1 W.L.R. 2436. The decision on appeal is discussed at para. 21–14, below.

21–11   The principle in *Re Daintrey* [1893] 2 Q.B. 116 is increasingly being confined narrowly. In *Cadle Co v Hearley* [2002] 1 Lloyds Rep 143 the judge refused to permit without prejudice correspondence to be admitted for the purpose of showing an acknowledgement of a debt. The *Daintrey* principle merely related to the admission of "independent unrelated facts" which were stated in without prejudice correspondence.

(3) The three party situation

21–13   The subsequent litigation in the two party situation need not relate to the same subject-matter: *Instance v Denny Bros Printing* [2001] EWCA Civ 939; [2002] R.P.C. 14, *per* Lloyd J. considering the speech of Lord Griffiths in *Rush and Tompkins*.

21–14   *Muller v Linsley and Mortimer* [1996] 1 P.N.L.R. 74 was followed without comment in *Dora v Simper, The Times*, May 26, 1999. In *Unilever v Procter & Gamble* [2001] 1 All E.R. 783, Robert Walker L.J. recognised the *Muller* decision, but said that it would often be the case that comments made at a negotiating meeting consisted of a mixture of admissions, assertions, offers and statements which could be interpreted as threats. It would often be impractical to unravel them as between those which were privileged and those which were not, and to seek to do so would undermine the privilege. See also the judgment of Lloyd J. in *Instance v Denny Bros Printing, The Times*, February 27, 2000 and *Murrell v Healy* [2001] 4 All E.R. 345 at 350, CA.

(4) When without prejudice documentation may be admitted in evidence

21–15   There is an authoritative review of the circumstances in which without prejudice correspondence may be admitted in evidence in the judgment of Robert Walker L.J. in *Unilever v Procter & Gamble* [2001] 1 All E.R. 783. See also *Knightstone Housing Association v Crawford*, unreported, October 27, 1999, EAT; *Somatra v Sinclair Roche and Temperley* [2000] 2 Lloyd's Rep. 673, CA and *The Giovanna* [1999] 1 Lloyd's Rep. 867.
     As to use of evidence from without prejudice negotiations on *ex parte* hearings, see *Somatra v Sinclair Roche and Temperley* [2000] 2 Lloyd's Rep.

673, *The Giovanna* [1999] 1 Lloyd's Rep. 867 and *Re Anglo Insurance Co*, unreported, November 8, 2000, *per* Neuberger J.

(5) Admissibility of without prejudice correspondence on issues of costs

See *UYB v British Railways Board*, [2000] 43 L.S.G. 602, CA.   **21–16**

(6) Admission of without prejudice communications to prevent impropriety

There have been a number of cases on this point; see *Knightstone Housing*   **21–17**
Association v Crawford, unreported, October 27, 1999, EAT, *Merrill Lynch v Raffa*, unreported, May 15, 2000, *Kooltrade v XTS*, [2001] F.S.R. 158.

In *WH Smith Ltd v Peter Colman* [2001] F.S.R. 91 CA the Court of Appeal said that the "unambiguous impropriety" test was not satisfied merely because a party was putting forward an implausible or inconsistent case, or facing an uphill struggle if the litigation continued.

The extent to which without prejudice privilege can be waived was considered by the Court of Appeal in *Somatra v Sinclair Roche & Temperley* [2000] 2 Lloyd's Rep. 673. Somatra sued their previous solicitors for negligence. The solicitors counterclaimed for their fees and obtained a freezing injunction. They referred to without prejudice meetings pursuant to their duty of disclosure on the application without notice. In fact, the negotiations were covertly taped by Somatra who sought to use the admission of the negotiations by the solicitors as a waiver entitling them to use them at trial. The Court of Appeal held that as the solicitors had put the without prejudice material in issue on the Mareva application, the other party were free to make use of their tapes in evidence.

4.—PRIVILEGE AGAINST SELF-INCRIMINATION

(1) The privilege against self-incrimination

See the restatement of the rule in *R. v Herts CC, Ex p. Green Industries Ltd*   **21–18**
[2000] 2 W.L.R. 373 at 377, *per* Lord Hoffmann. Also see *Microsoft Corporation v CX Computer Pty Ltd* [2002] F.C.A. 3, Australian Federal Court.

(2) When does the privilege apply?

This is another area in which the Human Rights Act has led to a number of   **21–20**
cases. The ECHR jurisprudence is set out in *Saunders v UK* (1997) 23 E.H.R.R. 313 at 337, para. 67, *Le Compte Van Leuven and de Mayers v Belgium* [1982] 5 E.H.R.R. 183. However, in civil cases the courts have not been applying different principles here since the Human Rights Act, save in determining whether the privilege has been abrogated by statute: see 21–21 below. In *V v C*, Court of Appeal, 16 October 2001, the defendant refused to put in a defence on the ground that it might assist the crown in criminal proceedings against him. The Court of Appeal said that the privilege against self-incrimination did not give him the right

not to put in a defence. By not putting in a defence what the defendant was doing was in effect asking the court to exercise its jurisdiction to stay the litigation pending criminal proceedings; on the facts, the court declined to do so.

In *Bell Cablemedia v Simmons* [2002] F.S.R. 34 CA the defendant was accused of taking bribes and returned on request the claimants' laptop, leaving in it by mistake a diskette which was said to provide damning evidence of his wrongdoing. He sought to prevent the diskette being adduced by the claimants in evidence, relying on the privilege against self-incrimination. The Court of Appeal pointed out that he had returned it voluntarily (albeit in error) and there was no principle which precluded the claimants from relying on it.

See also 21–29 below.

21–20   NOTE 87. As to self-incrimination under foreign law, see *Re BCCI SA*, unreported, December 6, 1999, *Surzur Overseas v Koros* [1999] 2 Lloyd's Rep. 611; *Brannigan v Davison* [1997] A.C. 238; *Morris v Banque Arab & International D'Investissement SA* [2001] 1 B.C.L.C. 275; (2000) 97(42) L.S.G. 43.

21–20   NOTE 89. The privilege can be claimed in contempt proceedings: *Memory Corp Plc v Sidhu (No.2)* [2000] Ch. 645; [2000] 2 W.L.R. 1106.

21–21   Where there is an express abrogation of the privilege, no problem arises in construing the statute and the only issue is the effect of Article 6 of the ECHR. Where the statute is unclear as to whether the privilege has been abrogated, or whether the material may be used in subsequent criminal proceedings, the court must construe the statute in accordance with the principles set out by the House of Lords in *R. v Herts CC, Ex p. Green Industries Ltd* [2000] A.C. 412. See also *Brown v Stott* [2001] 2 All E.R. 97, PC. The court will now adopt where possible a construction which does not provide an express abrogation of the privilege in cases involving a "criminal charge" where Article 6(2) of the Convention applies. So it will be important to determine whether what is in issue is a criminal charge or penalty. It was not in directors' disqualification proceedings: see *Re Westminster Property Management, Official Receiver v Stern* [2001] 1 All E.R. 633, CA. A financial penalty by way of confiscation order under the Drug Trafficking legislation was not imposed on persons charged with a criminal offence and thus the greater protection under s.6(2) of the Convention was not available: *McIntosh v Lord Advocate* [2001] 2 All E.R. 638, PC.

(6) Orders prohibiting use of potentially incriminating material

21–27   Note that the Youth Justice and Criminal Evidence Act 1999 amends a number of these statutes to provide that material obtained pursuant to these regulatory powers of investigation cannot be used at a subsequent criminal trial.

(7) Claiming the privilege

21–28   NOTE 20. See *Re Great Futures International*, unreported, March 22, 2001, *per* Neuberger J.

21–28   NOTE 21. See *Memory Corp v Siddhu* [2000] Ch. 645.

(8) The European Convention of Human Rights

21–29   An accused is entitled under Article 6 to remain silent and not to contribute to incriminating himself: see *Funke v France* [1993] 1 C.M.L.R. 897.

In *Saunders v United Kingdom* [1997] 23 E.H.R.R. 313, the Court of Human Rights held that the use of DTI transcripts in evidence was a breach of Article 6. The court distinguished the requirement for a person to produce relevant evidence in support of the case against him, such as documents, which was compatible with the Convention, with an infringement of the right to remain silent, which was not. See also *IJL v UK, The Times,* October 13, 2000, ECHR.

This distinction was emphasised in *R. v Herts County Council, Ex p. Green Environmental Industries Ltd* [2000] A.C. 412, HL. The local authority served on the applicant notices requesting information in respect of the discovery of large quantities of clinical waste found on the applicants' sites, and refused to undertake that the answers would not be used against them in subsequent prosecution. The applicants challenged the notices, issued under s.71(2) of the Environmental Protection Act 1990. The House of Lords held that the Article 6 protection did not arise at the stage of validity of the notices, and s.71(2) precluded the claiming of privilege against self-incrimination. There was no reason why the authority should not use the answers in reaching a decision as to whether to prosecute. Article 6 arose in the context of the criminal trial, and the question whether the answers should be admitted was for the trial judge.

In order to bring legislation in line with Article 6, the statutory discretion of criminal trial judges to exclude evidence has been widened see s.78 of the Police and Criminal Evidence Act 1984 and the Schedule to the Youth Justice and Criminal Evidence Act 1999.

See subsequently *R. v Central Criminal Court, Ex p. Bright* [2001] 2 All E.R. 244, DC, and *Secretary of State for Trade and Industry v Bright, The Times,* April 11, 2001, *per* Ferris J.

CHAPTER 22

LOSS AND ABUSE OF PRIVILEGE

1.—WAIVER OF PRIVILEGE

(2) Confidentiality and privilege

22–02   See *Brown v Bennett, The Times,* June 13, 2000 *per* Neuberger J.
As to the distinction between confidentiality and privilege, see also *TSB v Robert Irving and Burns* [1999] Lloyd's Rep. I.R. 528, the Court of Appeal decision is also reported at [2000] 2 All E.R. 826.

(3) Express waiver of privilege: general principles

22–03   A rather different type of waiver of privilege (in cases where there is a conflict of interest) can be seen in the unusual case of *TSB v Robert Irving and Burns* [1999] Lloyd's Rep. I.R. 528, the Court of Appeal decision is also reported at [2000] 2 All E.R. 826.

(4) Privilege belongs to the client

22–04   See now the 7th edition of the *Guide to Professional Conduct of Solicitors* (1999).

(5) When is privilege lost?

(j) *Documents referred to in expert reports and instructions to the expert*

22–15   See *Taylor v Bolton HA*, unreported QBD, January 14, 2000, *per* Morland J.

(l) *To what proceedings does waiver extend*

22–17   As to waiver in relation to without prejudice communications, see *Somatra v Sinclair Roche & Temperley* [2000] 2 Lloyd's Rep. 673, CA discussed at para. 21–17, above.

2.—WAIVER OF PRIVILEGE: WAIVER EXTENDING TO COLLATERAL OR
ASSOCIATED DOCUMENTS

(5) Waiver of privilege on taxation of costs

In *Giambrone v JMC Holidays Ltd* [2002] EWHC 495 Nelson J. held that **22–25**
privilege was not lost when privileged documents were supplied to the costs
judge under CPR PD 40.2(i) and 40.2.14. The procedure is for the judge to direct
a witness statement and for him to be shown the documents, so that he may
decide whether to put the party to its election either to disclose the documents to
the other party and to rely on them, or to decline to disclose the documents and
merely rely on the witness statement. To the same effect is the decision of
Pumfrey J. in *South Coast Shipping v Havant BC* [2002] 3 All E.R. 779, Ch D.
Also see *Dickinson v Rushmer* (2002) 152 New L.J. 58, Ch D.

(6) Wasted costs proceedings

In *Metcalf v Mardell* [2002] 3 W.L.R. 172 the House of Lords considered the **22–26**
position of a barrister faced with an application for a wasted costs order who was
precluded from giving a full answer by his client's privilege which had not been
waived. The court must proceed in such circumstances with great care and should
not make an order unless satisfied there was nothing the barrister could say if
unconstrained, in resisting the application.

4.—WAIVER OF PRIVILEGE: INADVERTENT DISCLOSURE

(2) Inadvertent Disclosure in the course of proceedings

The Court of Appeal reviewed the cases including *Breeze v John Stacey and* **22–32**
Sons [1999] 96 (28) LSG 27 in *Al Fayed v Commissioner of Police for the*
Metropolis [2002] EWCA Civ 78; *The Times*, June 17, 2002. The principles
relating to inadvertent disclosure in the course of proceedings applied both to
privilege and public interest immunity. The fact that the solicitor in question took
a view in good faith was a relevant pointer in deciding how a reasonable solicitor
would have acted. However, this was an equitable jurisdiction and thus there
were no rigid rules. The basis of the court's decision whether to permit reliance
on the document under CPR 31.20 should be exercised on the same principles as
were established from the cases.

5.—LOSS OF PRIVILEGE THROUGH FRAUD

(1) No privilege in iniquity

When a client phoned his solicitor's office and demanded to know who priced **22–34**
the quote for his conveyancing because he wanted to "rip someone's throat out"

he could not claim privilege for the statement as it was tantamount to a threat to kill. The decision of the judge to contrary effect was reversed: *C v C* [2001] 3 W.L.R. 446, CA.

(2) To what sort of fraud does the role apply?

22-35   See *The David Agmashenebeli*, unreported, January 2, 2001, *per* Colman J. Also see *Idoport Pty Ltd v National Australia Bank Ltd* [2001] N.S.W.S.C. 22, New South Wales Supreme Court, considering s.125 of the Evidence Act 1995.

CHAPTER 23

THE IMPLIED UNDERTAKING

1.—THE UNDERTAKING

(3) Express undertaking

As to means of protecting confidential documents required to be disclosed, see **23–05**
Premier Profiles Ltd v Tioxide Europe Ltd Moore-Bick J., September 20,
2002.

(5) Granting leave to use the documents

See *Bourns v Raychem (No. 2)* [2000] F.S.R. 841, CA.   **23–07**

(7) Termination of the undertaking

In *Killick v PriceWaterhouseCooper*, unreported, October 11, 2000, Ferris J. **23–09**
said that the CPR had not altered the *Riddick v Thames Board Mills* decision, and
the position has not been altered by CPR, r.31.22. In deciding whether to give
leave it is, however, relevant to look at what documents could be obtained on an
order for non-party disclosure under CPR, r.31.17.

In *Barings plc v Coopers & Lybrand* [2000] 3 All E.R. 910, CA the judge in **23–10**
Barings directors disqualification proceedings had read many of the voluminous
documents in the trial bundles but it was impossible to tell (for the purpose of
determining whether the documents could be used in subsequent proceedings)
whether the judge had actually read Board of Banking Supervision transcripts
exhibited to an affidavit. The judge could not be cross-examined as to what he
had read. So the only practical solution was that the onus was on the person who
wished to show that the documents had not come into the public domain because,
for example, the judge had not in fact read them. There was always a power
under CPR, r. 31.22 restricting or prohibiting subsequent use of a document
which is treated as having come into the public domain as a result of being "read
to or by the court" at a hearing held in public.
The Court of Appeal set out guidelines with particular application to patent
cases where there was an application under CPR 31.22 for documents to remain
confidential after trial, in *Lilly Icos Ltd v Pfizer (No 2)* [2002] 1 W.L.R. 2253,
CA. Assertions of confidentiality were not good enough; there needed to be
specific evidence as to why a party would be damaged.

(8) The implied undertaking in criminal cases

NOTE 55. An appeal in *Preston BC v McGrath* was dismissed: see *The Times*, **23–12**
May 19, 2000.

CHAPTER 24

FACTS EXCLUDED BY PUBLIC POLICY

1.—Exclusion of Evidence by Public Policy

(2) The development of public interest immunity to the present day

24–09   The ECHR considered public interest immunity in *Rowe and Davis v UK, The Times*, March 1, 2000. The procedure must be adversarial and equality of arms was one of the fundamental prerequisites of a fair trial. The right to an adversarial trial meant, at least in a criminal case, that both prosecution and defence had to be given the opportunity to have knowledge of and comment on the observations filed and the evidence adduced by the other party. The entitlement to disclosure was not however an absolute right as in any criminal proceedings there might be competing interests such as national security, protection of witnesses and the like which had to be weighed against the rights of the defendant. Only such measures restricting the rights of the defence which were strictly necessary were permissible under Article 6. Difficulties caused to the defence had to be counterbalanced by the procedures followed by the judicial authorities. It was for the national courts to assess whether the evidence justified non-disclosure. It was for the ECHR to ascertain whether the decision-making procedure applied complied with the requirements of adversarial proceedings and of equality of arms: see *Brandsetter v Austria*, unreported, August 28, 1991, Series A, No. 211, *Edwards v UK* (1993) 15 EHRR 417, *Doorson v Netherlands* (1996) 22 EHRR 330; *Van Mechelen v Netherlands* (1998) 25 EHRR 647.

In *R. v Smith (Joe), The Times*, December 20, 2000, the Court of Appeal held there was no breach of Article 6 in the procedure involving a preliminary *ex parte* ruling by the judge as to public interest immunity. Also see *R. v Botmeh* [2002] 1 W.L.R. 531, CA; *Altan v UK* (2002) 34 E.H.R.R. 33, E.Ct.H.R.

(3a) Consequences of a finding of public interest immunity

24–10A   Normally, if an application to suppress evidence on the grounds of public interest immunity is successful no use may be made of the evidence in the ensuing proceedings. In *R. v Smith* [2001] 1 W.L.R. 1031, the Court of Appeal held that it was not a violation of the "equality of arms" principle implicit in Article 6 for the judge to use information received during an *ex parte* public interest immunity investigation and not disclosed to the defence to determine whether the police had reasonable suspicion to arrest the defendant and therefore under the procedure laid down in PACE to take a non-intrusive sample without the defendant's consent.

(4) Claiming immunity: Criminal Cases

See *Phipson*, paras 9–51, 9–52 not Chap. 10.   **24–11**

NOTE 47. In *Jasper v UK* (2000) 30 EHRR 441 para. 61 the E.Ct.HR. emphasized   **24–11** that the "balancing exercise is weighted in favour of disclosing material in recognition of the importance of achieving the fullest possible disclosure of relevant material."
Also see *R. v Botmeh* [2002] 1 W.L.R. 531, CA.

(5) Claiming immunity: Civil Cases

In appropriate cases the immunity may be resolved in advance of the trial: see   **24–13** *Kinsella v Chief Constable of Nottingham, The Times*, August 24, 1999 *per* Tucker J. On the judge inspecting the documents to determine the claim see *Alcoota v CLC* [2001] N.T.S.C. 30, Supreme Court of the Northern Territory.

2.—Categories of Documents which may be Subject to Immunity

(4) Workings of central government

Also see *Commonwealth of Australia v CFMEU* (2000) 98 F.C.R. 31; *Alcoota*   **24–19** *v CLC* [2001] N.T.S.C. 30; *NTEIU v Commonwealth of Australia* [2001] F.CA. 610, Australian Federal Court.

(5) Proper functioning of the public service

Also see *R. v Brushett* [2001] Crim.L.R. 471, CA; *Gunn-Russo v Nugent Care*   **24–20** *Society,* unreported, Administrative Court, July 20, 2001.

(6) The police

Also see *R. (Green) v Prosecution Service* [2002] EWCA Civ 389, CA.   **24–21**

(7) Confidentiality and confidential relationships

Also see *Long v Attorney-General* [2001] 2 N.Z.L.R. 529, N.Z.H.Ct.; *Straka*   **24–22** *v Humber River Regional Hospital* (2000) 193 D.L.R. (4th) 680, Ontario CA.

(8) Protection of sources and informants

If the public interest comes down in favour of excluding evidence to prevent   **24–23** identification of an informer, the judge has no discretion to avoid excluding the evidence by holding the trial in camera: *Powell v Chief Constable of North Wales Constabulary, The Times*, February 11, 2000, CA.

The Human Rights Act 1998 has ushered in a case specific approach in relation to the disclosure of the identity of informants in civil cases. In *Chief Constable of Greater Manchester v McNally* [2002] EWCA Civ 14 [2002] Crim.L.R. 832; *The Times*, March 6, 2002, the Court of Appeal upheld a decision to order the police, who were the defendants in an action for wrongful arrest, false imprisonment and malicious prosecution, to disclose whether a witness was a police informer.

(g) Information leading to the detection of crime

24–23   In *R. v Looseley* [2001] UKHL 53; [2001] 1 WLR 2060 para. 125 Lord Scott said that it was well established that the prosecution must disclose information, including the identity of an informer, that may prove the accused's innocence. If the prosecution is unwilling to disclose the identity of an informer, the prosecution will usually have to be abandoned. However, if entrapment is alleged and there is an issue as to whether police officers had sufficient grounds for suspecting an individual of involvement in crime in order to justify an undercover operation "the police should not . . . . be expected to disclose the source of their suspicions if to do so would reveal the identity of an informant or prejudice their ability to obtain similar information in the future."

In *Chief Constable of Greater Manchester Police v McNally* [2002] EWCA Civ 14; [2002] Crim.L.R. 832; *The Times,* March 6, 2002, the Court of Appeal said that material relating to the identity of informers could be the subject of public interest immunity in civil cases as well as criminal, particularly in wrongful imprisonment and malicious prosecution cases. In performing the balancing act between the interest in protecting the informer and the right to a fair trial, the court would now need to have in mind Articles 2 and 8 of the Convention.

Also see *Carnduff v Rock* [2001] 1 W.L.R. 1786, CA.

24–24   NOTE 90. *R. v Dervish* [2001] EWCA Crim 2789; [2002] 2 Cr.App.R. 6.

(11) Records relating to children

24–26   The immunity that attaches to social service documents about children is not absolute. If the records are wanted for criminal proceedings involving allegations of sexual abuse, documents that might prove innocence or avoid a miscarriage of justice such as false allegations by the complainant in the past and anything that suggested that some other adult had indulged in similar activity with the child should be disclosed but not documents that would enable endless cross-examination as to credit on very peripheral matters to take place: *R. v Brushett*, December 21, 2000, unreported, CA. This flexible and pragmatic approach, the court held in Brushett, reconciles the principles laid down in *R. v Keane* (1994) 99 Cr.App.R. 1 with *R. v Reading Justices Ex p. Berkshire County Council* [1996] 1 Cr.App.R. 239 and complies with the requirements of Article 6 of the ECHR.

In *R (A Child)* [2002] 1 F.L.R. 755, in which a local authority sought public law orders, Charles J. said in that the "general statements that one sees in textbooks and hears that social work records are covered by public interest immunity . . . should now be consigned to history". The grounds for claiming public interest immunity must "set out with particularity the harm that it is alleged will be caused to the public interest . . . if material which passes the threshold test for disclosure is disclosed with or without appropriate redaction in the relevant proceedings." If a claim for non-disclosure is based on article 8 a compelling case for non-disclosure must be made and any non-disclosure must go no further than strictly necessary.

(12) Waiver of public interest immunity

In *Al-Fayed v Commissioner of Police of the Metropolis* [2002] EWCA Civ **24–27** 780; (2002) 99 (30) L.S. G. 39 the Court of Appeal said that where a party had inspected documents subject to public interest immunity which had been mistakenly disclosed Civil Procedure Rules 1998 Pt 31 r.31.20 and the principles laid down in *Guinness Peat Properties Ltd v Fitzroy Robinson Partnership* [1987] 1 W.L.R. 1027 apply.

3.—EXCLUSION OF EVIDENCE RELEVANT TO THE ADJUDICATIVE PROCESS

(5) Jurors

NOTE 13. On the issues of whether jury secrecy is compatible with Article 6 of **24–32** the ECHR and the scope of the jury secrecy rule see *R. v Pan, R. v Sawyer* [2001] S.C.C. 42, June 29, 2001, SCC; *R. v Quereshi* [2002] 1 Cr.App.R.433, *R. v Mirza* [2002] EWCA Crim 1235.

NOTE 14. In *R. v Allan*, April 6, 2001, unreported, CA, it is mentioned that the Court of Appeal had allowed the police to investigate communications that took place between jurors and court staff during a previous trial of the appellant.

4.—TELEPHONE INTERCEPTS

The provisions on telephone interception in the Interception of Communica- **24–33** tions Act 1985 have been superseded by the Regulation of Investigatory Powers Act 2000 (henceforth RIP Act) for matters arising since October 2000. The new Act deals with interception of all forms of communication without consent through public and private telecommunications systems and public postal systems. The definition of a public telecommunications system (s.2) is suffi- ciently wide to include any Internet service provider, mobile phone service or web server. The Act thus applies to all new forms of communication such as e-mail, instant messaging, voicemail, faxes, satellite telephones and radio-pagers. Intentional interception is generally a criminal offence under s.1 of the RIP Act unless:

   a. done pursuant to a warrant issued by the Secretary of State (or, in an emergency, a senior official) (s.7) or

   b. those conducting the interception have reasonable grounds for believing that the interception is with the consent of the sender and intended recipient of the communication (s.3(1)): where the sender but not the intended recipient (or vice versa) has consented, authorisation must be obtained under Pt II of the Act (s.3(2)) or

c. the interception involves a private telecommunication system and is by, or with the consent of, the person with the right to control it (s.1(6)).

Material intercepted under a warrant may be disclosed to the prosecutor in criminal proceedings to enable the prosecutor to assess whether a prosecution would be fair (s.15(4)(d)). Under the 1985 Act this was not permitted: *R. v P* [2001] 2 All E.R. 58 at 71–73. It is arguable, though unlikely, that disclosure to the prosecution without disclosure to the defence contravenes the "equality of arms" principle implicit in Article 6. Normally no mention may be made in legal proceedings of the existence of an interception warrant or the data collected under it by any party. Section 17 of the RIP Act provides:

"(1) Subject to s.18, no evidence shall be adduced question asked, assertion or disclosure made or other thing done in, for the purposes of or in connection with any legal proceedings which (in any manner)–

   (a) discloses in circumstances from which its origin in anything falling within subs.(2) may be inferred, any of the contents of an intercepted communication or any related communications data or
   (b) tends (apart from any such disclosure) to suggest that anything falling within subs.(2) has or may have occurred or be going to occur.

(2) The following fall within this subsection–

   (a) conduct by a person falling within subs.(3) that was or would be an offence under s.1(1) or (2) of this Act or under s.1 of the Interception of Communications Act 1985;
   (b) a breach by the Secretary of State of his duty under s.1(4) of this Act;
   (c) the issue of an interception warrant or of a warrant under the Interception of Communications Act 1985;
   (d) the making of an application by any person for an interception warrant, or for a warrant under that Act;
   (e) the imposition of any requirement on any person to provide assistance with giving effect to an interception warrant.

(3) The persons referred to in subs.(2)(a) are–

   (a) any person to whom a warrant under this Chapter may be addressed;
   (b) any person holding office under the Crown;
   (c) any member of the National Criminal Intelligence Service;
   (d) any member of the National Crime Squad;
   (e) any person employed by or for the purposes of a police force;
   (f) any person providing a postal service or employed for the purposes of any business of providing such a service and
   (g) any person providing a public telecommunications service or employed for the purposes of any business of providing such a service.

(4) In this section "intercepted communications" means any communication intercepted in the course of its transmission by means of a postal service or telecommunication system."

The exceptions, which are set out in s.18, relate in the main to statutory offences protecting the integrity of postal and telecommunication systems, immigration appeals and the Official Secrets Acts.

In *Morgans v DPP* [2000] 2 W.L.R. 386, the House of Lords overruled *R. v Rasool* [1997] 2 Cr.App.R. 190 and held that intercepts carried out by consent were inadmissible in evidence if they were communications falling within s.1(1) of the 1985 Act. See also *R (NTL Group Ltd) v Crown Court at Ipswich* [2002] 3 W.L.R. 1173 (interception of emails).

CHAPTER 25

THE RULE AGAINST HEARSAY

1.—THE RULE AT COMMON LAW

(3) Application of the rule

(b) *Previous identifications*

25–14   In *R. v Ward* [2001] Crim.L.R. 316 (transcript: New Law Online, case
3001211101), the Court of Appeal was confronted with an apparently novel
situation in which the identification had been by the defendant himself. A police
officer had stopped a vehicle that was involved in the crime and one of the
occupants had identified himself to the officer as Michael Kevin Ward and given
Ward's correct date of birth and address. The officer could not in court identify
the defendant as the person who had previously identified himself. The Court of
Appeal ruled that the officer's evidence was clearly hearsay and rejected a
submission that it was being put forward only to establish the fact that the
statement of identity had been made. However, the court went on to hold that the
identification was a statement adverse to the defendant's interests and so hearsay
evidence of it was admissible. The court noted the obvious circularity as the
hearsay evidence was only admissible if the identification had been a statement
adverse to the interests of its maker—which depended on whether the Ward had
been its maker, the proof of which matter was the reason for seeking to admit the
hearsay evidence in the first place. Another approach to the problem might have
been to make a proleptic assumption of admissibility and then evaluate the worth
of the admission: *cf.* in a completely different context, the approach to a
somewhat analogous problem of circular reasoning in *Mackender v Feldia*
[1967] 2 Q.B. 590, CA.

CHAPTER 26

HEARSAY IN CIVIL PROCEEDINGS

1.—INTRODUCTION

The machinery of the Civil Evidence Act 1995 applies to anti-social behaviour **26–02** orders as they are civil, not criminal in nature: *R. (McCann) v Manchester Crown Ct* [2002] UKHL 39; [2002] 3 W.L.R. 1313, HL.

3.—SAFEGUARDS: SECTIONS 2–4

In *McPhilemy v Times Newspapers*, unreported, June 6, 2000, the Court of **26–05** Appeal made clear that the CPR had not altered the *Filiatra Legacy* rule.

HEARSAY IN CRIMINAL PROCEEDINGS

2.—CRIMINAL JUSTICE ACT 1967, s.9 AND CRIMINAL JUSTICE ACT 1988, ss.23–26

(9) "A statement made by a person in a document"

27–13   *R. v Derodra* [2000] 1 Cr.App.R. 41, CA. According to Sir John Smith, "Documentary Evidence in Criminal Proceedings" in (1999) 149 N.L.J. 1550 the construction adopted in *Derodra* cannot be right.

(15) Witnesses who cannot be found

27–19   In deciding whether "all reasonable steps have been taken to find" the maker of the statement it is proper for the judge to consider the importance of the witness and the resources of the police, but not the seriousness of the offence with which the defendant is charged: *R. v Coughlan*, March 2, 1999, (CA, unreported).

(16) Witnesses in fear or kept out of the way

27–20   Article 6 of the European Convention on Human Rights requires the judge to give reasons for admitting a statement under s.23(4): *R. v Clive Denton* [2001] 1 Cr.App.R. 227.

Fear that is relevant is fear at the time when the witness is expected to give oral evidence: *R. v H* [2001] All E.R. (D.) 150.

(19) Proof of requirements of admissibility

27–23   In *R. v Coughlan*, March 2, 1999, unreported, CA, the trial judge was criticised for relying upon double hearsay.

> "Before a court decides to allow a statement to be read . . . it is . . . essential that the court holds a full and proper enquiry to determine whether one or other of the threshold provisions of s.23 has been satisfied to the high standard of proof required in a criminal case. Courts should not pay lip service to these provisions. In the ordinary way a defendant is entitled to have any witness whom he chooses present in court to give oral

evidence so that the witness may be cross-examined. The exception is allowed but it must only be where it has been clearly established that the requirements of the Act are met." *Per* Tuckey L.J. in *R. v Coughlan*, March 2, 1999, (CA, unreported).

(20) The court's discretion under Criminal Justice Act 1988, s.26

NOTE 97. *R. v Medway* [2000] Crim.L.R. 415.   **27–24**

NOTE 98. *cf. W v DPP*, February 7, 2001, (DC, unreported).

(22) The court's discretion under Criminal Justice Act 1988, s.25

The s.25 discretion was exercised to prevent a defendant who applied during   **27–26**
a trial to adduce her medical records pursuant to s.24(1) to do so because the prosecution had been given no opportunity to consider them and take instructions on them. The Divisional Court said that the doctors who treated the defendant were still alive and could be expected, with the assistance of their notes, to remember the substance of their consultations with her: *O'Sullivan v DPP*, March 27, 2000, (DC, unreported).

(23a) Compatibility of Criminal Justice Act 1988, ss.23, 24 with Article 6 of the European Convention on Human Rights

Article 6(1) of the European Convention on Human Rights provides that   **27–27A**
everyone charged with a criminal offence has the right to a fair trial, and Article 6(3) provides that such a person has certain minimum rights which include (d) "to examine or have examined witnesses against him". Statements may be admitted under ss.23 and 24 of the Criminal Justice Act 1988 without violating Article 6: see *R. v Gokal* [1997] 2 Cr.App.R. 266; *R. v Rutherford* [1998] Crim.L.R. 490; *Trivedi v UK* (1997) 89 A.D.R. 136; *cf. R. v Thomas* [1998] Crim.L.R. 887. But not in all circumstances: see *R. v Radak* [1999] 1 Cr.App.R. 187 (see para. 27–24). In *McKenna v H.M. Advocate* [2000] S.C.C.R. 159 the following principles were extracted from the relevant Strasbourg authorities:

"(1) The admissibility of evidence is a matter for national law . . .

(2) Guarantees in Article 6(3)(d) are specific aspects of the right to a fair trial . . .

(3) It is a function of the European Court of Human Rights to ascertain if the national proceedings regarded as a whole (including any evidence taken) has resulted in a fair trial . . .

(4) Hearsay evidence is not in itself incompatible with Article 6 of the Convention . . .

(5) In Asch [v. Austria (1993) 15 E.H.R.R. 597] it was acknowledged that it was sometimes impossible to lead evidence of witnesses directly. However, all evidence must be produced at a public hearing with a view to adversarial argument . . .

(6) The rights of the defence must be respected and this will normally require the accused to be given an adequate opportunity to challenge and question the witness . . . [I]f a witness is dead, direct questioning is impossible but a challenge can be made by leading other evidence, including evidence about the credibility of the witness . . .

(7) It is clear from the cases that hearsay evidence should not be the main or only evidence against the accused (*Kostovski* [*v Netherlands* (1989) 12 E.H.R.R. 434] para. 44 and A sch, para. 30) . . . " *Per* Lord Caplan.

Whether hearsay evidence can be admitted under the Criminal Justice Act 1988 without violating Convention rights is discussed at length in B. Emmerson & A. Ashworth, *Human Rights and Criminal Justice* (London, 2001), paras 15–108 et seq.

(23b) The reach of Criminal Justice Act 1988, s.24

27–27B   In *Chester-Nash v CPS*, April 18, 2000, unreported, DC, the prosecution relied upon a written statement by a fingerprint officer that fingerprints that another officer had testified had been found at the scene of the crime matched those on an exhibit that bore the accused's name. The Divisional Court held that, although this statement was correctly admitted under s.24 of the Criminal Justice Act 1988, it could not be relied upon to prove that the accused's fingerprints were at the scene of the crime: it could be used only to prove that the fingerprints from the scene of the crime matched those on the exhibit. A statement was required from those who had made the exhibit that the fingerprints labelled as belonging to the accused were those of the accused. The justices were wrong to use s.24 to cure the gap caused by the break in the evidential chain.

3.—Mechanical Instruments and Readings; Computers

(1) Readings of mechanical instruments

27–28   Section 68 of the Police and Criminal Evidence Act 1984 has been abolished by s.60 of the Youth Justice and Criminal Evidence Act 1999 with effect from April 14, 2000 (SI 2000/1034, art.2(a)).

(7) Evidence required to comply with s.69(1)

27–34   The conditions of admissibility laid down in s.69(1)(b) of the Police and Criminal Evidence Act 1984 can be proved by inferences from an admissible statement that does not qualify as a certificate: *R. v Kolton* [2000] Crim.L.R. 761.

4.—Evidence at Former Trials

(4) Opportunity for cross-examination

27–40   Inability to cross-examine the witness who gave evidence at the former trial does not contravene Articles 6(1) and 6(3)(d) of the European Convention on Human Rights if there are sufficient safeguards to ensure a fair trial: *H. M. Advocate v Nulty* [2000] S.C.C.R. 431.

CHAPTER 28

ADMISSIONS

2.—FORMAL ADMISSIONS FOR PURPOSES OF TRIAL

(1) Civil cases

In *Thomas v Davies* [2000] C.L.Y. 353, CC, the court held that as a matter of   **28–05**
law the defendant could resile from an admission made by his insurers, and
should the admission in correspondence that they were "now prepared to
concede liability" fall within CPR, r.14.1(5), it was a suitable case for the
exercise of its discretion. In *Browning v Oates* [2002] 5 C.L.Y. 53 CC however
the defendant was not permitted to resile from an admission of liability made by
loss adjusters because it was now too late for the other party to gather the
necessary evidence. The burden of proof rests upon the party seeking to
withdraw the admission of liability (see *Hackman v Hounslow LBC* [2000]
C.L.Y. 354, CC).

(2) Criminal Cases

On the circumstances in which it is appropriate for a court to allow the   **28–07**
withdrawal of a formal admission under s.10(4) of the Criminal Justice Act 1967,
see *R. v Kolton* [2000] Crim.L.R. 761, CA which indicates that leave is unlikely
to be granted unless there is cogent evidence that an admission made with the
benefit of legal advice was the product of a mistake or misunderstanding. In
contrast to s.10(4) of the Criminal Justice Act 1967, an acceptance reached under
s.3 of the Drug Trafficking Offences Act 1986 cannot be withdrawn at a later
stage of the proceedings: *R. v Emmett,* unreported, February 16, 1996, CA.

3.—PRINCIPLES COMMON TO ADMISSIONS IN CIVIL CASES AND TO CONFESSIONS IN CRIMINAL CASES

(5) Form of the admission

(b) *Written*

A response to a notice under s.172 of the Road Traffic Act 1988 which   **28–15**
required the registered keeper of a vehicle to state who had been driving it on a

[101]

particular occasion amounts to a formal admission for the purposes of proving the fact that a response had indeed been made and what it was. However, it was not admitted to prove the truth of the assertion that another person had been driving: *DPP v Wilson* [2001] EWHC 198, [2002] R.T.R. 37, QBD. The compatibility of s.172 with the European Convention on Human Rights has been considered in a several recent cases including *DPP v Wilson; Brown v Procurator Fiscal, Dunfermline* [2000] J.C. 328, High Ct of Justiciary, reversed by *Brown v Stott* [2001] 2 W.L.R. 817, PC. The House of Lords held in *R. v Hertfordshire County Council, Ex p. Green Environmental Industries Ltd* [2000] 2 A.C. 412 that a somewhat similar power did not violate the privilege against self-incrimination.

4.—Informal Admissions—Client, Solicitor, Counsel and Witnesses

(1) Civil cases

28–19   In *Sollitt v DJ Broady Ltd* [2000] C.P.L.R. 259, CA, a solicitor had actual authority, and if not, ostensible authority, to make admissions in a letter on behalf of the defendant. The court refused to allow the defendant to resile from an admission made under a mistake where this would cause serious prejudice to the claimant who had relied upon it. This prejudice has to be proved, it is not presumed: *Gale v Superdrug Stores plc* [1996] 1 W.L.R. 1089, CA. On the abandonment of a claim by counsel at trial, see *Worldwide Corporation Ltd v Marconi Communications Ltd,* unreported, June 22, 1999, CA.

CHAPTER 29

AGENCY, PARTNERSHIP, COMPANIES, COMMON PURPOSE, ACTING IN A CAPACITY

3.—CORPORATIONS

(2) Liability in other cases

The "identification principle" was confirmed as the sole basis of corporate liability for gross negligence manslaughter in *A.-G.'s Reference (No. 2 of 1999)* [2000] Q.B. 796. Liability under the proposed offence of corporate killing (see *Reforming the Law on Involuntary Manslaughter: The Government's Proposals* (Home Office 2000)) would be based on the acts and omissions of a significantly broader range of personnel than the identification principle allows.   **29–09**

4.—ACTS AND DECLARATIONS IN PURSUANCE OF A COMMON PURPOSE

The co-conspirators rule was analysed and applied in clear stages by the New Zealand High Court in *R. v Mahutoto (No. 2)* [2001] 2 N.Z.L.R. 115 and cites *Phipson* among its authorities.   **29–10**

The High Court of New Zealand in *R. v Mahutoto (No. 2)* [2001] 2 N.Z.L.R. 115 at 122 explains that the concept of ratification rather than agency justifies the admission of a co-conspirator's declarations against people who were not part of the common purpose at the time they were spoken: **29–11**

> "When a person decides to join a conspiracy after its inception, he or she is taken to have accepted the plan as it has developed and the steps that have already been taken towards arranging the intended unlawful acts. He or she is therefore taken as impliedly ratifying those steps already taken by the co-conspirators in furtherance of the common purpose."

CHAPTER 30

STATEMENTS IN THE PRESENCE, AND DOCUMENTS IN THE POSSESSION, OF A PARTY

2.—STATEMENTS

Reply, denial, silence

30–07 Part of the above passage from Parkes was quoted and applied by the New Zealand Court of Appeal in holding that a party was bound by an agent's admissions forwarded by the party without first being read: see *Juken Nissho Ltd v Northland R.C.* [2000] 2 N.Z.L.R. 556.

CHAPTER 31

CONFESSIONS

(2) Matters provable by confession

On the vexed question of whether a statement of name, address and birth date **31–02**
amounts to an admission, see *R. v Ward, Andrews & Broadley* [2001] Crim.L.R.
316, CA, in which it held that the statement, if the jury was satisfied that it was
made by the accused, was admissible as an exception to the hearsay rule. At trial,
Ward did not testify and the Court of Appeal accepted that the evidence was
prima facie hearsay. Another approach might be to use the state of mind
exception, people stating their belief in who they are being more often right than
wrong. This process entails an element of circularity since it assumes that the
statement was made by the person charged with the offence. It was claimed that
this was cured by the accuracy of the statements as to date of birth and address,
presumably as direct circumstantial evidence, but it is less than convincing that
only Ward would have known these relatively unremarkable details. The
statement may not appear to be adverse to the maker at the time but it is more
incriminating when the surrounding circumstances are taken into account.

(5) Admissibility under the Police and Criminal Evidence Act 1984, s.76

NOTE 21. Bicak contends in (2001) 65 J.Crim.L. 85 that s.76(2) did not replace **31–05**
the common law test of voluntariness but merely qualified it.

NOTE 32. See also *R. v Bow Street Magistrates, Ex p. Proulx* [2001] 1 All E.R. **31–07**
57 at 76–77, DC, in which the court explained "any" confession under s.76 in the
context of extradition proceedings as indicating "any such" as "such a"
confession as the applicant made. This formulation of the test may not give
sufficient weight to the abstract element of s.76(2)(b).

(6) Breach of provisions of the 1984 Act and the Codes of Practice

Consultation draft PACE Codes of Practice have recently been published and **31–09**
are available on the website: *www.homeoffice.gov.uk*. The main changes to Code
C that have been proposed concern the caution and the drawing of adverse
inferences from silence (and are dealt with in the supplement to chapter 32), the
custody officer's responsibility for deciding whether a person is fit to be
interviewed (para. 12.3) and provisions for determining whether an individual
could be at risk during an interview (Annex G).

The European Court of Human Rights has acknowledged in *Brennan v UK* **31–11**
October 16 2001 para. 53, [2002] Crim.L.R. 216, that the recording of interviews
and the presence of a solicitor constitute important safeguards against police
misconduct, but concluded that they are not indispensable preconditions to a fair
trial within the meaning of Art. 6(1).

31–11   NOTE 58. In *R. (D.P.P.) v Stratford Youth Court* [2001] E.W.C. Admin 615, 165 J.P. 761, it was held that a 17–year-old is not a juvenile for the purposes of Code C, but that the interviewing of a suspect of that age in the absence of an appropriate adult may raise issues under ss. 76 and 78 of PACE.

31–11   NOTE 60. See *R. v Aspinall* [1999] Crim.L.R. 741. The Court of Appeal also warns that the Human Rights Act will play a larger part in determining the operation of s.78 where police misconduct led to the absence of an appropriate adult and the waiver of the right to counsel.

(7) Discretionary exclusion of confessions

31–12   Where the accused was arrested for one offence and not informed that he was being questioned about a much more serious offence, and as a result did not seek legal advice, critical answers which he might not otherwise have given ought to have been excluded pursuant to s.78 (see *R. v Kirk* [2000] 1 W.L.R. 567 at 572, CA).

NOTE 69. The importance of access to legal advice as an element of procedural fairness was emphasised by the European Court in *Magee v UK* (2001) 31 E.H.R.R. 35, [2000] Crim.L.R. 681, a case where the presence of a solicitor at the initial stages of a long and intimidating interrogation would have acted as a counterweight to measures designed to sap the suspect's will. The European Court in *Brennan v UK* [2002] Crim.L.R. 216 has found that an accused's right to speak frankly with his lawyer in private is part of the basic requirements of a fair trial and follows from Art. 6(3)(c).

The major provisions of the Human Rights Act came into force on October 2, 2000 and now that Convention rights have force in domestic law, it is likely that considerable weight will be placed on such breaches when considering the exercise of the s.78 discretion, (see *R. v X, Y and Z, The Times*, May 23, 2000, CA. There is no principle of Convention law that unlawfully obtained evidence is inadmissible *per se*: *Schenck v Switzerland* (1988) 13 E.H.R.R. 242) just as a breach of constitutional rights was regarded as a major factor in favour of the exclusion of a confession in the Privy Council case of *Mohamed v State* [1999] 2 A.C. 111.

Entrapment continues to be a fertile basis for the mounting of challenges under s.78 of PACE, although the Court of Appeal has rejected such challenges in a number of drugs cases including *R. v Elwell, R. v Derby* [2001] EWCA Crim 1360; *R. v Haslock*, unreported, May 18, 2001, CA; *R. v Breen, R. v Barlow*, unreported, May 17, 2001, CA. The surge of appeals has been boosted by a number of cases involving "stings" perpetrated by private individuals or organisations such as newspapers (*R. v Shannon* [2001] 1 Cr.App.R. 168; *R. v Hardwicke & Thwaites* [2001] Crim.L.R. 220, CA) and trading standards officers or similar persons (*London Borough of Ealing Trading Standards v Woolworths* [1995] Crim.L.R. 59, QBD; *Taunton Dean Borough Council v Brice*, unreported, July 10, 1997, QBD). Private bodies sometimes resort to "extreme provocation" since they are not bound by the PACE Codes or formal codes of conduct concerning undercover investigations such as the Undercover Operations Code of Practice.

The latter Code, a response to the duties to be imposed upon public bodies under the Human Rights Act, applies to exercises conducted by the police, national crime squad, National Criminal Intelligence Service and Customs and Excise (see *www.ncis.co.uk*). However reprehensible such behaviour, when it is not perpetrated by an agent of the state, it has been difficult for the defence to challenge the subsequent use of such evidence in criminal proceedings under s.78 or to seek a stay of proceedings.

In *R. v Hardwicke & Thwaites*, for example, the jury upon finding the defendants guilty, added that had they been entitled to consider the "extreme provocation", the verdict would have been different. A stay of proceedings was however, ordered in *R. v Woods* [2000] C.L.Y. 916 where the conversations had been inadequately recorded and the police not brought into the investigation for some months. Decisions of the ECHR have also encouraged the challenge of the English law relating to entrapment, notably the case of *Teixeira de Castro v Portugal* (1999) 28 E.H.R.R. 101 in which it was held that the police had overstepped the mark by instigating a crime which would not otherwise have been committed in breach of Article 6. This decision has been distinguished by Lord Bingham in *Nottingham CC v Amin* [2000] 1 W.L.R. 1071 QBD as applied in *R. v Loosley*, unreported, April 30, 2000, CA, on the basis that the relatively passive behaviour of the police in hailing the accused's taxi simply provided him with the opportunity to commit an offence without prevailing upon him or overbearing his will.

Similarly, in *R. v Hardwick & Thwaites*, above, factors including the ample grounds for suspecting that the accused was dealing in drugs, his clear disposition and the fact that he was not caught in an isolated transaction, as well as the misconduct being perpetrated by private individuals, enabled the Court of Appeal to distinguish *Teixeira de Castro*. It seems that the traditional approach of English courts to alleged agent provocateur evidence, exemplified by *R. v Smurthwaite and Gill* [1994] 1 All E.R. 898, CA is set to continue, the significance of *Teixeira de Castro* being minimised (see *Attorney-General's Reference (No. 3 of 2000)* [2001] 2 Cr.App.R. 472). However, the House of Lords in *R v Loosely, Attorney-General's Reference (No.3 of 2000)* [2001] 1 WLR 2060 reversed part of the decision in *Attorney-General's Reference (No. 3 of 2000)* because the police had incited a crime and offered an unusual inducement to the defendant to deal in heroin for the first time.

Undercover operations sometimes entail covert recordings based on intrusive surveillance, and these methods may also be used to gather evidence in cases where no entrapment is involved, as in *R. v Khan* where a listening device was attached to the suspect's house, enabling incriminating conversations to be recorded and used against him. The Police Act 1997, Pt III, which authorises covert entry upon or interference with property or wireless telegraphy by the police, Customs officers and others, was a response to the lack of statutory regulation of such practices highlighted by the House of Lords ([1997] A.C. 558) and the ECHR in *Khan v UK* (2000) 31 E.H.R.R. 45. The lack of regulation was held to amount to a breach of Article 8(1), but did not automatically render the admission of the evidence was automatically unfair under Article 6 (following *Schenk v Switzerland* (1988) 13 E.H.R.R. 242). In Khan, the accused had enjoyed ample opportunity at trial to contest the authenticity of the tapes and the fairness of using them.

In the important judgment of *PG and JH v UK* September 25, 2001 [2002] Crim.L.R.308, the European Court of Human Rights applied *Khan* to another unregulated installation of a covert listening device in a private home. It also ruled that a recording of a suspect's voice procured by similar means in a police cell was a further violation of Art. 8 even though its purpose was to obtain a "voice sample" for analysis rather than the contents of the conversation. It did not, however, regard the "metering" of telephone calls on the basis of statutory authority to violate Art. 8. Evidence derived from metering had been held to be admissible by the House of Lords in *R. v Preston* [1994] A.C. 130.

The Interception of Communications Act 1985 which covered the interception of post or public telecommunication has now been replaced by the Regulation of Investigatory Powers Act 2000 which covers a wider range of telecommunications and also deals with surveillance and the use of agent provocateurs (see *Mirfield* in [2001] Crim.L.R. 91 on the evidential aspects of RIPA). Section 17 of RIPA, like s.9 of the Interception of Communications Act 1985, explicitly renders inadmissible evidence tending to disclose that an interception warrant has been issued, or that it was reasonably believed that one party to the communication consented to the interception (the two legitimate telephone interception methods), or that an unlawful interception had been conducted.

On whether this ban extends to the material obtained by any interception, lawful or not, the House of Lords in a series of decisions (including *R. v Preston* [1994] 2 A.C. 130 and *R. v Effik* [1995] 1 A.C. 309) culminating in *Morgans v DPP* [2001] 1 A.C. 315 has decided that in the case of the 1985 Act such evidence is generally inadmissible (*cf. R. v Rasool* [1997] 1 W.L.R. 1092, CA; *R. v Owen* [1999] 1 W.L.R. 949, CA). Intercepts carried out abroad under positive lawful authority, as opposed to unregulated interceptions of communications considered in cases such as *Malone v UK* (1984) 7 E.H.R.R. 14 and *Khan* [1997] A.C. 558 are, however, admissible even if one or both parties to the conversation is in the United Kingdom (*R. v P.* [2001] 2 All E.R. 58, HL). This does not breach Article 6 because the discretionary control conferred by s.78 was held to be adequate by the European Court in Khan. See also *R. v Bailey, Brewin and Ganji* [2001] EWCA Crim 733.

In a number of Crown Court cases described by Cape [2002] Crim.L.R.471, evidence of police interviews has been excluded under s.78 on the basis that the accused had received incompetent or inadequate advice or assistance. This argument was unsuccessfully advanced in *R. v Wahab* [2002] EWCA 1570.

(8) Function of judge and jury

31–13   NOTE 89. These cases were applied by the Privy Council in *Timothy v The State* [2001] 1 W.L.R. 485. The trial judge's decision on a *voire dire* to determine the admissibility of a confession should not be revealed to the jury since it may cause unfair prejudice to the defendant by conveying the impression that the judge has reached a concluded view on the credibility of the relevant witnesses and the defendant—*R. v Mitchell* [1998] A.C. 695, 703 (HL), affirmed *Adams & Lawrence v R.* [2002] UKPC 14, paras 12–15.

(9) Procedure: the Crown Court

31–15   NOTE 98. The solution adopted in *R. v Langley* [2001] Crim.L.R. 651, CA was for the court to order a retrial. The defence, probably for tactical reasons, had not sought a *voir dire* but attempted to undermine the evidence of the confession in cross-examination of a police witness. Facts emerged which, had the defence known of them earlier, might well have led it to challenge the admissibility of the confession on the *voir dire*.

(10) Procedure: Magistrates' Courts

The Court of Appeal has stated in *Flannery v Halifax Estate Agencies Ltd* **31–16**
[2000] 1 W.L.R. 377 that a judge in civil proceedings is under a duty to explain
why he has reached his decision and where arguments are advanced on both
sides, give reasons why he preferred one case over the other. The scope of the
duty varies in the circumstances but in the instant case a failure to supply reasons
was a breach of due process and an independent ground of appeal since the losing
party was effectively deprived of his chance of appeal. While it was not raised in
the judgment, this reasoning may well extend to the conduct of a *voir dire* and
would be consistent with the right to a fair trial enshrined in the European
Convention on Human Rights. See also *English v Emery Reimbold & Strick Ltd*
[2002] EWCA Civ 605, [2002] 1 W.L.R. 2409, CA.

For a case in which it would have been appropriate for justices to exclude
evidence under s.78(1) see *D.P.P. v Jimale* [2001] Crim.L.R. 139 (DC).

(11) Burden of Proof

While s.76(2) expressly imposes a burden of proof on the prosecution, the s.78 **31–17**
discretion is to be exercised whenever the court concludes that the evidence
should not be admitted and it has been held in *R. v Governor of Brixton Prison
Ex p. Saifi* [2001] 4 All E.R. 168, 187 that the concept of burden of proof has no
part to play. *Per* Rose L.J., "The prosecution desiring to adduce and the defence
seeking to exclude evidence will each seek to persuade the court about impact on
fairness. We regard the position as neutral and see no reason why s.78 should be
understood as requiring the court to consider upon whom the burden of proof
rests."

(12) Practice before the jury

(b) *Tape-recordings*

The Police and Criminal Evidence Act 1984 (Tape-Recording of Interviews) **31–19**
(Amendment) Order 2001 (SI 2001/2480), which came into force on August 1,
2001, extends the requirement that the police in England and Wales tape record
their interviews to the questioning of suspects about possible offences under the
Official Secrets Act 1911. A Code of Practice on the visual recording of
interviews in police stations under s.60A(1) of PACE came into operation on 7
May 2002 under SI 2002/1266.

(14) Cross-examination on inadmissible confession

In *R. v Corelli* [2001] EWCA Crim 971, the Court of Appeal indicated that *R.* **31–25**
v Myers did not preclude an involuntary confession being put in cross-
examination to the co-accused who had made it, nor was it inconsistent with *Lui
Mei Lin v R.* and *R. v Rowson*.

(17) Admissibility of facts discovered as a result of an excluded confession

NOTE 56. *Lam Chi Ming* was applied by the Privy Council in *Timothy v The* State **31–29**
[2000] 1 W.L.R. 485 at 490–493 and the House of Lords in *R. v Hertfordshire
C.C., Ex p. Green Industries Ltd* [2000] 2 A.C. 412 at 421–422.

(19) "Mixed statements" ...

31–31   On the distinction between mixed and wholly exculpatory statements see *Hall,* [2001] Archbold News 10.5.

(21) Lies of the accused

31–35   "The steady and almost unstoppable stream of reported decisions and appeals . . . on the subject of lies told by a defendant and the directions which should be given by the trial judge when he does so" (*R. v Middleton* [2001] Crim.L.R. 251) has prompted the Court of Appeal to emphasise that the underlying purpose of the *Lucas* direction is to avoid the risk that the jury might adopt "an inadmissible chain of reasoning", namely that telling lies means the accused must be guilty. Where there is no risk of the jury following the prohibited line of reasoning, a *Lucas* direction is unnecessary, but in appropriate cases, such as *R. v Sylvester and Walcott* [2002] EWCA Crim 1327, an appeal may be allowed in part because no *Lucas* direction was provided. It is inherently unlikely that such a direction would be appropriate in relation to lies which the jury conclude must have been told to them in his evidence, since this is usually covered by general directions of law on the burden and standard of proof.
    In *R. v Barnett* [2002] EWCA Crim 454, [2002] 2 Cr.App.R. 11, where an accused charged with handling stolen goods gave three completely contradictory accounts, his lies, though tending to undermine the defence that he did not know the property was stolen, had little significance as direct evidence of guilt and hence did not attract a *Lucas* direction. In neither *Barnett* nor *Rahming v R.* [2002] UKPC 23 para. 10, where the accused did not testify, did the prosecution rely on his lies as supporting an inference of guilt. The Court of Appeal in *Middleton* noted that the addition of a *Lucas* direction could often be circular and therefore confusing. While emphasising that it did not intend to reformulate principle or undermine existing authorities, the Court of Appeal advocated an analysis of the principle underlying the *Lucas* direction, rather than recourse to "laboriously trawling through hosts of reported and unreported cases" most of which were simple illustrations.
    In some circumstances it may be appropriate to combine a direction under s.34 of the Criminal Justice and Public Order Act regarding the accused's failure to mention a relevant matter when questioned by the police with a *Lucas* direction on lies (*R. v O(A)* [2000] Crim.L.R. 617, CA; *R. v Rodrigues* [2001] EWCA Crim 444, distinguishing *R. v Harron* [1996] Crim.L.R. 581). See below, para. 32–07. For the proper phrasing of a *Lucas* direction in the context of a co-accused see *R. v Burley, Molnar and Stanton* [2001] EWCA Crim 731.

(24) Admissions under compulsory process of law

31–39   The question of whether a statute which confers a power to ask questions or obtain documents or information excludes the privilege against self-incrimination is one of construction and often implied from the purpose of the Act (see *R. v Director of Serious Fraud Office, Ex p. Smith* [1993] A.C. 1 at 32, *per* Lord Mustill, endorsed by Lord Hoffmann in *R. v Hertfordshire C.C., Ex p. Green Industries Ltd* [2000] 2 A.C. 412 at 421). In *R. v Hertfordshire C.C., Ex p. Green Industries Ltd* at 419–421, Lord Hoffmann regarded the case for implied exclusion of the privilege under s.71(2) of the Environment Protection Act 1990 as even stronger than in the cases of the Banking and Companies Acts. The power was not conferred merely to enable the gathering of evidence against offenders but for the broad public purpose of protecting health and the environment, which would be frustrated were people with vital information entitled to refuse to answer. Moreover, a request under s.71(2) did not itself form even a preliminary part of any criminal proceedings, nor was the nature of the questioning prone to abuse.

The use in criminal proceedings of incriminatory evidence so obtained was subject to the exclusionary discretion under s.78 of the Police and Criminal Evidence Act and the statute did not implicitly revoke s.78 as it had been interpreted as so doing in *Saunders v UK* (1997) 23 E.H.R.R. 313. The question of trial fairness did not arise as answers had not been tendered in evidence against those individuals questioned under s.71(2). The House of Lords found the s.71(2) procedure to be compatible with the privilege against self-incrimination as described in *Saunders v UK* which was confined to the use of evidence at a criminal trial and not concerned with the use of compulsory powers at the preliminary, examination stage. The distinction between seeking information for purely administrative or extra judicial reasons and seeking it for the purposes of launching a prosecution will require further development in later cases (see *R. v Bright* [2001] 1 W.L.R. 662 at 693–694, DC) and in those decided after October 2, 2000 the guidance of the House of Lords may not be as persuasive because of the operation of s.2(1) of the Human Rights Act 1998.

In another case before the European Court of Human Rights, which the Government conceded was indistinguishable from *Saunders v UK*, the court held that the legal obligation upon the applicants to provide information to DTI inspectors did not necessarily contravene Article 6 of the Convention. This turned upon the use made of the resulting information by the prosecution at trial: see *IJL, GMR & AKP v UK* [2001] Crim.L.R. 133; 9 B.H.R.C. 222.

The House of Lords has concluded in *R. v Allen (No.2)*[2001] UKHL 45, [2001] 3 W.L.R. 843, distinguishing *Saunders v UK*, that it is not contrary to Articles 6 or 8 of the ECHR to require an individual to provide information to the Inland Revenue for the purposes of tax assessment.

Delete this paragraph.   **31–40**

After the decision in *Saunders*, Parliament amended s.434(5) of the Com- **31–41** panies Act so that evidence obtained by DTI Inspectors could not be used in prosecutions for certain offences. Similar provisions in other statutes were also amended to the same effect by s.59 and Sch. 3 of the Youth and Criminal Justice Act 1999. Where it applies, this provision has the effect of prohibiting the use of answers given under compulsion in any subsequent criminal trial except when the defendant himself relies on the answers or where charges are brought against a person as a result of his failure to comply with a statutory requirement to answer questions. In *R. v Kearns* [2002] EWCA Crim 748, [2002] 1 W.L.R. 2815; *The Times*, April 4, 2002, CA this was held to mean that information now demanded under s.354(3)(a) of the Insolvency Act 1986 did not infringe the defendant's rights to silence and not to incriminate himself.

The Court of Appeal observed that the decisions of the European Court of Human Rights drew a clear distinction between the statutory power to compel a person to give information for the purposes of an administrative or regulatory procedure and the subsequent use of such information in criminal proceedings against the person who was obliged to give it. It further restricted the scope of Article 6 by endorsing the approach previously taken by the Court of Appeal in *Attorney-General's Reference (No 7 of 2000)* [2001] EWCA Crim 888; [2001] 2 Cr.App.R 286. It had held, following *Saunders v UK, ibid.* at paras 68–69, that while legitimate objection might be made to evidence that the defendant had been forced to create by the use of compulsory powers, the delivery of documents to the official receiver under compulsion, that is evidence already in existence and so brought to the attention of the court, could not render a trial unfair. That is because the existence and quality of such evidence were independent of any order to produce it that was made against the will of the accused person.

31–43A Section 172 of the Road Traffic Act 1988 provides that where the driver of a vehicle is alleged to be guilty of one of the more serious motoring offences to which the section applies, the person keeping the vehicle is obliged to give such information as to the identity of the driver as may be required by the police. It also imposes a duty on "any other person" asked by the police to give information leading to the identification of the driver. The penalty for non-compliance is not as onerous as some compulsory questioning provisions and includes a fine, currently, of no more than £1000, and mandatory endorsement of an individual's licence.

The compatibility of s.172 with Article 6 of the European Convention on Human Rights was considered by the Privy Council in the Scottish case of *Brown v Stott* [2001] 2 W.L.R. 817 (reversing the decision of the High Court of Judiciary in *Brown v Stott (Procurator Fiscal, Dunfermline)* 2000 S.C. (J.C.) 328) which held unanimously that the accused's rights to a fair trial were not infringed even though s.172 led to an admission which was relied upon at trial. It was observed that the jurisprudence of the European Court established that, while overall fairness of the trial cannot be compromised, the constituent rights within Article 6, such as the right not to incriminate oneself and the right to silence are not themselves absolute, and s.172 when properly applied did not represent a disproportionate response to the serious social problem of motor vehicle misuse. A number of factors were identified by Lord Bingham in [2001] 2 W.L.R. 817 at 836–837. See also Lord Steyn at 841–842 as supporting this conclusion:

(1) Section 172 provides for the posing of a single, simple question, the answer to which is not incriminatory of itself, and the penalty for refusing to answer is moderate and non-custodial.

(2) The requirement that the accused be made to answer was no more objectionable than being compelled to undergo a breath test, a require-ment that had not been criticised. The distinction drawn in *Saunders v UK* (1997) 23 E.H.R.R. 313 at paras 68–69 between a statement and other material having an existence independent of the will of the suspect was acknowledged but not regarded as particularly persuasive. The latter category includes breath, blood, urine samples, and in *JB v Switzerland* extended to evidence obtained from a compulsorily installed tacograph (*cf. Attorney-General's Reference (No. 7 of 2000)*, [2001] EWCA Crim 888; [2001] 1 W.L.R. 1879 in which this distinction was described as jurisprudentially sound).

(3) All who own or drive motor vehicles realise that they by doing so are subjecting themselves to a regulatory regime imposed for similar reasons

for the control of firearms, and this regime was not applicable to the wider public.

Brown was applied in England by the Divisional Court in *DPP v Wilson* [2001] EWHC Admin. 198, [2002] R.T.R. 37. It concerned s.172(b) of the Road Traffic Act rather than s.172(a) which had been considered in *Brown*. The Court in Wilson held that were no grounds to exclude the evidence under s.78 of PACE given that it requires fairness to both sides and the measure was a proportionate one to combat a serious social problem. The European Court of Human Rights, however, later delivered an important decision in *Heaney & McGuinness v Ireland*, December 21, 2000, para. 58 [2001] Crim.L.R. 481. (See also *Quinn v Ireland*, December 21, 2000, ECHR, paras 56–59 and the later ECHR case of *JB v Switzerland*, May 3, 2001, paras 64–71 which will have to be taken into account by English Courts.) The Court found in the former case that the threat of a six-month prison sentence had destroyed the essence of the right to silence and expressed approval of *Funke v France* (1993) 16 E.H.R.R. 297. In *Funke*, the penalty for non-cooperation had been merely financial, but was held to be a threat of criminal sanction nonetheless. Just as significantly in the context of s.172, a strong public interest in the authorities obtaining the information did not prevent their methods breaching Article 6.

In *Heaney & McGuinness*, the statute required persons detained on suspicion of specific terrorist offences to account for their movements and conduct during that particular time. Some commentators suggest that *Heaney & McGuinness v Ireland* leaves the status of s.172 of the Road Traffic Act in doubt (see *Ashworth* in [2001] 5 Archbold News 5) and may invalidate the current English approach to limited incursions upon the privilege against self-incrimination. In practice this may not be the case as the courts are left with some discretion when determining whether the right to silence has been effectively destroyed and a well-reasoned approach to the problem may be developed.

CHAPTER 32

RESTRICTIONS ON THE RIGHT TO SILENCE—INTRODUCTION

1.—THE NATURE OF THE RIGHT

32–01   This chapter deals with the right to silence in criminal cases. The right to silence does not extend to give a defendant as a matter of right the same protection in civil proceedings, and the Crown might, as a result of civil proceedings, obtain evidence to which it would not otherwise have had access—*Secretary of State for the DTI v Crane, The Times*, June 4, 2001, Ch D.

3.—PRE-TRIAL SILENCE

32–04   It has been held in *R v Dervish* [2001] EWCA Crim 2789, [2002] 2 Cr.App.R. 6 that an inference can be drawn from silence upon being charged under s.34(1)(b) even if s.34(1)(a) is inapplicable because the interview itself has been excluded due to breaches of the PACE Codes of Practice and the failure of the police to inform the suspect's solicitor of the true facts. The Court of Appeal held that the two limbs of s.34 are independent, the word "or" between the two sub paragraphs simply indicating that in either circumstance consideration can be given to the drawing of the adverse inference. Nor did s.34 exclude the possibility of the inference being drawn at each separate stage and in some circumstances forensic weight could be attached to a double inference combining the two sub paragraphs. While the defence objected that this approach to s.34(1)(b) gave the police the benefit of a "back-up" inference in the event of the interview being excluded, the Court of Appeal was content for this to be dealt with by the trial judge determining whether such an inference would in all the circumstances be unfair. It should not be permitted in circumstances where the safeguards contained in PACE and the Codes had been nullified or there had been bad faith by the police.

32–04   NOTE 15. *Add*: R. Leng, "Silence Pre-trial, Reasonable Expectations and the Normative Distortion of Fact-Finding" (2001) 5 E & P 240.

The Judicial Studies Board specimen directions on ss. 34, 36 and 37 are   **32–05** available from its website: *www.jsboard.co.uk.*

NOTES 25 AND 32. *R. v McGarry* is now reported at [1999] 1 Cr.App.R. 377.

A proper foundation must be laid before a s.34 inference can be drawn. In *R.*   **32–05** *v B(MT)* [2000] Crim.L.R. 181, CA, the appellant when asked by the police why his accuser should fabricate a story of rape, denied knowing any reason. At trial the alleged victim admitted during evidence in chief that she hated the appellant; he later testified that the witness was motivated by jealousy. The Court of Appeal allowed the appeal on the basis that the judge had not ascertained whether or not the appellant knew of the jealousy at the time of the interview, and it was only if he knew by that time that an adverse inference could be drawn from his failure to mention it. The inference would presumably be relatively mild as the accused's evidence did little to advance his case.

A bare admission at trial of an element of the prosecution case, while a fact relied upon by the Crown, is not the assertion of a fact by the accused: *R. v Betts & Hall* [2001] 2 Cr.App.R. 257 at 264.

A broad view of a "fact" under s.34 was adopted in *R. v Milford* [2001] Crim.L.R. 330, CA.

On the related question of judicial comment on the failure of the defence to call a particular witness, which may be influenced by legislative changes permitting comment on silence during interview, see *R. v Khan* [2001] EWCA Crim 486.

Restrictions on the drawing of adverse inferences from silence where the   **32–06** suspect desires, but has not yet received, legal advice appeared in s.58 of the Youth Justice and Criminal Evidence Act as a response to the decision of the ECHR in *Murray v UK* (1996) 22 E.H.R.R. 29. Another development is the proposed amendments to PACE Code C to reflect the type of caution which the accused should receive once s.58 comes into force. In short, if the suspect wants legal advice, and until it is received, he must be cautioned according to the familiar terms used before the Criminal Justice and Public Order Act 1994. The various situations in which the "old" and "new" cautions should be administered are set out by Zander in (2002) 152 NLJ 1035. The Consultation draft PACE Codes are available on the website: *www.homeoffice.gov.uk.*

The most significant development in this area of the law is undoubtedly   **32–07** *Condron v UK* (2001) 31 E.H.R.R. 1; [2000] Crim.L.R. 679 which is discussed by Jennings, Ashworth and Emmerson in [2000] Crim.L.R. 879. The European Court of Human Rights found that the applicants' right to a fair trial had been violated by a s.34 direction which failed to strike the required balance between the right to silence and the drawing of adverse inferences. A similar problem with the s.34 direction had also arisen in *R. v Milford* [2001] Crim.L.R. 330, CA and *R. v Morgan* [2001] EWCA Crim 445. The fact that a s.34 direction was not given despite earlier indications from the judge that it would be did not prevent the trial from being fair. In *Condron* it was impossible to gauge the role played by the appellants' silence at interview in the decision to convict but the jury should have been told not to draw an adverse inference if they were satisfied that the men did not speak because their solicitor advised them to make no comment, believing them to be unfit for interview.

A passage in the later European Court case of *Averill v UK* (2001) 31 E.H.R.R. 36; 8 B.H.R.C. 430, para. 49, suggests that there may exist other sufficient reasons apart from reliance upon legal advice for the accused remaining silent during police questioning. The Court of Appeal in *R. v Morgan* [2001] EWCA Crim 445 has interpreted the requirement found in paragraph 61 of the judgment in *Condron* that the jury consider the plausibility of the appellants' explanation for electing to make no comment as meaning that the jury should be directed not to draw an adverse inference from silence unless it could sensibly be attributed to a non-innocent explanation, drawing an analogy with the *Lucas* direction regarding lies. *R. v Francom* [2001] Cr.App.R. 237 was however a case of non-direction rather than misdirection, and distinguished *Condron* for this reason. In some circumstances, it may be appropriate to give the jury both a s.34 direction and a *Lucas* [1981] Q.B. 720 direction on lies.

In *R. v O(A)* [2000] Crim.L.R. 617, CA, the appellant, convicted of rape, is alleged to have denied in an interview with the police that he ever had intercourse with his stepdaughter, who had had an abortion, although he confirmed that he had admitted to her mother that he was the father. DNA testing proved that he was the father but it appears that he was not told this at the time. At trial, *O* claimed that he had confined his denial to a specific period and admitted that consensual intercourse had taken place some days later, a date more likely to have resulted in the pregnancy. If the accused had not lied in the interview, his failure to mention the later act of consensual intercourse was relevant to the jury, subject only to a s.34 direction not being given if he had unequivocally revealed the fact before the interview. See also *Beckles v United Kingdom, The Times,* October 15, 2002 ECHR (direction violated Article 6).

32–07   NOTE 40. The view taken in *Condron* must be reviewed in the light of the European Court of Human Rights decisions in *Condron v UK* and *Averill v UK* that a lawyer's advice may be a legitimate reason for declining to answer police questions and such an explanation should be given appropriate weight by the jury when deciding whether an adverse inference should be drawn.

32–07   NOTE 41. On the issue of legal advice to remain silent now see *R. v Milford* [2001] Crim.L.R. 330, CA; *R. v Morgan* [2001] EWCA Crim 445.

32–08   It seems that the reasoning in *R. v Mountford* [1999] Crim.L.R. 575, however logical, was subsequently rejected in *R. v Hearne* [2000] 6 Archbold News 2 on the basis that it was to be confined to its special facts, and if of general application would deprive s.34 of much of its effect. The jury in *R. v Gill* [2001] 1 Cr.App.R. 160 at 163–164 was placed in the same position as in *Mountford* in that in resolving the issue of whether *Gill* could have been expected to mention the fact at the time, they could only be sure he was lying and reject his explanation if they concluded that his possession of the drugs was for the purpose of dealing rather than personal use. The jury should not therefore have been invited to consider s.34. *Hearne* was preferred to *Gill* and *Mountford* by the Court of Appeal in *R. v Gowland-Wynn* [2001] EWCA Crim 715; [2002] 1 Cr.App.R. 41. See also *R. v Daly* [2001] EWCA Crim 2643; [2002] 2 Cr.App.R. 14.

6.—SCOPE OF SECTION 35

R. v Cowan [1996] 1 Cr.App.R. 1 requires that the jury be directed to look for   **32–13**
a prima facie case before drawing an adverse inference under s.35 from the
accused's failure to testify but it was held in *R. v Doldur* [2000] Crim.L.R. 178,
CA that different considerations apply in the case of s.34. There the issue is
whether the failure to provide an explanation at an earlier stage of the
investigation is suspicious, and the defence evidence will be available to be
considered along with the prosecution evidence at the time that the jury has to
make its decision. On the other hand, in the s.34 case of *R. v Gill* [2001]
Cr.App.R. 160 at 166–167, the Court of Appeal applied a number of factors in
Cowan including the need for the jury to find a case to answer before determining
whether adverse inferences were justified. The UK Government in *Condron v UK*
(2001) 31 E.H.R.R. 1, ECHR at para. 38 also argued that s.34 required a prima
facie case but this point was not resolved by the European Court of Human
Rights.

In *Telfner v Austria* (2002) 34 EHRR 7; [2001] Crim.L.R. 821 the applicant
was convicted of a traffic offence although the police had not been able to
discover which member of the family had been driving the vehicle. He pleaded
not guilty and denied having driven the car at the time but did not provide any
further information. The ECHR criticised the court for relying upon a police
report so weak that it did not amount to a prima facie case, to require the
applicant to refute the case against him, and his failure to do so led it to conclude
that he had been driving and hence his conviction. Here the link between Article
6(2) and the presumption of innocence was emphasised and it was wrong to place
the burden of proof on the defence.

The Judicial Studies Board's specimen directions concerning the defendant
who does not give evidence at trial are available from its website:
www.jsboard.co.uk.

CHAPTER 33

JUDICIAL DISCRETION TO ADMIT OR EXCLUDE EVIDENCE

1.—CRIMINAL PROCEEDINGS

(8) Police and Criminal Evidence Act 1984, s.78

33–10   For academic comment on s.78, see K. Grevling, "Fairness and the exclusion of evidence under s.78(1) of the Police and Criminal Evidence Act" in (1997) 113 L.Q.R. 667; A. Choo and S. Nash, "What's the Matter with Section 78?" in [1999] Crim.L.R. 929.

(11) The meaning of s.78(1)

33–13   In *R. v Looseley* [2001] UKHL 53; [2001] 1 WLR 2060 Lord Nicholls said that the phrase "fairness of the proceedings" is "directed mainly at matters going to fairness in the actual conduct of the trial; for instance the reliability of the evidence and the defendant's ability to test its reliability. But, rightly, the courts have been unwilling to limit the scope of the wide and comprehensive expression strictly to procedural fairness." (para. 12). The section has been generously interpreted and this has enabled the ECHR to regard it as a significant protection to for the accused: "in the great majority of situations if the evidence would be excluded under common law as being obtained in abuse of process or under Article 6 of the European Convention, it is most unlikely to be held admissible under s.78 of PACE." *per* Lord Woolf, *R. v Mason* [2002] EWCA Crim 385 at [49].

(12) "The circumstances in which the evidence was obtained"

(a) *Eavesdropping cases*

33–15   For the consequences of eavesdropping (including interception of communications) breaching Article 8 (respect for private life), see para. 33–21, below.

The admissibility of covertly recorded conversations in a police cell between suspected offenders whilst under arrest was considered in *R. v Mason* [2002] EWCA Crim 385. In this case the police had failed to follow Home Office guidelines which were found to apply by analogy. Moreover, there was a breach of Article 8 in that the surveillance was not "in accordance with law" (Article 8(2)). Lord Woolf said that a contravention of Article 8 is something that the trial judge must take into account when exercising the s.78 discretion but admitting

[118]

the evidence will not necessarily violate the Article 6: "The European Court of Human Rights recognizes that to insist on the exclusion of evidence could in itself result in a greater injustice to the public than the infringement of Article 8 creates for the appellants" (para. 67). It had been right to admit the evidence because the police had acted in good faith, nothing unlawful had been done (the police had merely arranged a situation which was likely to result in the appellants volunteering confessions) and there was nothing unfair in relying on the tapes. If the appellants had wanted to challenge the reliability and quality of the evidence, they should have supported the challenge by independent expert evidence. Lord Woolf indicates that intrusive covert surveillance should not be undertaken unless it is impossible to obtain evidence by more conventional means (a condition satisfied in this case) but, it is submitted, even a disproportionate interference with Article 8 will not necessarily make the trial at which the covertly obtained evidence is admitted unfair and, as Lord Woolf states, the remedy for a violation of Article 8 does not have to consist of the exclusion of evidence (para. 67).

For a critique of *R. v Chalkley* [1998] 2 Cr.App.R. 79, see A. Choo and S. **33–17**
Nash, "What's the Matter with Section 78?" in [1999] Crim.L.R. 929.

(b) *Offences instigated*

In *R. v Looseley* [2001] UKHL 53; [2001] 1 WLR 2060. Lord Nicholls said **33–18**
that when considering an application by the defence to exclude evidence from an agent provocateur under s.78 "courts should distinguish clearly between an application to exclude evidence on the ground that the defendant should not be tried at all" (which should be handled as an application to stay the proceedings) and "an application to exclude evidence on the grounds of procedural fairness" (para. 18). In the latter case, the question is whether admitting the evidence will adversely affect the fairness of the proceedings. Evidence from an agent provocateur should be excluded "if there is good reason to question the credibility of evidence given by an agent provocateur, or which casts doubt on the reliability of other evidence procured by or resulting from his actions, and that question is not susceptible of being properly or fairly resolved in the course of the proceedings from available, admissible and "untainted" evidence" *per* Potter L.J. *R. v Shannon* [2001] 1 WLR 51, 69 (cited in *Looseley supra* with approval by Lord Hoffman at para. 43 and Lord Hutton at para. 103).
If the trial judge refuses to exclude evidence under s.78 because of entrapment, the Court of Appeal said in *R. v Elwell* [2001] All ER (D) 248, the defence will not be allowed to admit evidence of the entrapment as part of its case because this would amount to an invitation to the jury to consider entrapment as a defence, which it is not.
For an analysis of Strasbourg jurisprudence on entrapment and Article 6 of the European Convention, see B. Emmerson & A. Ashworth, *Human Rights and Criminal Justice* (London, 2001), paras 15–35 et seq.

NOTE 72. See also *R. v Looseley* [2001] UKHL 53; [2001] 1 WLR 2060. **33–18**

(14) European Convention on Human Rights

Breach of Article 8 (respect for private life) is, of itself, irrelevant to questions **33–21**
of admissibility at trial. The issue is whether Article 6 (the right to a fair trial) has

been breached: *Khan v UK* (2000) 8 B.H.R.C. 310, paras 29–39. In *R. v P* [2002] 1 A.C. 146, Lord Hobhouse said that Article 6 does not entitle a defendant "to have unlawfully obtained evidence excluded just because it was so obtained. What he is entitled to is an opportunity to challenge its use and admission in evidence and a judicial assessment of the effect of its admission upon the fairness of the trial as is provided for by section 78". See also *R. v Loveridge*, [2001] 2 Cr.App.R. 591, CA; *R. v Wright* [2001] EWCA Crim 1394.

No principle of common law or of European Convention on Human Rights law prohibits the use of unlawfully obtained evidence (provided that there has been no ill-treatment of the accused such as to violate Article 3): *BOC Ltd v Barlow* [2001] All E.R. (D.) 53, CA. Article 6, in conjunction with Article 13, however, requires an effective procedure for challenging the admissibility of illegally obtained evidence: *Schenk v Switzerland* (1991) 13 E.H.R.R. 242, para. 47. For a detailed discussion of the Convention case law see B. Emmerson & A. Ashworth, *Human Rights and Criminal Justice* (London, 2001), para. 15–06 et seq. When the admissibility of unlawfully obtained evidence is challenged in an English criminal trial, the issue is whether the evidence can be admitted without rendering the trial as a whole unfair. In *Attorney-General's Reference (No.3 of 1999)* [2001] 2 A.C. 91, the House of Lords held that a trial was not unfair where evidence was admitted that was based on information obtained as a result of the failure to destroy a DNA sample in accordance with the requirements of s.64(3B)(b) of the Police and Criminal Evidence Act 1984. For a fuller discussion of how English courts should exercise their discretion under s.78 in cases of unlawfully obtained evidence in the post-Human Rights Act era see B. Emmerson & A. Ashworth, *Human Rights and Criminal Justice* (London, 2001), paras 15–22 et seq. See also *Taylor-Sabori v United Kingdom*, App. No. 47114/99, *The Times*, October 31, 2002 (interception of pager messages—violation of Article 8).

NOTE 95. Case note (2000) 4 E. & P. 268.

(16) Procedure

33–23   Section 78 confers a power to exclude evidence in terms wide enough for it to be exercised on the court's own motion: *R. v Governor of Brixton Prison, Ex p. Saifi* [2001] 1 W.L.R. 1134.

(17a) Extradition proceedings

33–24A   At common law a magistrate has no discretion to refuse to admit admissible evidence in committal proceedings: *R. v Conway* (1990) 91 Cr.App.R. 143. Lord Hoffmann, however, said in *R. v Governor of Brixton Prison, Ex p. Levin* [1997] A.C. 741 at 748 that s.78 applied. The issue on an application to exercise s.78 is whether the admission of the disputed evidence would have an adverse effect on the fairness of the extradition proceedings themselves, not whether it would have an adverse effect on the fairness of the trial after the defendant's return: the magistrate should assume that the trial judge in the foreign court can ensure a fair trial. The test by which to decide whether to exclude evidence is whether admitting it "would outrage civilized values". A refusal to exclude evidence under s.78 was upheld in *R. v Bow Street Magistrates' Court, Ex p. Proulx* [2001]

1 All E.R. 57 at 89 and *R. v Governor of Brixton Prison, Ex p. Saifi* [2001] 1 W.L.R. 1134. An apparent breach of the law of the country seeking extradition is a matter relevant to the exercise of the s.78 discretion but, according to Lord Nolan in *R. v Khan* [1997] A.C. 558, a court is not obliged to decide whether or not there has been a breach of foreign law. This proviso is criticised in para. 33–25, below, but the criticism is perhaps directed only to cases in which s.78 is applied in the course of a trial. Also see Case Note (1998) 2 E. & P. 198.

(18) Burden of proof

In *R. v Governor of Brixton Prison, Ex p. Saifi* [2001] 1 W.L.R. 1134, an **33–25** extradition application, the Court of Appeal rejected the argument that the prosecution have to disprove allegations under s.78 to the criminal standard, or, indeed, that the concepts of onus and burden of proof have any application. Lord Justice Rose observed at para. 52:

> "No doubt it is for that reason that there is no express provision as to the burden of proof, and we see no basis for implying such a burden. The prosecution desiring to adduce and the defence seeking to exclude evidence will each seek to persuade the court about impact on fairness. We regard the position as neutral and see no reason why section 78 should be understood as requiring the court to consider upon whom the burden of proof rests."

In extradition proceedings an investigation in the nature of a full trial to resolve disputed facts was neither practical nor desirable and was not intended by the terms of s.78. In exercising the s.78 discretion the court must have regard to all the circumstances which could reasonably have a bearing on the issue of fairness including ones not raised by the defence.

> "The weight to be attached to an individual circumstance may increase or decrease because of the presence of other related or unrelated circumstances. The preponderance of all the circumstances may show that the admission of the evidence would have such an adverse effect on fairness as to require its exclusion." (para. 58).

(20) Interviews and confessions

If a mentally ill person is deprived of the safeguards meant to be afforded to **33–27** vulnerable persons, a confession is likely to be excluded under s.78, *e.g. R. v Aspinall* (1999) 49 B.M.L.R. 82.

Although the Codes of Practice do not apply directly to prison officers, failure to abide by the spirit of the Codes may lead to the exclusion of a confession under s.78: *R. v Martin Taylor*, unreported, March 16, 2000, CA. There may be circumstances where a Youth Court should exclude a confession by a young person under s.78 who was interviewed in the absence of an appropriate adult even though there was no breach of the Code because the accused had reached the age of 17. Courts should be aware of the pressure for a young person to get things over and done with: *R. v Stratford Youth Court* [2001] All E.R. (D.) 364, DC.

(21) Identification evidence

NOTE 31. *R. v Forbes* [2001] 1 A.C. 473 at 487; *R. v Popat (No.2)* (2000) 164 J.P. **33–28** 65, CA.; *R. v Nunes* [2001] EWCA Crim 2283.

(22) Evidence under Police and Criminal Evidence Act 1984, s.74 of a conviction

33–29 NOTE 33. *R. v Dixon* (2000) 164 J.P. 721, CA.

(23) Other examples

33–30 Magistrates should be slow to exclude evidence of the taking of a specimen under the Road Traffic Act 1988 because of a technical shortcoming in the procedure carried out at the roadside: *DPP v Kay* [1999] R.T.R. 109.

In *R. v PR* [2001] 1 W.L.R. 1314, the Court of Appeal suggested that where similar fact evidence is admissible, the trial judge still has a discretion under s.78 to decide whether to admit it and, if so, whether to admit it in its entirety. Query: if similar fact evidence is admissible because of its high probative value, it seems unlikely that a judge could exercise discretion to wholly exclude it under s.78.

(25) Abuse of process

33–32 NOTE 41. In *R. v Sutherland* Nottingham Cr Ct January 29, 2002 the police had covertly recorded conversations in an exercise yard. In so doing they had ignored the conditions for intercepting legally privileged communications laid down in the *Draft Code of Practice on Covert Surveillance*. In the circumstances (violation of private conversations protected by s.58 PACE between detainees and their solicitors), the police conduct also contravened Article 6 of the ECHR and therefore s.6(1) of the HRA. Both as a matter of principle and because there could be no equality of arms in the circumstances, Newman J. stopped the trial.

33–32 NOTE 44. *R. v Hardwicke* [2001] Crim.L.R. 220, CA (stay refused: lawlessness by investigative journalist distinguished from executive lawlessness). *R. v Looseley* [2001] UKHL 53; [2001] 1 WLR 2060 where Lord Nicholls said at para. 16 that "the grant of a stay, rather than the exclusion of evidence at the trial, should normally be regarded as the appropriate response in a case of entrapment . . . A prosecution founded on entrapment would be an abuse of the court's process." See also Lord Hoffmann at para. 42 and Lord Hutton para. 104. The case is also important for establishing that proactive conduct by police officers should not be viewed as constituting incitement or instigation, and therefore according to *Teixeira de Castro v Portugal* (1999) 28 EHRR 101, a contravention of Article 6, where the conduct is, in the words of McHugh J. in *Ridgeway v R* (1995) 194 CLR 19, 92, "consistent with the ordinary temptations and stratagems that are likely to be encountered in the course of criminal activity". Other factors that may have to be taken into account include the nature of the offence, the reason for the particular police operation and the nature and extent of police participation in the crime. The stronger the inducement and the more persistent and forceful the police overtures, the more likely the court will conclude that the police have induced the crime. The defendant's criminal record is unlikely to be relevant unless linked to factors grounding reasonable suspicion of criminal activity. "Since the English doctrine assumes the defendant's guilt and is concerned with the standards of behaviour of the law enforcement officers, predisposition is irrelevant to whether a stay should be granted or not" *per* Lord Hoffmann (para. 68). All law lords agreed that these principles were consistent

with the ECHR's decision in *Teixeira de Castro v Portugal* (1999) 28 EHRR
101.

NOTE 45. Guidance was given on how to approach an application to stay   **33–32**
proceedings because of the loss of video tape evidence useful to the defence in
R. v Feltham Magistrates' Court [2001] 1 W.L.R. 1279. The Divisional Court
said that no stay should be imposed unless the defendant could show on the
balance of probabilities that the defence would suffer serious prejudice to the
extent that the accused could not receive a fair trial or the prosecution had
behaved so badly (either by acting in bad faith or because of some serious fault)
that it was unfair to try the defendant.
   On the procedure to be followed when application is made to stay a
prosecution as an abuse of process see the *Practice Direction (Crown Court:
Abuse of Process Applications)* [2000] 1 W.L.R. 1134.

2.—CIVIL PROCEEDINGS

(1) Discretion prior to the civil justice reforms

   On the absence of a common law discretion to exclude evidence in civil   **33–34**
proceedings see *Arab Monetary Fund v Hashim (No.2)* [1990] 1 All E.R. 673 at
681.

RES GESTAE

2.—RELEVANT FACTS AS PART OF THE *RES GESTAE*

(1) Category 1 in *Ratten v R.*

34–03   The admissibility at common law of a fact as part of the *res gestae* when no issue of hearsay arises usually depends on nothing more than its relevance: *Bull v R.* (2000) 171 A.L.R. 613, HCA, *per* McHugh, Gummow and Hayne JJ. Relevance in this context, it is submitted, means direct and not circumstantial relevance. It is this that distinguishes evidence disclosing misconduct by the accused that is admitted as part of the *res gestae* (*e.g. O'Leary v The King* (1946) 73 C.L.R 566 and para. 34–06, below) from similar fact evidence (see para. 17–20).

34–06   NOTE 16. See also *R v North* [1999] DCR 1063; 1999 NZDCR LEXIS 39.

3.—DECLARATION AS PART OF *RES GESTAE* RECEIVED AS ORIGINAL EVIDENCE

(1) Two categories of declarations

34–09   It has been suggested that using the *res gestae* rule to admit declarations that are not hearsay is unnecessary and confusing: S. J. Odgers, "Res Gestae Regurgitated" in (1989) 12 UNSWLR 262.

(2) Declarations which are facts in issue or relevant facts

34–10   A statement by the accused that explains his actions and is admissible against him as part of the *res gestae* is not generally admissible evidence against a co-defendant: *Hamill v H.M. Advocate* [1999] S.L.T. 963, HC.

4.—Spontaneous Statements as Exceptions to the Hearsay Rule

(3) Cases prior to *Ratten v R.*

NOTE 53. The decision in *Bedingfield* is defended on its facts by D. Wilde, **34–15** "Hearsay in Criminal Cases: *Res Gestae* And Dying Declarations: *R. v. Bedingfield Revisited*" in (2000) 4 E. & P. 107.

(6) *R. v Andrews*

NOTE 83. For a critique of *R. v Andrews* [1987] A.C. 281, see D. Ormerod, **34–22** "Redundant Res Gestae" [1998] Crim.L.R. 301 an article which examines the Law Commission's proposal (*Evidence in Criminal Proceedings: Hearsay and Related Topics*, Report No. 245 (1997)) to retain the *res gestae* exceptions to hearsay.

NOTE 86. In *R. v West*, September 14, 1999, unreported, CA, a witness was **34–22** permitted to give evidence that she overheard the victim shout the accused's name. The victim was a witness for the prosecution and this evidence supported her credibility.

In *Furbert v R.* [2000] 1 W.L.R. 1716, the Privy Council held that evidence tendered by a co-defendant of a statement by the deceased shortly after he was shot as to the identity of his assailant was of no relevance and therefore inadmissible because he could not, on the evidence, have seen who shot him.

NOTE 87. See too *R. v Harris* [2002] EWCA Crim 1597 where prosecution **34–22** evidence of a telephone conversation between a child and the police was excluded because of the possibility that what she had said might have been distorted by earlier conversations between the child and other adults. Details of these conversations were not before the jury.

CHAPTER 35

COMMON LAW EXCEPTIONS TO THE RULE AGAINST HEARSAY:
STATEMENTS BY DECEASED PERSONS

1.—GENERAL

(4) Miscellaneous

35–06   The admission into evidence (here pursuant to s.259 of the Criminal Procedure
(Scotland) Act 1995) of statements of a deceased witness which strongly
inculpate an accused does not violate the accused's rights under Article 6(1) and
(3)(d) of the European Convention on Human Rights 1950: *McKenna (Michael)
v H.M. Advocate* 2000 J.C. 291; *H.M. Advocate v Bain* [2001] Scot. HC 31; 2002
S.L.T. 340, both High Court of Justiciary (Appeal). As to the timing of objections
to admission of such evidence in criminal trials, see *H.M. Advocate v Bain.*

2.—DECLARATIONS AGAINST INTEREST

(5) The interest

35–11   The manner in which an admitted debt is paid does not constitute a sufficient
interest for this purpose: *R. v Moore and Hawkins* [1999] EWCA Crim 2131,
CA.

6.—DYING DECLARATIONS IN CASES OF HOMICIDE

(3) Homicide of declarant

35–62   In *R. v Kelly* (2001) 132 Can CC 122 the New Brunswick Court of Appeal
rejected an attempt to admit hearsay evidence of a deceased witness in a non-
homicide case.

[126]

CHAPTER 36

COMMON LAW EXCEPTIONS TO THE RULE AGAINST HEARSAY: STATEMENTS IN PUBLIC OR OFFICE DOCUMENTS, CORPORATION BOOKS AND PUBLISHED WORKS; ANCIENT DOCUMENTS AS EVIDENCE OF ANCIENT POSSESSION

5.—OFFICIAL CERTIFICATES, LETTERS AND RETURNS

(4) Examples of certificates

Also see *Attorney-General for the Cayman Islands v Roberts* [2002] UKPC **36–37** 18; [2002] 1 W.L.R. 1842 (certificate certifying substance to be cocaine).

6.—CORPORATION, COMPANY AND BANKERS' BOOKS

(4) Bankers' books

The words "other records" are not apt to cover records kept by a bank of **36–46** conversations between its employees, however senior, and its customer, but cover records of the same kind as ledgers, day books, cash books and account books which are the means by which a bank records day-to-day financial transactions: *Re Howglen Ltd* [2000] 1 All E.R. 376.

Section 9 of the Bankers' Books Evidence Act 1879 has been amended by various enactments and reads as follows:

(1) In this Act the expressions "bank" and "banker" mean—

    (a) a deposit-taker;] [and]
    (b) ... ;
    (c) the National Savings Bank;
    (d) ....

(1A) "Deposit taker" means—

(a) a person who has permission under Pt 4 of the Financial Services and Markets Act 2000 to accept deposits; or

(b) an EEA firm of the kind mentioned in para. 5(b) of Sch. 3 to that Act which has permission under para. 15 of that Schedule (as a result of qualifying for authorisation under para. 12(1) of that Schedule) to accept deposits or other repayable funds from the public.

(1B) But a person is not a deposit-taker if he has permission to accept deposits only for the purpose of carrying on another regulated activity in accordance with that permission.

(1C) Subs.(1A) and (1B) must be read with—

(a) s.22 of the Financial Services and Markets Act 2000;
(b) any relevant order under that section; and
(c) Sch. 2 to that Act.

(2) Expressions in this Act relating to "bankers' books" include ledgers, day books, cash books, account books and other records used in the ordinary business of the bank, whether those records are in written form or are kept on microfilm, magnetic tape or any other form of mechanical or electronic data retrieval mechanism.

In *R. v Moisan* (2001) 141 Can CC (3rd) 213 an Alberta Queen's Bench Court held that a bank's video surveillance footage was a "copy of any entry in any book or record kept in any financial institution" within ss.29 and 30 of the Canada Evidence Act, R.S.C. 1985.

(a) *Production of original books*

36–47   NOTE 2. "Special cause" may include use as exculpatory evidence in a criminal trial to which the bank is neither accused nor complainant: *R. v Moisan* (2001) 141 Can CC (3rd) 213, Alberta Queen's Bench.

(b) *Inspection*

36–48   As to requirements for valid orders under s.7 see *Blanchfield v Hartnett* [2002] I.E.S.C. 39 *per* Fennelly J., Supreme Court of Ireland.

(c) *Meaning of "bank"*

36–50   See the amended s.9 of the Bankers' Books Evidence Act 1879 at 36–46 above.

7.—Published Histories, Maps, Dictionaries, Tables, etc.

(1) Histories

36–53   Judicial notice will not be given to historical documents if they contain disputed adjectival facts, or are too controversial or uncertain: *R. v Blais* (2001)

198 D.L.R. (4th) 220, Man CA. Also see *Law Society of British Columbia v Gravelle* (2001) 200 DLR (4th) 82, B.C.C.A. (reliance on historical texts and archives to determine whether notaries were probating wills in England prior to November 19, 1858).

(5) Scientific and professional, etc., records

Section 10 of the Civil Evidence Act 1995 is not currently in force in England **36–59** and Wales and has been prospectively repealed in Northern Ireland by the Civil Evidence (Northern Ireland) Ord. 1997, SI 1997/2983 (NI 21), art.13(2), Sch. 2.

CHAPTER 37

OPINION AND EXPERT EVIDENCE

2.—EXCEPTIONS

(2) Opinions of experts

(a) *General*

37–09   NOTE 42. Add Redmayne, *Expert Evidence and Criminal Justice* (OUP, 2000); L. Meintjes-Van der Walt, "Ruling on expert evidence in South Africe: A comparative analysis" (2001) 5 E & P 226.

37–11   For the expert witness' immunity from suit, see *Stanton v Callaghan* [2000] 1 Q.B. 75. See also *Raiss v Paimano* [2000] N.P.C. 101 and New Law Online, case 2010814601, in which it was held that the immunity was not lost through dishonesty.

(b) *Ultimate issue*

37–14   In *R. v Gilfoyle* [2001] 2 Cr.App.R. 57, the Court of Appeal declined to receive the evidence of a psychologist who had recently carried out a "psychological autopsy" on the victim. The appellant's wife had been found hanged in their garage. The prosecution case was that the appellant had tried to disguise the murder as a suicide. One matter relied on at trial by the prosecution was the absence of anything in the victim's personality or behaviour to suggest that she might commit suicide. The psychologist was an expert in the analysis of human behaviour. He had, since the trial, made a fresh study (the "psychological autopsy") of the state of mind of the victim prior to her death, which suggested that there was convincing support for the deceased having committed suicide. The Court of Appeal declined to receive this fresh evidence for a number of reasons having to do with the immaturity of the science, but also because the task of "assessing levels of happiness or unhappiness" is properly one for the jury, involving no matters outwith their collective experience (and so not being a matter properly within the province of expert evidence at all).

However, in *R. v O'Brien, The Times,* February 16, 2000, the Court of Appeal held that expert evidence regarding the defendant's personality and propensity to make false confessions could be admitted even though the defendant was not suffering from a recognised mental illness. He suffered from a personality disorder. The test for admission had to do not with the categorisation of the disorder but its propensity to render a confession unreliable. However, such expert evidence was to be limited to disorders where there was a substantial deviation from the norm and a history indicative of abnormality that pre-dated the confession.

NOTE 17. In *R. v Gilfoyle* [2001] 2 Cr.App.R. 57, the Court of Appeal (*per* Rose   **37–14** L.J.) expressed the view (*obiter*) that there may well be mental conditions falling short of mental illness, in relation to which the jury would require expert evidence.

(3) Expert evidence in civil proceedings

(b) *The new system summarised*

(ii) EXPERT'S DUTY TO THE COURT

CPR, r.35.14, which permitted an expert to seek directions from the court,   **37–24** even without notifying the parties, has been amended with effect from March 25, 2002. Now the expert must (unless the court otherwise directs) provide a copy of any proposed request for directions to the parties before filing it with the court (see 44–221).

(iii) EXPERT'S REPORTS

CPR, Pt 35 Practice Direction—Experts and Assessors was substantially   **37–26** revised and renumbered with effect from March 2002 (see 44–208). In considering questions of expert evidence the court is entitled to take into account the Codes of Guidance of any relevant professional body: *Peet v Mid-Kent Healthcare Trust (Practice Note)* [2002] 1 W.L.R. 210, C.A. Particularly useful in this context are the *Code of Guidance for Experts and those instructing them* (Academy of Experts, 1 June 2001 revision) and *Code of Guidance on Expert Evidence: A Guide for Experts and those instructing them for the purpose of Court proceedings* (Expert Witness Institute, December 2001). For proceedings in the Commercial Court, see Commercial Court Guide (6th ed., 2002), para. H2.

(iv) COURT'S GENERAL CONTROL OF EXPERT EVIDENCE

The principles on allowing expert evidence were reviewed in detail by Evans-   **37–28** Lombe J. in *Barings Plc v Coopers & Lybrand* [2001] Lloyd's Rep. Bank 85. It is for the party seeking to call expert evidence to satisfy the court that expert evidence is available which would have a bearing on the issues which the court has to decide and would be helpful to the court in coming to a conclusion on those issues. The evidence of the experts should be exchanged and filed well in advance of the hearing. It clearly serves the purposes of effective case management that, as far as possible, issues relating to the admissibility of expert evidence be disposed of well before the trial starts so that significant costs can be saved. The judge derived the following propositions from the authorities [at 45]:

"Expert evidence is admissible under section 3 of the Civil Evidence Act 1972 in any case where the court accepts that there exists a recognised expertise governed by recognised standards and rules of conduct capable of influencing the court's decision on any of the issues which it has to decide and the witness to be called satisfies the court that he has a sufficient familiarity with and knowledge of the expertise in question to render his opinion potentially of value in resolving any of those issues. Evidence meeting this test can still be excluded by the court if the court takes the view that calling it will not be helpful to the court in resolving any issue in the case justly. Such evidence will not be helpful where the issue to be decided is one of law or is otherwise one on which the court is able to come to a fully informed decision without hearing such evidence".

For a case where the Court of Appeal reversed (in part) the judge's decision not to allow expert evidence, see *Mann v Messrs Chetty and Patel (a firm)* [2000] EWCA Civ 267. In that case the Court of Appeal stated that in deciding whether to allow expert evidence the Court has to make a judgment on at least three matters:

    (a) how cogent the proposed expert evidence will be;

    (b) how helpful it will be in resolving any of the issues in the case; and

    (c) how much it will cost and the relationship of that cost to the sums at stake.

The difficulties for a judge at the case management stage of deciding what is expedient and proportionate are recognised and illustrated by *Mann v Messrs Chetty and Patel* above. The problems are even more demanding in a case where a single joint expert has been appointed: see *Kranidiotes v Paschali* [2001] EWCA Civ 347, CA. In that case the court substituted a cheaper expert than the one originally appointed by the court.

The last sentence of this paragraph requires some qualification. The court will refuse permission to rely on expert evidence when a previous application has been refused and there has been no material change of circumstances: *Jameson v Smith* [2001] EWCA Civ 1264, [2001] 6 C.P.L.R. 489, CA.

The parties are expected to apply for permission to adduce expert evidence well before trial. The court will refuse permission if it is sought just before trial and to grant it would cause injustice to an opponent: *Calenti v North Middlesex NHS Trust*, March 2, 2001 (unreported) QBD (Buckley J.); *Dew Pitchmastic Plc v Birse Construction Ltd* 78 Con L.R. 162, QBD (T&CC). Permission may be granted even if sought late in the day where appropriate: *Hanley v Stage and Catwalk Ltd* [2001] EWCA Civ 1739, CA (permission granted to both sides shortly before trial); *Holmes v SGB Services Plc* [2001] EWCA Civ 354, CA (permission granted to call further expert and trial adjourned in light of report of the single joint expert). The court may also extend time for service of a report: *Meredith v College Valuation Services Ltd* [2001] EWCA Civ 1456, CA.

A party is not obliged to produce his expert's report to his opponent if he decides not to adduce it. This is the case even where the expert's selection had not been opposed using the procedure in the Pre-Action Protocol for Personal Injury Claims, paras 3.14–3.21: *Carlson v Townsend* [2001] 1 W.L.R. 2415, CA.

(v) Restriction and Control of Expert Evidence

(iii) *Single joint expert*

In *Daniels v Walker* [2000] 1 W.L.R. 1382, the Court of Appeal (*per* Lord   **37–39**
Woolf M.R.) set out guidance on the steps to be taken where a party was
dissatisfied with a single joint expert's report. Lord Woolf drew a distinction
between substantial cases (such as that before him) and cases of modest value. In
the latter type of case, it may be that the cost of obtaining a further report from
another expert would be disproportionate to the value of the claim. If it were,
then the most that should be allowed is for the dissatisfied party to put a question
to the joint expert who has already prepared a report. However, in cases where
a substantial amount was at stake, whilst the appointment of a single joint expert
was ideally the first step, it would not always be the last. A party should, if they
so wished, be allowed to obtain further information before deciding whether they
wished to challenge any part of the report. They would then have to decide
whether to resolve any disagreement by posing further questions to the joint
expert or by obtaining their own expert report.

In a case where the party obtained its own expert report, it was desirable that
the experts then held a meeting to see if any of the issues between them could be
resolved. Oral evidence from the experts was to be seen as a last resort. An
argument was also addressed to the court based on Article 6 of the European
Convention on Human Rights: the refusal of the trial judge to allow the defendant
to instruct their own expert was a breach of the defendant's Article 6 right in that
it amounted to a barring of an essential part of the claim. Lord Woolf gave this
argument short shrift and took the opportunity to issue a general warning to
counsel in future cases to take a responsible attitude to running human rights
arguments. Lord Woolf clearly felt that such arguments were superfluous given
that the overriding objective of the CPR is to deal with cases *justly*. It may be
observed that it is a slightly odd culmination of the history of the fearless
advocate in the cause of human rights to say that he has to be careful not to take
a point based on the Human Rights Act 1998 which the court thinks a bad one
lest he "discredit" (Lord Woolf's word) the legislation.

Following *Daniels*, Neuberger J. in *Cosgrove v Pattison* [2001] 2 C.P.L.R. 177
went on to list nine factors which were, in his opinion, relevant when deciding
whether or not to allow a party who was dissatisfied with the joint expert to call
their own expert:

   (i) the nature of the issues,

   (ii) the number of issues between the parties,

  (iii) the reason the new expert is wanted,

  (iv) the amount at stake,

   (v) the effect of permitting further expert evidence to be called on the
conduct of the trial,

  (vi) any delay in making the application,

 (vii) any delay that instructing and calling the new expert will cause,

(viii) any special features of the case,

(ix) the overall justice to the parties.

See also *Mutch v Allen* [2001] 2 C.P.L.R. 200 and *Holmes v SGB Services Plc* [2001] EWCA Civ 354, CA.

It should be noted that in *Oxley v Penwarden* [2001] C.P.L.R. 1, the Court of Appeal emphasised that there was no presumption that a single joint expert should be appointed in all cases. There clearly were cases, such as the present (a medical negligence case where the central issue was causation) where a joint expert would not be appropriate. Mantell L.J. considered that, in such a case, were a single joint expert ordered, and the parties unable to agree a nomination (as was likely) then the judge would bear the burden of selecting an expert himself. In an area where there was more than one school of thought, the choice would effectively decide an essential question in the case without the opportunity for challenge.

37–39   NOTE 4. By chance there has now been a controlled experiment relating to the comparative merits of the two systems. In the UK/EC Report of the *Surveys of the M.V. Derbyshire* (March 1998) certain conclusions were reached by an expert investigator who was fully qualified and wholly independent: his sole aim was to establish the truth of the way in which the *Derbyshire* was lost. At the Re-opened Formal Investigation in the Loss of the *M.V. Derbyshire*, the conclusion of this expert was challenged by parties who were able to call their own witnesses to give a contradictory opinion and by their advocates to cross-examine the expert. For many weeks of the hearing, he adhered to the theory he had propounded (despite being cross-examined on at least three occasions by several counsel and having access to the written factual and expert material of those parties). Eventually, he accepted that the explanation which he had given in all good faith was not the correct one. The truth was established because parties with an interest to serve focused on the contentious findings more intensely than an independent and disinterested expert could do.

(vi) EXPERT EVIDENCE IN CRIMINAL PROCEEDINGS

37–42   The requirement that an expert be a truly independent witness has caused problems in two recent cases. In *Field v Leeds City Council* [2001] 2 C.P.L.R. 129, the council sought to call one of its own employees to act as its expert in a claim made against them as a housing authority for disrepair. The court was strongly influenced by public policy considerations: the defendant would have to meet its legal costs out of the ring-fenced funds it had available for housing repairs. Lord Woolf M.R. held that the simple fact of employment did not disqualify the employee from acting as an expert witness for his employer. An employee was capable of being independent. However, before a person could give evidence as an expert, the court had to be satisfied on two counts: (i) that the person had the relevant expertise in an area in issue, and (ii) that the person was fully aware of the primacy of an expert's duty to the court. In the present case there was not enough information before the court as to the particular employee's experience, and the actual nature of his employment, to decide whether he was qualified to give expert evidence. Furthermore, if the council wished to use him, it would be incumbent on them to show that the proposed expert had full knowledge of his duties to the court and, in particular, the requirement of objectivity.

The fact of the expert's employment may go to the weight the judge assigns to his evidence (*per* May L.J.). However, a seemingly contrary approach was taken by Evans-Lombe J. in *Liverpool Roman Catholic Archdiocesan Trust v Goldberg, (No.3)* [2001] 1 W.L.R. 2337. In that case, in which *Field* was not cited in the judgment, the defendant (who was a barrister) wished to call a friend and colleague from the same chambers to give expert evidence on his behalf. The proposed expert stated in his report that he did not believe that his relationship with the defendant would affect his evidence, though he admitted that his personal sympathies were engaged to a greater extent than would be normal for an expert witness. Evans-Lombe J. held that this relationship disqualified the friend from being called to give expert evidence as the evidence should be *seen* to be the independent product of the expert. His Lordship did not, apparently, doubt that the friend was in fact capable of the requisite degree of independence. However, on grounds of public policy, his evidence should not be admitted because the relationship between the expert and the defendant was such as "a reasonable observer might think was capable of affecting the views of the expert so as to make them unduly favourable to that party". In so holding, Evans-Lombe J. departed from the initial opinion of Neuberger J. (before whom the application to exclude had been made and who had stood the matter over to trial) that the evidence was admissible, the relationship between the expert and the defendant going only to the weight to be ascribed to the evidence.

With respect, it must be doubted whether the decision of Evans-Lombe J. in the above case can be other than *per incuriam*, given the decision of the Court of Appeal in *Field*: Stanley Burton J., *Admiral Management Services Ltd v Para-Protect Ltd* [2002] EWHC 233; [2002] 1 W.L.R. 2722 at [33]. The relationship of employer-employee is surely a relationship which a "reasonable observer" would think capable of affecting the evidence of an expert/employee. However, the decision in *Field* leaves no room for a principle that "justice must be seen to be done". All it requires is that justice must in fact be done—as long as the judge is satisfied that the expert is fully aware of the primacy of his duty to the court, the effect that a relationship between the expert and a party may have on the suspicions of a reasonable observer are irrelevant.

(6) Compellability of expert witnesses

In *Brown v Bennett, The Times,* November 2, 2000, the Claimants issued a **37–49** witness summons against their own expert who they were no longer able to pay. At the application of the expert, Neuberger J. set aside the summons, saying that only in an exceptional case would an expert who could not be paid be compelled to testify. In *R. v Davies (Keith), The Times,* March 4, 2002, CA it was held wrong to permit the Crown to call the defendant's own psychiatric expert, who he had declined to call. This was because the evidence was inextricably dependent on privileged material and fell within s.10(1)(b) of the Police and Criminal Evidence Act 1984. Furthermore, the defendant was entitled to protection from inadvertently incriminating himself. It may be a breach of confidence for an expert to send a copy of his report to a third party without his client's consent: *De Taranto v Cornelius* [2001] EWCA Civ 1511, CA.

(8) Subject of expert testimony: obscene articles, science, art, trade, technical terms, handwriting, foreign law identity

(i) Facts

37–61   It is debatable whether the science of lip reading has sufficiently developed to permit the use of expert evidence. Despite the reservations expressed by A. Campbell-Tiech in an article, "Lip reading as expert evidence", [2002] 4 Archbold News, such evidence has been admitted by a number of judges.

(j) Identity

37–62   In *R v Dallagher* [2002] EWCA Crim 1903; [2002] Crim.L.R. 821; *The Times*, August 21, 2002 ear print expert evidence was held to be admissible, albeit the conviction in that case was set aside.

In *R. v O'Doherty* [2002] Crim.L.R. 761 the Court of Appeal in Northern Ireland stated that on the present state of scientific knowledge no prosecution should be brought one plank of which is voice identification evidence, subject to defined exceptions. The court also gave guidance on warnings to the jury in such cases. See also D. Ormerod, "Sounding out Expert Voice Identification" [2002] Crim.L.R. 771.

37–62   NOTE 22. See also *R. v Hookway* [1999] Crim.L.R. 750 in which it was held by the Court of Appeal that facial mapping evidence standing alone could afford a case that could properly be left to the jury.

(9) Subjects on which experts may not testify

(a) Construction of documents: statutory terms

37–64   NOTE 35. See also *LHS Holdings Ltd v Laporte Plc* [2001] 2 All E.R. (Comm) 563, CA: expert evidence on the meaning of a phrase in a contractual dispute notice was not permitted because it was directed not towards explaining technical language (there was none) but towards establishing that the notice did not set out reasonable details of the grounds of dispute as was contractually required. That question was for the court alone to answer.

(b) Professional conduct

37–65   Expert evidence is receivable to elucidate the rules and practices of any profession where there is a "recognised expertise governed by recognised standards and rules of conduct" (*per* Evans-Lombe J. in *Barings Plc v Coopers & Lybrand* [2001] Lloyd's Rep. Bank 85). It is not necessary that there exists some professional institute governing the profession, nor even a written code of practice or rules. Indeed, Evans-Lombe J. was of the opinion that it is in cases where there is no written code that expert evidence is often most necessary. In the case before the court, his Lordship held that expert evidence on the management of investment banks involved in futures and derivatives trading was admissible, there existing a sufficient body of expertise with recognised standards in that area. In *R. v Wahab* [2002] EWCA Crim 1570 [at 43], the Court of Appeal highlighted the inappropriate deployment of expert evidence from one solicitor, criticising a solicitor retained on behalf of a suspect who was challenging the reliability of his confession on the basis of incompetent advice; the judge did not need expert legal evidence.

(c) *English law: morals: human nature*

NOTE 42. See also *R. v Gilfoyle* [2001] Cr.App.R. 57, CA.   **37–66**

CHAPTER 38

JUDGMENTS

2.—Judgments as Giving Rise to Estoppels in Subsequent Proceedings

(1) All judgments are impeachable on certain grounds

(a) Not final

38–05   The Court of Appeal in *Taylor v Lawrence* [2002] EWCA Civ 90; [2002] 3 W.L.R. 640 has recognised that it has power to re-open an appeal which it has already determined by way of a final judgment in order to avoid real injustice in exceptional circumstances. The court will only do so where there is no alternative remedy by way of appeal to the House of Lords. Permission of the court is required in order to make an application. In *Seray-Wurie v Hackney LBC* [2002] EWCA Civ 909, the Court of Appeal extended this exceptional discretion to decisions of the High Court when it is sitting as an appellate court. In order to exercise this power it must be clearly established that a significant injustice has occurred and there is no alternative effective remedy.

(4) Judgments in civil cases as affecting parties and privies

(a) Introductory

38–15   NOTE 20. See generally *Johnson v Gore Wood* [2002] 2 A.C. 1 HL.

(b) Merger

(iv) Different Parties and Parties in Different Capacities

38–21   NOTE 51. Add *The Irina Zharkikh* [2001] 2 Lloyd's Rep. 319 (N.Z.H.Ct. in Admiralty), following *The Rena K* [1979] QB 377.

(v) ARBITRATION AND MERGER

Where a claim which can be the subject of the *in rem* procedure is referred to   **38–22**
arbitration and is the subject of an award, the *in rem* procedure cannot then be
invoked by way of an action on the award: *The Bumbesti* [1999] 2 Lloyd's Rep.
481.

NOTE 64. Add *The Irina Zharkikh* [2001] 2 Lloyd's Rep. 319 at 327 (N.Z.H.Ct.   **38–22**
in Admiralty), where it was observed that the cases seem to draw a distinction
between claims for damages which are settled by arbitral award (in which case
there is judicial unanimity that the underlying cause of action merges with the
arbitral award) and claims for debt (where the prevailing view is, rather, that
there is no merger).

(c) *Res Judicata Estoppels*

(iii) SAME PARTIES OR THEIR PRIVIES

See generally *Johnson v Gore Wood* [2001] 2 W.L.R. 72, HL. See also Watt,   **38–25**
"The Danger and Deceit of the Rule in *Henderson v Henderson*: a New
Approach to Successive Actions Arising From The Same Factual Matter" [2000]
19 C.L.J. 287.

Privity of interest

NOTE 36. See generally *Johnson v Gore Wood* [2002] 2 A.C. 1 HL.   **38–29**

(iv) SAME SUBJECT-MATTER

Same issue in the subsequent case

NOTE 56. See also *S.G.I. Ltd v Deakin*, May 23, 2001, New Law Online, case   **38–33**
201059503.

(vii) ISSUE ESTOPPEL

Foreign courts

NOTE 96. See *Baker v McCall*, New Law Online, case 2990916002, September   **38–40**
22, 1999.

(viii) FRESH EVIDENCE AND OTHER SPECIAL CIRCUMSTANCES

In *S.G.I. Ltd v Deakin*, May 23, 2001, New Law Online, case 201059503,   **38–42**
Aldous L.J. appears to have had in mind a unified approach to issue estoppel and
Henderson v Henderson abuse of process. Having quoted from the judgment of
Lord Bingham in *Johnson v Gore Wood* [2002] 2 A.C. 1, Aldous L.J. applied
these comments in the context of issue estoppel. In deciding whether relitigation
of an issue decided in earlier proceedings is an abuse of process, the court should
decide, "whether, in all the circumstances, a party is misusing or abusing the

process of the court by seeking to raise before it the issue which could have been raised before" (*per* Aldous L.J. quoting the words of Lord Bingham in *Johnson*). With respect, and as is clear from the passage quoted, Lord Bingham was referring only to *Henderson v Henderson* abuse—where an issue was not raised in the earlier proceedings—and was not commenting on the correct approach in cases of issue estoppel—where the issue had been decided in the earlier proceedings. See, by way of contrast, the judgment of May L.J. in the same case where he gives a summary of the differences of approach to cause of action estoppel (absolute bar), issue estoppel (likely but not inevitably a bar) and *Henderson v Henderson* abuse (requires a "broad merits based procedural judgment" to decide whether a bar).

(ix) THE WIDER SENSE OF *RES JUDICATA*

38–43   See generally Lord Bingham's speech in *Johnson v Gore Wood & Co* [2002] 2 A.C.1 H.L.

(x) ABUSE OF PROCESS

Claims which could and should have been brought previously

38–44   In *Time Group Limited v Computer 2000 Distribution Limited* [2002] EWHC 126 (TCC), Bowsher J. summarised some of the principles in the following terms at [83]:

"a. The decision "should be a broad merits based judgment which takes account of the public and private interests involved and also takes account of all the facts of the case, focussing attention on the crucial question whether, in all the circumstances, a party is misusing or abusing the process of the court by seeking to raise before it the issue which could have been raised before". See *per* Lord Bingham in *Johnson v Gore Wood*.

b. The categories of abuse of process are not closed: *per* Lord Diplock in *Hunter v Chief Constable of the West Midlands Police* [1982] AC 529 at 536D, and *per* Stuart-Smith LJ in *Ashmore v British Coal* [1990] QB 338 at 352D, and *per* Sir David Cairns in *Bragg v Oceanus Mutual* [1982] 2 Lloyds Rep. 132, 137, 138–139.

c. It is a serious matter to dismiss an action for abuse of process of the court.

d. However, when abuse is repeated, the court has a duty, not a discretion, to dismiss the action: *per* Lord Diplock *ibid*.

e. There is no presumption against successive actions in contract raising similar issues. There are cases where it is perfectly proper to bring successive actions for breach of contract raising similar issues against different parties: *per* May L.J. in *Manson v Vooght* [1999] BPIR 376 at 387–388.

f. There are cases where it is perfectly proper to bring an action against a defendant intending that the only effective recovery shall be from a third party joined by that defendant.

g. The onus of proof of abuse is on the party alleging abuse of the process of the court: *per* Lord Bingham in *Johnson v Gore Wood* at page 90.

h. There is a public interest in finality in litigation including the public interest in efficiency and economy in the conduct of litigation: *ibid*."

In addition it should be noted that there is a well established principle of **38–44A**
practice that if a litigant has brought an action or application against another and
has failed, then he may be precluded from bringing a fresh action or application
until he has paid the costs of the previous proceeding: *Morton v Palmer* (1882)
9 QBD 89 at 92 (Cave J.); *Thames Investment and Securities plc v Benjamin*
[1984] 1 W.L.R. 1381. The principle which enables the court to require the
payment of the costs of a previous unsuccessful action is one which applies
whether the claimant is a company or an individual: *Sinclair v British
Telecommunications plc* [2001] 1 W.L.R. 38 at 45. This jurisdiction is fully wide
enough to make an order against a claimant in the second action who is the
successor in title of the claimant in the first action (*Sinclair v British Telecommunications plc* [2001] 1 W.L.R. 38 at 46) or where the claimant company
was the alter ego of the claimant in the second action (*Barakot v Epiette* [1998]
1 B.C.L.C. 283, CA).

NOTE 14. But see *J.A. Pye (Oxford) Ltd v South Gloucestershire District Council*   **38–45**
[2000] N.P.C. 112, CA, (Transcript: New Law Online, case 1001010102) in
which Otton L.J. held that *Seddon* turned on its own special facts.

Elements of abuse

NOTE 22. But see *J.A. Pye (Oxford) Ltd v South Gloucestershire D.C.* [2000]   **38–47**
N.P.C. 112, CA. See also *Sweetman v Shepherd* [2000] C.P.L.R. 378.

Previous litigation ending in compromise. In *Johnson v Gore Wood & Co*   **38–50**
[2001] 2 W.L.R. 72, the House of Lords also rejected the argument that the rule
in *Henderson v Henderson* does not apply where the first action had culminated
in a compromise and not a judgment.

Special circumstances

In *Johnson v Gore Wood & Co* [2002] 2 A.C. 1, HL, Lord Bingham's view was   **38–51**
that it is preferable to ask whether in all the circumstances a party's conduct is
an abuse than to ask whether the conduct is an abuse and then, if it is, to ask
whether the abuse is excused or justified by special circumstances. In allowing
re-litigation of a claim, the court may decide to impose conditions under the
powers set out at CPR, r.3.1(3) and r.24.6; *Sweetman v Shepherd* [2000] C.P.L.R.
378. A change of circumstances may justify the bringing of a further action. In
Gairy v A-G of Granada [2002] 1 AC 167, the Privy Council qualified the *res
judicata* and abuse of process principles in the following terms at [27]:

> "There is authority, which was not challenged, that a consent order may found a plea
> of *res judicata* even though the court has not been asked to investigate and pronounce
> on the point at issue (see *Spencer Bower, Turner & Handley, Res Judicata*, 3rd ed
> (1996), Ch.2, para.38), and it may well be abusive to raise in later proceedings an issue
> or claim which could and in all the circumstances should have been raised in earlier
> proceedings. But these are rules of justice, intended to protect a party (usually, but not
> necessarily, a defendant) against oppressive or vexatious litigation. Neither rule can
> apply where circumstances have so changed as to make it both reasonable and just for
> a party to raise the issue or pursue the claim in question in later proceedings".

Impecuniosity. However in *Johnson v Gore Wood & Co* [2002] 2 A.C. 1, Lord   **38–54**
Bingham, whilst accepting that lack of funds would not ordinarily excuse a

failure to raise in earlier proceedings an issue which could and should have been raised then, did not regard it as necessarily irrelevant, particularly if it appears that the lack of funds has been caused by the party against whom it is sought to claim.

Application of abuse of process beyond the parties

38–56   Where there are co-defendants in an action, it is not an abuse of process for a defendant who refrains from seeking an indemnity or contribution from a co-defendant in that action to bring subsequent proceedings for that purpose; *per* Kennedy L.J. in *Sweetman v Shepherd* [2000] C.P.L.R. 378, and see *Baker v McCall* [2000] C.L.C. 189.

    See also *J.A. Pye (Oxford) Ltd v South Gloucestershire District Council* [2000] N.P.C. 112.

Collateral attack

38–57   NOTE 48. See generally *Arthur J.S. Hall & Co v Simons* [2002] 1 A.C. 615, HL. You cannot sue the police for beating a confession out of you (*Hunter v Chief Constable*) but you can sue the barrister who fails to elicit the fact in cross-examination.

Effects beyond the parties

38–58   Unsurprisingly, the *Hunter* doctrine of abusive collateral attack played a central role in the decision of the House of Lords in *Arthur J.S. Hall & Co v Simons* [2002] 2 A.C. 615 to remove the advocate's immunity from suit. The operation of the rule in *Hunter* was regarded by the majority of their Lordships as providing the necessary safeguards to prevent litigants using an action against their former advocate as a means of launching a collateral challenge against previous criminal conviction. Lord Hoffmann gave the most extensive analysis of the purpose of the *Hunter* doctrine. In criminal cases, public policy demands that there not be conflicting decisions, since this would bring the system for the administration of justice into disrepute (this is subject to the rare exceptional cases where the existence of conflicting decisions would not, because of special circumstances, have this effect). In the case of a previous conviction, the rule in *Hunter* is sufficient to prevent a litigant bringing an action for negligence against a former legal adviser which might result in two different courts coming to conflicting decisions on the litigant's guilt. A separate rule of advocate's immunity is therefore otiose. However, in civil cases, the issues are normally only of interest to the parties involved. "There is no public interest objection to a subsequent finding that, but for the negligence of his lawyers, the losing party would have won" (*per* Lord Hoffmann, *ibid*, at 706).

    It is not clear from the speech of Lord Hoffmann whether he regarded the *Hunter* doctrine as having any role to play in preventing challenges to previous civil judgments. From his exposition of the public policy rationale behind *Hunter*, it would seem that the doctrine is confined to challenges to earlier convictions. However, both Lord Steyn (at 679) and Lord Browne-Wilkinson (at 685) conceived that there might be some residual role for the *Hunter* doctrine in cases of challenges to earlier civil judgments, but their Lordships did not expand upon these observations.

The nature and basis of the later claim

The Court of Appeal has attempted to place beyond doubt that it is the nature   **38–61**
and effect of the second proceedings that determines whether they are a challenge
to the original decision, and not the intention with which they are brought: *R. v
Belmarsh Magistrates' Court, Ex p. Watts* [1999] 2 Cr.App.R.188. Although the
case does not appear to have been cited to their Lordships in *Arthur J.S. Hall &
C. v Simons*, above, the reasoning of the majority in that case endorses the earlier
decision. The majority in *Arthur J.S. Hall* held that the ultimate question in
determining whether a collateral challenge was an abuse of process was to ask
whether conflicting decisions would bring the administration of justice into
disrepute (see *ibid.,* at 705, *per* Lord Hoffmann). However, Lord Hobhouse, in
the minority, interpreted the *Hunter* rule as applying to the purpose of the second
litigation. His Lordship said (correctly, it is submitted) that not every collateral
challenge would be an abuse of process (see *ibid.*, at 751). However, his rationale
for this was that, if the purpose of the second litigation was to secure damages
from a former legal adviser in respect of negligence then this was a proper
purpose and so was not an abuse of process. With respect, this cannot be correct.
A collateral challenge would not be an abuse if the resulting conflicting decisions
would not bring the law into disrepute; such cases are exceptional. Whatever the
litigant's purpose, and however legitimate, a collateral challenge whereby
conflicting decisions would bring the law into disrepute (almost always the case)
is an abuse of process.

Criminal cases

(c) *Autrefois acquit*

In March 2001, the Law Commission published their findings on the future of   **38–69**
the double jeopardy rule; Law Com. No.276. The principal recommendation is
that the double jeopardy rule should be subject to an exception but only where the
original acquittal was for murder or genocide (Recommendation 1). This
exception can be justified because of the unique nature of the crimes, the
abhorrence with which they are viewed: a manifestly illegitimate acquittal
damages the reputation of the criminal justice system in the eyes of the public
sufficiently to justify the proposed exception (para. 4.30). The exception should
apply retrospectively to past acquittals. However, it would only apply where new
evidence has emerged which is viewed by the court as compelling (Recommendation 3). A retrial should not be permitted on the basis of evidence which
was in the possession of the prosecution at the time of the original trial but which
could not be adduced then, but could now, because of a change in the law
(Recommendation 6).

It is to be noted that the Commissioners have not recommended that the
exception be extended to previous acquittals for manslaughter *in its present form.*
The Commissioners regard the present offence as being simply too broad in
terms of culpability. (The Commissioners recommended in Law Com. No.237
that the offence of manslaughter be split. A new offence of reckless killing
should cover the most serious cases. If such an offence were created, the double
jeopardy exception should be extended to it; see paras 4.37 to 4.40.)

The Government White Paper, *Access for All* (July 2002; CM 5563) at paras 4.63 to 4.66 proposes reform of the double jeopardy principles in the following terms:

"4.63 The double jeopardy rule means that a person cannot be tried more than once for the same offence. It is an important safeguard to acquitted defendants, but there is an important general public interest in ensuring that those who have committed serious crimes are convicted of them. The Stephen Lawrence Inquiry Report recognised that the rule is capable of causing grave injustice to victims and the community in certain cases where compelling fresh evidence has come to light after an acquittal. It called for a change in the law to be considered, and we have accepted that such a change is appropriate. The European Convention on Human Rights (Article 4(2) of Protocol 7) explicitly recognises the importance of being able to re-open cases where new evidence come to light.

4.64 We believe that the principles recommended by the Law Commission in its report last year provide the right basis for our reforms and we will bring forward legislation to implement many of its recommendations. Our reforms will go wider than the proposal that change should be limited to murder and certain allied offences. We believe that there are other cases where a re-trial would be justified if there were compelling fresh evidence giving a clear indication of guilt. For this reason we have decided that the change should extend to a number of other very serious offences such as rape, manslaughter and armed robbery. We do not expect these procedures to be used frequently, but their existence will benefit justice.

4.65 Our proposals will work as follows:

- Should fresh evidence emerge that could not reasonably have been available for the first trial and that strongly suggests that a previously acquitted defendant was in fact guilty, the Director of Public Prosecutions (DPP) will need to give his personal consent for the defendant to be re-investigated. He may also indicate that another police force should conduct the re-investigation. This will ensure that the rights of acquitted defendants are properly protected.
- Before submitting an application to the Court of Appeal to quash an acquittal, the DPP will need to be satisfied that there is new and compelling evidence and that an application is in the public interest and a re-trial fully justified.
- The Court of Appeal will have the power to quash the acquittal where:

  – there is compelling new evidence of guilt; and
  – the Court is satisfied that it is right in all the circumstances of the case for there to be a re-trial.

- There will be scope for only one re-trial under these procedures.

4.66 The power will be retrospective. That is, it will apply to acquittals which take place before the law is changed, as well as those that happened after."

Whilst Article 4(2) of Protocol 7 to the European Convention on Human Rights permits multiple prosecutions in limited circumstances, Article 14(7) of the International Covenant on Civil and Political Rights provides:

"No one shall be liable to be tried or punished again for an offence for which he has already been finally convicted or acquitted in accordance with the law and penal procedure of each country".

N.B. The United Kingdom has not ratified Protocol 7 to the ECHR.

(e) *Oppression*

38–72
There is a general jurisdiction to prevent oppression by the litigation of issues which are technically different but in the substance the same is matters which have already been disposed of: see *e.g. R. v Piggott and Litwin* [1999] 2 Cr.App.R.321, CA.

(f) *The prohibition on undermining an acquittal*

38–73 & 38–74
These sections have been rendered substantially obsolete by *R. v Z* [2000] 2 A.C. 483, HL, where the defendant had been convicted once and acquitted three times on charges of rape. The House of Lords held that evidence, including the acquittals, should have been admitted by the trial judge because the circumstances of all the previous cases were highly relevant to the instant charge. The rule against double jeopardy extended only to further *prosecutions* for offences of which the accused had been acquitted. See also para. 17–56A, above, and see [2001] Crim.L.R.222 and Law Commission Paper No.276, *Double Jeopardy and Prosecution Appeals.*

3.—JUDGMENTS AS EVIDENCE AGAINST STRANGERS

(2) At common law

Principle

(ii) FOR STRANGERS AGAINST PARTIES

38–78
In *Hawaz v The Thomas Cook Group Ltd* October 27, 2000, New Law Online, case 2001019305, the scope of the rule in *Hollington v F. Hewthorn & Co Ltd* [1943] 1 K.B. 587 was challenged. It was argued that the decision is only binding authority on the admissibility of previous *criminal* convictions. Whilst accepting that this originally would have been correct, the court held that the decision had been applied to *civil* judgments in subsequent cases by higher courts. Moreover, the reasoning of *Hollington* is logically applicable to earlier civil judgments; both criminal and civil judgments are technically expressions of opinion and inadmissible as such. The court affirmed that the principles adumbrated in *Hollington* remain applicable to findings in earlier civil cases as well as criminal.

38–78
NOTE 52. See also Lord Hoffmann's comment in *Arthur J.S. Hall v Simons* [2002] 1 A.C. 615 at 702 that the Court of Appeal in *Hollington v F. Hewthorn & Co Ltd* [1943] 1 K.B. 587 was "generally thought to have taken the technicalities of the matter much too far".

(3) Acquittals

Other exceptions

(iii) CONTRACT, ADMISSIONS, ACQUIESCENCE

38–84   In *Hawaz v The Thomas Cook Group Plc*, October 27, 2000, New Law Online, case 2001019305, the court rejected the submission that a failure to appeal a decision could be received as evidence of an admission of the correctness of that decision in subsequent proceedings. Keene J. found that *Eaton v Swansea Water Works* 17 QBD 267 was not authority for this general proposition but was confined to the context of easements where acquiescence might be an issue in the case. To hold otherwise would be fundamentally to undermine the rule in *Hollington v Hewthorn* in any case where there had been no appeal.

(5) Under the Police and Criminal Evidence Act 1984, ss.73 to 75

38–91   Foreign convictions, where admissible, may be proved under s.7 of the Evidence Act 1851 together with evidence as to the identify of the person convicted: *R. v Mauricia* [2002] EWCA Crim 676; [2002] 2 Crim.App.R. 27, CA.

38–92   Where evidence of a conviction is admissible by virtue of s.4, the materials referred to in s.75(1) are admissible for the purpose of identifying the facts on which the conviction was based: see *R. v Hinchcliffe* [2002] EWCA Crim 837; [2002] 4 Archbold News 1, CA.

CHAPTER 40

AUTHORSHIP AND EXECUTION: ATTESTATION: ANCIENT
DOCUMENTS: CONNECTED AND INCORPORATED DOCUMENTS:
ALTERATIONS AND BLANKS: REGISTRATION, STAMPS, ETC.

1.—GENUINENESS, AUTHORSHIP AND EXECUTION

(3) Deeds, signature, sealing and delivery

(b) *The law subsequent to the Law of Property (Miscellaneous
Provisions) Act 1989*

(i) SIGNATURE

But in *Shah v Shah* [2001] EWCA Civ 527; [2002] QB 35, the Court of Appeal **40–11**
held that, where joint mortgagors had tendered a deed bearing the signature of a
witness attesting to the mortgagors' signatures, when in fact the attesting
witness' signature had been added at a time shortly after the mortgagors had
signed the deed and not in their presence, the mortgagors were estopped from
denying the validity of the deed on the grounds of non-conformity with s.1 of the
Law of Property (Miscellaneous Provisions) Act 1989. See further above, para.
5–03.

(4) Documents requiring attestation

(d) *Wills*

Also see *Vallancourt Estate v Vallancourt* (2001) 195 D.L.R. (4th) 508.   **40–15**

2.—CONNECTED DOCUMENTS: INCORPORATION: REFERENCE

While an exchange of letters may be sufficient to satisfy s.2(3) of the Law of **40–24**
Property (Miscellaneous Provisions) Act 1989 and create an equitable mortgage,

where there was ambiguity in the letters this could not be resolved by extraneous evidence of prior oral agreement: *De Serville v Argee Ltd* (2001) 82 P. & C.R. D12.

40–24 NOTE 47. Also see *Jones v Forest Fencing Ltd* [2001] EWCA Civ 1700; [2001] N.P.C. 165. Accordingly the purported sale of a leasehold interest will not be enforceable if it does not comply with s.2: *Bircham & Co Nominees (No.2) Ltd v Worrell Holdings Ltd* [2001] EWCA Civ 775; (2001) 82 P. & C.R. 34; [2001] 47 E.G. 149, CA.

CHAPTER 41

CONTENTS OF DOCUMENTS GENERALLY: PRIMARY AND SECONDARY EVIDENCE, CONTENTS OF PARTICULAR DOCUMENTS: PUBLIC, JUDICIAL AND PRIVATE

(2) Principle

See *Masquerade Music Ltd v Springsteen* [2001] EWCA Civ 563, [2001] **41–03**
C.P.L.R. 369; [2001] E.M.L.R. 25, referred to under para. 41–34 below.

2.—SECONDARY EVIDENCE, FORMS OF

(7) No degrees of secondary evidence

(b) *Cases in which secondary evidence is admissible*

(v) SEARCH

In *Masquerade Music Ltd v Springsteen* [2001] EWCA Civ 563, [2001] **41–34**
C.P.L.R. 369; [2001] E.M.L.R. 25, Jonathan Parker L.J., who gave the only
reasoned judgment of the Court of Appeal, recognised that the "best evidence"
rule was dead, and stated, at para. 80, that the requirement that a party in
possession of the original of a document produce it in evidence was not founded
on any rule of law but was simply a reflection of the fact that, if the original was
available to him, he would be unable to account satisfactorily to the court for its
non-production when inviting the court to admit secondary evidence of its
contents with the practical consequence that the court would attach no weight to
the secondary evidence. Therefore he observed at para. 85 that the "admissibility" of any secondary evidence would be entirely dependent upon the weight
to be attached to it. At para. 87 he observed that, if the original was not produced,
the only requirement (in the absence of any allegation of bad faith or impropriety
on the part of the party in whose possession the original had been) imposed on
that party was to provide a reasonable explanation for the non-production of the
original. In the absence of such an explanation, the court would almost certainly
decline to accept any secondary evidence.

3.—Public Documents

(2) European Economic Communities

41–39   Section 1(2) of the European Communities Act 1972 has been amended to delete paragraph (f) and insert new paragraphs (k)–(p).

(4) Treaties, charters, letters patent, etc.

41–43   Now see the Civil Jurisdiction and Judgments Order 2001, SI 2001/3929.

(5) Proclamations and orders in council

41–44   The first clause of s.2 reads:

> "Prima facie evidence of any proclamation, order, or regulation issued before or after the passing of this Act by Her Majesty, or by the Privy Council, also of any proclamation, order, or regulation issued before or after the passing of this Act by or under the authority of any such department of the Government or officer or office-holder in the Scottish Administration as is mentioned in the first column of the schedule hereto, may be given in all courts of justice, and in all legal proceedings whatsoever, in all or any of modes herein-after mentioned; that is to say:"

Subs.(3) has been amended so that "officer(s)" now includes "office-holder(s)".

41–46   In *Hammond v Wilkinson* [2001] Crim.L.R. 323, the Divisional Court indicated that, where a defendant wished to challenge whether a statutory instrument had been proved in accordance with the Documentary Evidence Act 1868, such a challenge ought to be made timeously. The prosecution was entitled to re-open its case to put right a technical deficiency raised by the defence in its submissions by asking for a copy of the statutory instrument from the Stationery Office, but it was desirable that the resulting waste of costs should be avoided in future.

(8) General provisions as to proof of the authenticity and contents of public documents

(a) *Documents admissible if "purporting" to be duly signed, etc.*

41–50   Also see *R. v Bell* (2001) 152 Can CC (3rd) 534, British Columbia Court of Appeal (certificate of registration admissible under provincial and federal legislation as proof of accused's ownership of vehicle).

(10) Public inquisitions, maps, surveys, extents and report

41–54   See also *Trevelyan v Secretary of State* [2001] EWCA Civ 266; [2001] 1 W.L.R. 1264, CA.

4.—JUDICIAL DOCUMENTS

(1) Superior courts

See also s.136 of the Supreme Court Act 1981.   **41–63**

(2) Criminal proceedings

In *R. v C (W.B.)* (2001) 142 Can CC 490 (affirmed 153 Can CC 575) the   **41–65**
transcript of a previous guilty plea was admissible at common law as a record of
the proceeding. In *R. v Nandan* [2002] 2 N.Z.L.R. 783 Hammond J. for the Court
of Appeal at pp.787–788 stated that past convictions can be proven in a number
of ways, including by statutory certificate or by any other recognised method,
such as from the court record itself.

In *R. v Harris* [2001] Crim.L.R. 227 the Court of Appeal held that the wording   **41–66**
of s.74(3) showed that its purpose was not to define or enlarge the circumstances
in which evidence of the fact that the accused had committed the offence was
admissible, but was simply to assist in the mode of proof of that fact. The
admissible evidence included evidence relating both to essential and non-
essential issues arising in the course of the proceedings, so long as it was relevant
to any issue in the proceedings. The effect of the section is therefore, by
admitting evidence of the conviction, to shift the onus onto the defendant to
prove that he did not commit the offence, on the balance of probabilities.

(4) Appeals

Replace first sentence by: As to documentation required in the Court of Appeal   **41–70**
on the hearing of an appeal, see CPR, Pt 52 and the associated Practice
Direction—Appeals.

(8) Foreign and colonial proceedings

Foreign convictions may only be proven by means of the Evidence Act 1851,   **41–74**
s.7: *R. v Mauricia* [2002] EWCA Crim 676; [2002] 2 Cr.App.R. 27, CA (Crim
Div).

5. PRIVATE DOCUMENTS, WHEN REGISTERED, ENROLLED

(1) Civil Evidence Act 1995 and Criminal Justice Act 1988

Section 24 of the Criminal Justice Act 1988 has been amended. Paragraph (c)   **41–80**
of subs.1 has been repealed and a new subs.5 now reads:

"This section shall not apply to proceedings before a magistrates' court inquiring into
an offence as examining justices."

CHAPTER 42

EXCLUSION OF EXTRINSIC EVIDENCE IN SUBSTITUTION OF, TO CONTRADICT, VARY, OR ADD TO DOCUMENTS

1.—EVIDENCE IN SUBSTITUTION

(4) Private formal documents

42–05   See *De Serville v Argee Ltd* (2001) 82 P. & C.R. D12 (para. 40–24 above).

3.—EVIDENCE TO CONTRADICT, VARY OR SUBSTITUTE

(1) Principle

42–13   "The purpose of an entire agreement clause is to preclude a party to a written agreement from threshing through the undergrowth and finding in the course of negotiations, some (chance) remark or statement (often long-forgotten or difficult to recall or explain) upon which to found a claim, such as the present, to the existence of a collateral warranty. The entire agreement clause obviates the occasion for any such search, and the peril to the contracting parties posed by the need in its absence to conduct such a search. For such a clause constitutes a binding agreement between the parties that the full contractual terms are to be found in the document containing the clause and not elsewhere, and that, accordingly, any promises or assurances made in the course of the negotiations (which in the absence of such a clause, might have effect as a collateral warranty) shall have no contractual force, save in so far as they are reflected and given effect in the document. The operation of the clause . . . is to denude what would otherwise constitute a collateral warranty of legal effect . . . An entire agreement clause does not preclude a claim in misrepresentation, for the denial of contractual force cannot effect the status of a statement as a misrepresentation", *per* Lightman J. in *Innterpreneur Pub Co v East Crown Ltd* [2000] 2 Lloyd's Rep. 611, [2000] 3 E.G.L.R. 31 at 33.

See also *HIH Casualty and General Insurance v New Hampshire Insurance Co* [2001] EWCA Civ 735; [2001] 2 Lloyd's Rep 161; *Watford Electronics Ltd v Sanderson EFL Ltd* [2001] EWCA Civ 317, paras 38 et seq, [2001] 1 All E.R. (Comm) 696; *White v Bristol Rugby Ltd* [2002] I.R.L.R. 204.

4.—EXCEPTIONS TO THE RULE

(3) Private formal documents: terms of transaction

(b) *Collateral agreements and warranties*

NOTE 80. Add: But *cf.* note 4, above.   **42–25**

(6) Invalid or conditional documents: escrows: fraud: mistake: want of consideration, etc.

(g) *Wills*

Extrinsic evidence is admissible to show that a will or part of it were known   **42–42** of and approved by the deceased: *Fuller v Strum* [2001] EWCA Civ 1879; [2002] 1 W.L.R. 1097.

CHAPTER 43

ADMISSION OF EXTRINSIC EVIDENCE IN AID OF
INTERPRETATION AND TO REBUT PRESUMPTIONS

1.—INTERPRETATION

(2) Objects and limits of interpretation—the meaning of the words or the intention of the writer?

43–12   In *BCCI v Ali (No 1)* [2001] UKHL 8; [2002] 1 A.C. 251; [2001] 2 W.L.R. 735, Lord Nicholls expressly kept open the issue of the extent of the exclusion of evidence of the actual intention of the parties on the interpretation of a written agreement. In the same case Lord Hoffmann, at para. 39, said:

> "when, in *Investors Compensation Scheme Ltd v West Bromwich Building Society* [1998] 1 WLR 896, 913, I said that the admissible background included "absolutely anything which would have affected the way in which the language of the document would have been understood by a reasonable man", I did not think it necessary to emphasise that I meant anything which a reasonable man would have regarded as *relevant*. I was merely saying that there is no conceptual limit to what can be regarded as background. It is not, for example, confined to the factual background but can include the state of the law (as in cases in which one takes into account that the parties are unlikely to have intended to agree to something unlawful or legally ineffective) or proved common assumptions which were in fact quite mistaken. But the primary source for understanding what the parties meant is their language interpreted in accordance with conventional usage: "we do not easily accept that people have made linguistic mistakes, particularly in formal documents". I was certainly not encouraging a trawl through "background" which could not have made a reasonable person think that the parties must have departed from conventional usage."

Also see *Heaton v Axa Equity and Law Life Assurance Plc* [2002] UKHL 15; [2002] 2 A.C. 329; *MSC Mediterranean Shipping Co SA v Polish Ocean Lines (The Tychy) (No.2)* [2001] EWCA Civ 1198; [2001] 2 Lloyd's Rep. 403; *Daejan Properties Ltd v Bloom* [2000] E.G.C.S. 85; *Sinochem International Oil (London) Co Ltd v Mobil Sales and Supply Corp (No.1)* [2000] 1 All E.R. (Comm) 474; [2000] 1 Lloyd's Rep. 339; *Zoan v Rouamba* [2000] EWCA Civ 8; [2000] 1 W.L.R. 109 at paras 37–42.

2.—Rules as to Extrinsic Evidence

Rule 1

(2) Contracts

A compromise agreement in "full and final settlement" of A's claims against   **43–26**
C may not be effective to bar B's subsequent claims against C arising out of the
same facts, where there is identifiable loss: *Heaton v Axa Equity and Law Life
Assurance Plc* [2002] UKHL 15; [2002] 2 A.C. 329.

(3) Wills

(b) *Subject matter*

In P*rouse v Scheuerman* (2001) 197 D.L.R. (4th) 732 the British Columbia   **43–29**
Court of Appeal read into a will the words "all my estate" where the will named
a single beneficiary but failed to state the extent of property given.

(c) *Meaning of terms and other ambiguities*

In *Re Murray Estate* (2001) 197 D.L.R. (4th) 245 the Nova Scotia Court of   **43–30**
Appeal admitted extrinsic evidence of the closeness of the deceased's relation-
ships to particular named beneficiaries in order to determine the method of
division of the estate between them.

(4) Statutes

In *Stevenson v Rogers* [1999] QB 1028, it was held there was ambiguity or   **43–32**
"real doubt" whether the implied term as to merchantability contained in s.14(2)
of the Sale of Goods Act 1979 depended upon the sale being in the course of a
business; recourse to *Hansard* demonstrated that the term could be implied
whether or not the sale was in the course of a business. In *R. v Human
Fertilisation Authority, Ex p. Blood* [1999] Fam. 151, Sir Stephen Brown P. with
the consent of both parties used *Hansard* to determine whether a reference in
Sch. 3 of the Human Fertilisation and Embryology Act 1990 to gametes was
intended also to apply to the use of an embryo in the context of an argument
based on European Community law; it was intended to apply to both.
  In *R. v Mullen* [2000] QB 520, it was held, partly as a result of the conflicting
views expressed by the House of Lords in *R. v Martin* [1998] A.C. 917, and
partly because of a procedural absurdity which would otherwise result, that the
word "unsafe" in s.2(1) of the Criminal Appeal Act 1968 as amended was
sufficiently ambiguous to permit the court to have recourse to *Hansard*, and that
it had a broad meaning apt to embrace abuse of process in the Crown Court, as
well as in the Magistrates' Court. In *Oliver Ashworth (Holdings) Ltd v Ballard
(Kent) Ltd* [2000] Ch.12, Laws L.J. referred to the difference between the literal
and the purposive approach to the construction of legislation, and observed:

"Where there is a potential clash, the conventional English approach has been to give at least very great and often decisive weight to the literal meaning of the enacting approach enjoined for the interpretation of legislative measures of the European Union and in light of the House of Lords' decision in *Pepper v. Hart* [1993] A.C. 593. I will not here go into the details or merits of this shift of emphasis; save broadly to recognise its virtue and its vice. Its virtue is that the legislator's true purpose may be more accurately ascertained. Its vice is that the certainty and accessibility of the law may be reduced or compromised. The common law, which regulates the interpretation of legislation, has to balance these considerations."

43–34   In *R. v Secretary of State for the Environment, Ex p. Spath Holme Ltd* [2000] UKHL 61; [2001] 2 A.C. 349 at 391; [2001] 2 W.L.R. 15 at 31, Lord Bingham of Cornhill said:

"In *Pepper v. Hart* the House (Lord Mackay of Clashfern LC dissenting) relaxed the general rule which had been understood to preclude reference in the courts of this country to statements made in Parliament for the purpose of constructing a statutory provision. In his leading speech, with which all in the majority concurred, Lord Browne-Wilkinson made plain that such reference was permissible only where (a) legislation was ambiguous or obscure, or led to an absurdity; (b) the material relied on consisted of one or more statements by a minister or other promoter of the Bill together, if necessary, with such other parliamentary material as might be necessary to understand such statements and their effect; and (c) the effect of such statements was clear (see pp.640b, 631d, 634d). In my opinion, each of these conditions is critical to the majority decision.

(1) Unless the first of the conditions is strictly insisted upon, the real risk exists, feared by Lord Mackay of Clashfern L.C., that the legal advisers to parties engaged in disputes on statutory construction will be required to comb through Hansard in practically every case (see pp.614g, 616a). This would clearly defeat the intention of Lord Bridge of Harwich that such cases should be rare (p.617a) and the submission of counsel that such cases should be exceptional (p.597e).

(2) It is one thing to rely on a statement by a responsible minister or promoter as to the meaning or effect of a provision in a bill thereafter accepted without amendment. It is quite another to rely on a statement made by anyone else, or even by a minister or promoter in the course of what may be lengthy and contentious parliamentary exchanges, particularly if the measure undergoes substantial amendment in the course of its passage through Parliament.

(3) Unless parliamentary statements are indeed clear and unequivocal (or, as Lord Reid put it in *R. v. Warner* [1969] 2 A.C. 256, 279e, such as "would almost certainly settle the matter immediately one way or the other"), the court is likely to be drawn into comparing one statement with another, appraising the meaning and effect of what was said and considering what was left unsaid and why. In the course of such an exercise the court would come uncomfortably close to questioning the proceedings in Parliament contrary to Article 9 of the Bill of Rights 1688 and might even violate that important constitutional prohibition.

It has been argued that the stringent conditions laid down by the House in *Pepper v. Hart* were not satisfied in that very case; see *Bennion, Statutory Interpretation*, 3rd ed., 1997, pp.483–485. That is not a view I could accept; there was a difference of judicial opinion when the matter was first argued in the House and there were very clear statements on the point at issue by the responsible minister. But the case turned on a narrow point, the meaning of "the cost of a benefit" in section 63(2) of the Finance Act 1976. The minister gave what was no doubt taken to be a reliable statement on the meaning of that expression. Here the issue turns not on the meaning of a statutory expression but on the scope of a statutory power. In this context a minister might describe the circumstances in which the government contemplated use of a power, and might be pressed about exercise of the power in other situations which might arise. No doubt the minister would seek to give helpful answers. But it is most unlikely that he would seek to define the legal effect of the draftsman's language, or to predict all the circumstances in which the power might be used, or to bind any successor administration. Only if a minister were, improbably, to give a categorical assurance to Parliament that a power would not be used in a given situation, such that Parliament could be taken to have legislated on that basis, does it seem to me that a parliamentary statement on the scope of a power would be properly admissible.

I think it important that the conditions laid down by the House in *Pepper v. Hart* should be strictly insisted upon. Otherwise, the cost and inconvenience feared by Lord Mackay of Clashfern L.C., whose objections to relaxation of the exclusionary rule were based on consideration of practice not principle (see p.615g), will be realised. The worst of all worlds would be achieved if parties routinely combed through Hansard, and the courts dredged through conflicting statements of parliamentary intention (see p.631f), only to conclude that the statutory provision called for no further elucidation or that no clear and unequivocal statement by a responsible minister could be derived from Hansard".

See also Steyn, "*Pepper v Hart:* a Re-Examination" in (2001) 21 O.J.L.S. 59.

In *R. v Richmond London Borough Council, Ex p. Watson* [2001] Q.B. 370, the Court of Appeal held that the term "after-care services" in s.117 of the Mental Health Act 1983 was not ambiguous; there was only uncertainty in the penumbra of its meaning. Reference to *Hansard* was accordingly not permitted.

In *Inland Revenue Commissioners v Laird Group Plc* [2002] EWCA Civ 576; [2002] S.T.C. 722 the Court of Appeal held that it was not appropriate to refer to Parliamentary commentary in *Hansard* to construe a consolidating statute; the relevant provisions being unambiguous.

Also see *AE Beckett & Sons (Lyndons) Ltd v Midland Electricity Plc* [2000] EWCA Civ 312; [2001] 1 W.L.R. 281.

As a result of the enactment of the Human Rights Act 1998, in accordance   **43–35**
with the will of Parliament expressed in s.3, which requires the court to find an interpretation of a statutory provision compatible with the European Convention if it is possible to do so, it will sometimes be necessary for the courts to adopt a linguistic interpretation which may appear strained, involving both reading down the express language of the statute and the implication of provisions, so as to avoid, unless it is plainly impossible to do so, the need for the court to make a declaration of incompatibility: see *R. v A (No.2)* [2001] UKHL 25; [2001] 2 W.L.R. 1546 at 1563, *per* Lord Steyn.

Also see *R. v Lambert* [2001 UKHL 37; [2001] 3 W.L.R. 206; *Wilson v First County Trust Ltd (No 2)* [2001] EWCA Civ 633; [2001] 3 W.L.R. 42

3.—ADMISSION OF EXTRINSIC EVIDENCE TO REBUT PRESUMPTION
AFFECTING DOCUMENTS

(2) Satisfaction of portions and debts

(a) *Portions*

See also *Re Cameron* [1999] Ch. 386.   **43–67**

(6) Miscellaneous

43–76   *Hale v Norfolk County Council* [2000] EWCA Civ 290; [2001] Ch 717, CA.

MISCELLANEOUS STATUTES AND ORDERS

Phipson on Evidence (15th ed.) included in an appendix a number of miscellaneous statutes and orders relevant to the law of evidence, many of which have recently been amended. This appendix sets out those amendments, together with a range of relevant Civil Procedure Rules and Practice Directions. This appendix should be read in conjunction with the appendix in the 15th edition.

CRIMINAL PROCEDURE ACT 1865

Proof of conviction of witness for felony or misdemeanour may be given

6.—[(1)][1] A witness may be questioned as to whether he has been convicted of any felony or misdemeanour, and upon being so questioned, if he either denies or does not admit the fact, or refuses to answer, it shall be lawful for the cross examining party to prove such conviction; and[2] a certificate containing the substance and effect only (omitting the formal part) of the indictment and conviction for such offence, purporting to be signed by [the proper officer of the court where the offender was convicted][3] (for which certificate a fee of [25p] and no more shall be demanded or taken,) shall, upon proof of the identity of the person, be sufficient evidence of the said conviction, without proof of the signature or official character of the person appearing to have signed the same. **44–04**

[(2)][4] In subs.(1) "proper officer" means—

(a) in relation to a Magistrates' Court in England and Wales, the justices' Chief Executive for the court; and

(b) in relation to any other court, the clerk of the court or other officer having the custody of the records of the court, or the deputy of such clerk or other officer.]

---

[1] Numbered as such by Access to Justice Act 1999, s.90(1), Sch. 13, para. 3(1), (2): in force, April 1, 2001.

[2] Words from "and a certificate" to "signed the same" repealed, in relation to criminal proceedings, by Police and Criminal Evidence Act 1984, s.119, Sch. 7, Pt IV and SI 1989/1341, art.1(3): in force on a date to be appointed.

[3] Words in square brackets from "the proper officer" to "offender was convicted" substituted by Access to Justice Act 1999, s.90(1), Sch.13, para. 3(1), (2): in force, April 1, 2001.

[4] Subs.(2) inserted by Access to Justice Act 1999, s.90(1), Sch. 13, para. 3(1), (3): in force, April 1, 2001.

CIVIL EVIDENCE ACT 1968

Convictions as evidence in civil proceedings

44–06   **11.**—(5) Nothing in any of the following enactments, that is to say—

(a) [s.14 of the Powers of Criminal Courts (Sentencing) Act 2001] (under which a conviction leading to . . . discharge is to be disregarded except as therein mentioned);[5]

(6) In this section "court-martial" means a court-martial constituted under the Army Act 1955, the Air Force Act 1955 or the Naval Discipline Act 1957 . . . , and in relation to a court-martial "conviction", . . . , means a finding of guilty which is, or falls to be treated as, the finding of the court, and "convicted" shall be construed accordingly.[6]

Findings of adultery and paternity as evidence in civil proceedings

44–07   **12.**—(5)

[(d) . . . .];[7]

Conclusiveness of convictions for purposes of defamation actions

44–08   **13[8].**—(1) In an action for libel or slander in which the question whether [the plaintiff] did or did not commit a criminal offence is relevant to an issue arising in the action, proof that at the time when that issue falls to be determined, [he] stands convicted of that offence shall be conclusive evidence that he committed that offence; and his conviction thereof shall be admissible in evidence accordingly.

POLICE AND CRIMINAL EVIDENCE ACT 1984

Power of justice of the peace to authorise entry and search of premises

44–23   **8.**—[(6) This section applies in relation to a relevant offence (as defined in s.28D(4) of the Immigration Act 1971) as it applies in relation to a serious arrestable offence.][9]

---

[5] Words "section 14" to "Act 2001" substituted by Powers of Criminal Courts (Sentencing) Act 2000, s.165(1), Sch. 9, para. 36: in force, August 25, 2000. Words omitted repealed by Criminal Justice Act 1991, ss. 100, 101(2), Sch. 11, para. 5, Sch. 13.
[6] First words omitted repealed by Armed Forces Act 2001, s.38, Sch. 7, Pt 1: in force, February 28, 2002. Final words omitted repealed by Armed Forces Act 1996, ss. 5, 35(2), Sch. 1, Pt IV, para. 100, Sch. 7, Pt II.
[7] Repealed by Child Support, Pensions and Social Security Act 2000, s.85, Sch. 9, Pt IX: in force, April 1, 2001.
[8] Words in square brackets in s.13 substituted or inserted by Defamation Act 1996, s.12(1).
[9] Subs.(6) inserted by Immigration and Asylum Act 1999, s.169(1), Sch. 14, para. 80(1), (2): in force, February 14, 2000.

Special provisions as to access

9.—[(2A) Section 4 of the Summary Jurisdiction (Process) Act 1881 (c 24)   **44–24** (which includes provision for the execution of process of English courts in Scotland) and s.29 of the Petty Sessions (Ireland) Act 1851 (c 93) (which makes equivalent provision for execution in Northern Ireland) shall each apply to any process issued by a circuit judge under Sch. 1 to this Act as it applies to process issued by a magistrates' court under the Magistrates' Courts Act 1980 (c 43).][10]

[Searches and examination to ascertain identity][11]

54A.—[(1) If an officer of at least the rank of inspector authorises it, a person   **44–31A** who is detained in a police station may be searched or examined, or both—

(a) for the purpose of ascertaining whether he has any mark that would tend to identify him as a person involved in the commission of an offence; or
(b) for the purpose of facilitating the ascertainment of his identity.

(2) An officer may only give an authorisation under subs.(1) for the purpose mentioned in paragraph (a) of that subsection if—

(a) the appropriate consent to a search or examination that would reveal whether the mark in question exists has been withheld; or
(b) it is not practicable to obtain such consent.

(3) An officer may only give an authorisation under subs.(1) in a case in which subs.(2) does not apply if—

(a) the person in question has refused to identify himself; or
(b) the officer has reasonable grounds for suspecting that that person is not who he claims to be.

(4) An officer may give an authorisation under subs.(1) orally or in writing but, if he gives it orally, he shall confirm it in writing as soon as is practicable.
(5) Any identifying mark found on a search or examination under this section may be photographed—

(a) with the appropriate consent; or
(b) if the appropriate consent is withheld or it is not practicable to obtain it, without it.

(6) Where a search or examination may be carried out under this section, or a photograph may be taken under this section, the only persons entitled to carry out the search or examination, or to take the photograph, are—

---

[10] Subs.(2A) inserted by Criminal Justice and Police Act 2001, s.86(1): in force, August 1, 2001.
[11] s.54A inserted by Anti-terrorism, Crime and Security Act 2001, s.90(1): in force, December 14, 2001.

(a) constables; and

(b) persons who (without being constables) are designated for the purposes of this section by the chief officer of police for the police area in which the police station in question is situated;

and s.117 (use of force) applies to the exercise by a person falling within paragraph (b) of the powers conferred by the preceding provisions of this section as it applies to the exercise of those powers by a constable.

(7) A person may not under this section carry out a search or examination of a person of the opposite sex or take a photograph of any part of the body of a person of the opposite sex.

(8) An intimate search may not be carried out under this section.

(9) A photograph taken under this section—

(a) may be used by, or disclosed to, any person for any purpose related to the prevention or detection of crime, the investigation of an offence or the conduct of a prosecution; and

(b) after being so used or disclosed, may be retained but may not be used or disclosed except for a purpose so related.

(10) In subsection—

(a) the reference to crime includes a reference to any conduct which—
   (i) constitutes one or more criminal offences (whether under the law of a part of the United Kingdom or of a country or territory outside the United Kingdom); or
   (ii) is, or corresponds to, any conduct which, if it all took place in any one part of the United Kingdom, would constitute one or more criminal offences;
      and

(b) the references to an investigation and to a prosecution include references, respectively, to any investigation outside the United Kingdom of any crime or suspected crime and to a prosecution brought in respect of any crime in a country or territory outside the United Kingdom.

(11) In this section—

(a) references to ascertaining a person's identity include references to showing that he is not a particular person; and

(b) references to taking a photograph include references to using any process by means of which a visual image may be produced, and references to photographing a person shall be construed accordingly.

(12) In this section "mark" includes features and injuries; and a mark is an identifying mark for the purposes of this section if its existence in any person's case facilitates the ascertainment of his identity or his identification as a person involved in the commission of an offence.]

Intimate searches

55.—(1) Subject to the following provisions of this section, if an officer of at **44–32** least the rank of superintendent [inspector][12] has reasonable grounds for believing—

(a) that a person who has been arrested and is in police detention may have concealed on him anything which—
  (i) he could use to cause physical injury to himself or others; and
  (ii) he might so use while he is in police detention or in the custody of a court; or
(b) that such a person—
  (i) may have a Class A drug concealed on him; and
  (ii) was in possession of it with the appropriate criminal intent before his arrest,

he may authorise an intimate search of that person.

(2) An officer may not authorise an intimate search of a person for anything unless he has reasonable grounds for believing that it cannot be found without his being intimately searched.

(3) An officer may give an authorisation under subs.(1) above orally or in writing but, if he gives it orally, he shall confirm it in writing as soon as is practicable.

(4) An intimate search which is only a drug offence search shall be by way of examination by a suitably qualified person.

(5) Except as provided by subs.(4) above, an intimate search shall be by way of examination by a suitably qualified person unless an officer of at least the rank of superintendent [inspector][13] considers that this is not practicable.

[(14A) Every annual report under s.57 of the Police Act 1997 (reports by Director General of the National Crime Squad) shall contain information about searches authorised under this section by members of the National Crime Squad during the period to which the report relates.][14]

Right to have someone informed when arrested

56.—(2) Delay is only permitted—   **44–33**

(a) in the case of a person who is in police detention for a serious arrestable offence; and
(b) if an officer of at least the rank of superintendent [inspector][15] authorises it.

[(5A) An officer may also authorise delay where the serious arrestable offence is a drug trafficking offence [or an offence to which Pt VI of the Criminal Justice

---

[12] Word "superintendent" repealed and "inspector" substituted by Criminal Justice and Police Act 2001, s.79: in force on a date to be appointed.
[13] *ibid.*
[14] Subs.(14A) inserted by Police Act 1997, s.134(1), Sch. 9, para.47: in force, April 1, 1998.
[15] Word "superintendent" repealed and word "inspector" substituted by Criminal Justice and Police Act 2001, s.74: in force on a date to be appointed.

Act 1988 applies (offences in respect of which confiscation orders under that Part may be made)] and the officer has reasonable grounds for believing—

[(a) where the offence is a drug trafficking offence, that the detained person has benefited from drug trafficking and that the recovery of the value of that person's proceeds of drug trafficking will be hindered by telling the named person of the arrest; and

(b) where the offence is one to which Pt VI of the Criminal Justice Act 1988 applies, that the detained person has benefited from the offence and that the recovery of the value of the property obtained by that person from or in connection with the offence or of the pecuniary advantage derived by him from or in connection with it will be hindered by telling the named person of the arrest].][16]

[(5A) An officer may also authorise delay where he has reasonable grounds for believing that—

(a) the person detained for the serious arrestable offence has benefited from his criminal conduct, and

(b) the recovery of the value of the property constituting the benefit will be hindered by telling the named person of the arrest.

(5B) For the purposes of subs.(5A) above the question whether a person has benefited from his criminal conduct is to be decided in accordance with Pt 2 of the Proceeds of Crime Act 2002.]

[(10 Nothing in this section applies to a person arrested or detained under the terrorism provisions.][17]

Access to legal advice

44–35   **58.**—[(8A) An officer may also authorise delay where the serious arrestable offence is a drug trafficking offence [or an offence to which Pt VI of the Criminal Justice Act 1988 applies] and the officer has reasonable grounds for believing—

[(a) where the offence is a drug trafficking offence, that the detained person has benefited from drug trafficking and that the recovery of the value of that person's proceeds of drug trafficking will be hindered by the exercise of the right conferred by subsection (1) above; and

(b) where the offence is one to which Pt VI of the Criminal Justice Act 1988 applies, that the detained person has benefited from the offence and that the recovery of the value of the property obtained by that person from or in connection with the offence or of the pecuniary advantage derived by him from or in connection with it will be hindered by the exercise of the right conferred by subs.(1) above].][18]

---

[16] Subs.(5A) substituted, by subsequent subss. (5A), (5B), by the Proceeds of Crime Act 2002, s.456, Sch. 11, paras 1, 14(1), (2): in force on a date to be appointed.
[17] Subs.(10) substituted, for subss.(10), (11) as originally enacted, by the Terrorism Act 2000, s.125(1), Sch. 15, para. 5(1), (5): in force, February 19, 2001 (except in relation to a person detained prior to that date).
[18] Subs.(8A) substituted, by subsequent ss.(8A), (8B) by Proceeds of Crime Act 2002, s.456, Sch. 11, paras. 1, 14(1), (3): in force on a date to be appointed.

[(8A) An officer may also authorise delay where he has reasonable grounds for believing that—

(a) the person detained for the serious arrestable offence has benefited from his criminal conduct, and
(b) the recovery of the value of the property constituting the benefit will be hindered by the exercise

(8B) For the purposes of subs.(8A) above the question whether a person has benefited from his criminal conduct is to be decided in accordance with Pt 2 of the Proceeds of Crime Act 2002.]

[(12) Nothing in this section applies to a person arrested or detained under the terrorism provisions.][19]

[Visual recording of interviews][20]

60A.—[(1) The Secretary of State shall have power—   **44–36A**

(a) to issue a code of practice for the visual recording of interviews held by police officers at police stations; and
(b) to make an order requiring the visual recording of interviews so held, and requiring the visual recording to be in accordance with the code for the time being in force under this section.

(2) A requirement imposed by an order under this section may be imposed in relation to such cases or police stations in such areas, or both, as may be specified or described in the order.

(3) An order under subs.(1) above shall be made by statutory instrument and shall be subject to annulment in pursuance of a resolution of either House of Parliament.

(4) In this section—

(a) references to any interview are references to an interview of a person suspected of a criminal offence; and
(b) references to a visual recording include references to a visual recording in which an audio recording is comprised.]

Fingerprinting

61.—(1) Except as provided by this section no person's fingerprints may be   **44–37**
taken without the appropriate consent.

(2) Consent to the taking of a person's fingerprints must be in writing if it is given at a time when he is at a police station.

(3) The fingerprints of a person detailed at a police station may be taken without the appropriate consent—

---

[19] Subs.(12) substituted, for subss. (12)–(18) as originally enacted, by Terrorism Act 2000, s.125(1), Sch. 15, para. 5(1), (6): in force, February 19, 2001 (except in relation to a person detained prior to that date).
[20] Inserted by Criminal Justice and Police Act 2001, s.76(1): in force, June 19, 2001.

    (a) if an officer of at least the rank of superintendent [inspector]²¹ authorises them to be taken; or

    (b) if—

        (i) he has been charged with a recordable offence or informed that he will be reported for such an offence; and

        (ii) he has not had his fingerprints taken in the course of the investigation of the offence by the police.

[(3A) Where a person charged with a recordable offence or informed that he will be reported for such an offence has already had his fingerprints taken as mentioned in paragraph (b)(ii) of subs.(3) above, that fact shall be disregarded for the purposes of that subsection—

    (a) the fingerprints taken on the previous occasion do not constitute a complete set of his fingerprints; or

    (b) some or all of the fingerprints taken on the previous occasion are not of sufficient quality to allow satisfactory analysis, comparison or matching (whether in the case in question or generally).]²²

(4) An officer may only give an authorisation under subs.(3)(a) above if he has reasonable grounds—

    (a) for suspecting the involvement of the person whose fingerprints are to be taken in a criminal offence; and

    (b) for believing that his fingerprints will tend to confirm or disprove his involvement [or will facilitate the ascertainment of his identity (within the meaning of s.54A), or both]

[but an authorisation shall not be given for the purpose only of facilitating the ascertainment of that person's identity except where he has refused to identify himself or the officer has reasonable grounds for suspecting that he is not who he claims to be].²³

[(4A) The fingerprints of a person who has answered to bail at a court of police station may be taken without the appropriate consent at the court or station—

    (a) the court, or

    (b) an officer of at least the rank of inspector,

authorises them to be taken.

(4B) A court or officer may only give an authorisation under subs.(4A) if—

    (a) the person who has answered to bail has answered to it for a person whose fingerprints were taken on a previous occasion and there are reasonable grounds for believing that he is not the same person; or

---

²¹ Word "superintendent" repealed and word "inspector" substituted by Criminal Justice and Police Act 2001, s.78(2): in force on a date to be appointed.
²² Subs.(3A) inserted by Criminal Justice and Police Act 2001, s.78(3): in force on a date to be appointed.
²³ Words in square brackets inserted by Anti-terrorism, Crime and Security Act 2001, s.90(2)(a) and (b): in force, December 14, 2001.

(b) the person who has answered to bail claims to be a different person from
a person whose fingerprints were taken on a previous occasion.][24]

(5) An officer may give an authorisation under subss.(3)(a) [or (4A)][25] above
orally or in writing but, if he gives it orally, he shall confirm it in writing as soon
as is practicable.
(6) Any person's fingerprints may be taken without the appropriate consent if
he has been convicted of a recordable offence.[26]

[(a) he has been convicted of a recordable offence;
 (b) he has been given a caution in respect of a recordable offence which, at
the time of the caution, he has admitted; or
 (c) he has been warned or reprimanded under s.65 of the Crime and Disorder
Act 1998 (c 37) for a recordable offence].

(7) In a case where by virtue of subss.(3) or (6) above a person's fingerprints
are taken without the appropriate consent—

(a) he shall be told the reason before his fingerprints are taken; and
(b) he reason shall be recorded as soon as is practicable after the fingerprints
are taken.

[(7A) If a person's fingerprints are taken at a police station, whether with or
without the appropriate consent—

(a) before the fingerprints are taken, an offence shall inform him that they
may be subject to a speculative search; and
(b) the fact that the person has been informed of this possibility shall be
recorded as soon as is practicable after the fingerprints have been
taken.]

(8) If he is detained at a police station when the fingerprints are taken, the
reason for taking them [and, in the case falling within subs.(7A) above, the fact
referred to in paragraph (b) of that subsection] shall be recorded on his custody
record.
[(8A) Where a person's fingerprints are taken electronically, they must be
taken only in such manner, and using such devices, as the Secretary of State has
approved for the purposes of electronic fingerprinting.[27]
(9) Nothing in this section—

(a) affects any power conferred by para.18(2) of Sch. 2 of the Immigration
Act 1971 [, s.141 of the Immigration and Asylum Act 1999 or regulations
made under s.144 of that Act];[28] and

---

[24] Subss.(4A), (4B) inserted by Criminal Justice and Police Act 2001, s.78(4): in force on a date to
be appointed.
[25] Words "or (4A)" inserted by Criminal Justice and Police Act 2001, s.78(5): in force on a date to
be appointed.
[26] Words in italics repealed and paras (a)–(c) substituted by Criminal Justice and Police Act 2001,
s.78(6): in force on a date to be appointed.
[27] Subs.(8A) inserted by Criminal Justice and Police Act 2001, s.78(7): in force on a date to be
appointed.
[28] Words in square brackets inserted by Immigration and Asylum Act 1999, s.169(1), Sch. 14, para.
80(1), (4): in force on a date to be appointed.

[(b) applies to a person arrested or detained under the terrorism provisions].[29]

Intimate samples

44–38 **62.**—(1) [Subject to s.63B below,][30] an intimate sample may be taken from a person in police detention only—

(a) if a police officer of at least the rank of superintendent [inspector][31] authorises it to be taken; and
(b) if the appropriate consent is given.

[(1A) An intimate sample may be taken from a person who is not in police detention but from whom, in the course of the investigation of an offence, two or more non-intimate samples suitable for the same means of analysis have been taken which have proved insufficient—

(a) if a police officer of at least the rank of superintendent [inspector][32] authorises it to be taken; and
(b) if the appropriate consent is given.]

(2) An officer may only give an authorisation [under subss.(1) or (1A) above] if he has reasonable grounds—

[under subss.(1) or (1A) above] if he has reasonable grounds—
(a) for suspecting the involvement of the person from whom the sample is to be taken in a [recordable offence]; and
(b) for believing that the sample will tend to confirm or disprove his involvement.

(3) An officer may give an authorisation under subss.(1) [or (1A)] above orally or in writing but, if he gives it orally, he shall confirm it in writing as soon as is practicable.
(4) The appropriate consent must be given in writing.
(5) Where—

(a) an authorisation has been given; and
(b) it is proposed that an intimate sample shall be taken in pursuance of the authorisation,

an officer shall inform the person from whom the sample is to be taken—

(i) of the giving of the authorisation; and
(ii) of the grounds for giving it.

---

[29] Subs.(9)(b) substituted by the Terrorism Act 2000, s.125(1), Sch. 15, para. 5(1), (7): in force, February 19, 2001 (except in relation to a person detained prior to that date).
[30] Words in square brackets inserted by Criminal Justice and Court Services Act 2000, s.74, Sch. 7, Pt II, paras 76, 78: in force, July 2, 2001.
[31] Word "superintendent" repealed and word "inspector" substituted by Criminal Justice and Police Act 2001, s.80(1): in force on a date to be appointed.
[32] *ibid.*

(6) The duty imposed by subs.(5)(ii) above includes a duty to state the nature of the offence in which it is suspected that the person from whom the sample is to be taken has been involved.

(7) If an intimate sample is taken from a person—

(a) the authorisation by virtue of which it was taken;
(b) the grounds for giving the authorisation; and
(c) the fact that the appropriate consent was given,

shall be recorded as soon as is practicable after the sample is taken.

[(7A) If an intimate sample is taken from a person at a police station—

(a) before the sample is taken, an officer shall inform him that it may be the subject of a speculative search; and
(b) the fact that the person has been informed of this possibility shall be recorded as soon as practicable after the sample has been taken.]

(8) If an intimate sample is taken from a person detailed at a police station, the matters required to be recorded by subss.(7) [or (7A)] above shall be recorded in his custody record.

(9) An intimate sample, other than a sample of urine [or a dental impression], may only be taken from a person by a registered medical practitioner [or a registered nurse][33] [and a dental impression may only be taken by a registered dentist].

(10) Where the appropriate consent to the taking of an intimate sample from a person was refused without good cause, in any proceedings against that person for an offence—

(a) the court, in determining—
(i) whether to commit that person for trial; or
(ii) whether there is a case to answer; and
[(aa) a judge, in deciding whether to grant an application made by the accused under—
(i) s.6 of the Criminal Justice Act 1987 (application for dismissal of charge of serious fraud in respect of which notice of transfer has been given under s.4 of that Act); or
(ii) para. 5 of Sch. 6 to the Criminal Justice Act 1991 (application for dismissal of charge of violent or sexual offence involving child in respect of which notice of transfer has been given under s.53 of that Act); and]
(b) the court or jury, in determining whether that person is guilty of the offence charged,

may draw such inferences from the refusal as appear proper...

(11) Nothing in this section affects [ss. 4 to 11 of the Road Traffic Act 1988].

(12) Nothing in this section applies to a person arrested or detained under the terrorism provisions; and subs.(1A) shall not apply where the non-intimate

---

[33] Words "or a registered nurse" inserted by Criminal Justice and Police Act 2001, s.80(2): in force on a date to be appointed.

samples mentioned in that subsection were taken under para. 10 of Sch. 8 to the Terrorism Act 2000.][34]

Other samples

44–39   **63.**—(1) Except as provided by this section, a non-intimate sample may not be taken from a person without the appropriate consent.

(2) Consent to the taking of a non-intimate sample must be given in writing.

(3) A non-intimate sample may be taken from a person without the appropriate consent if—

(a) he is in police detention or is being held in custody by the police on the authority of a court; and

(b) an officer of at least the rank of superintendent [inspector][35] authorises it to be taken without the appropriate consent.

[(3A) A non-intimate sample may be taken from a person (whether or not he falls within subs. (3)(a) above) without the appropriate consent if—

(a) he has been charged with a recordable offence or informed that he will be reported for such an offence; and

(b) either he has not had a non-intimate sample taken from him in the course of the investigation of the offence by the police or he has had a non-intimate sample taken from him but either it was not suitable for the same means of analysis or, though so suitable, the sample proved insufficient.

(3B) A non-intimate sample may be taken from a person without the appropriate consent if he has been convicted of a recordable offence.]

(3C) A non-intimate sample may also be taken from a person without the appropriate consent if he is a person to whom s.2 of the Criminal Evidence (Amendment) Act 1997 applies (persons detained following acquittal on grounds of insanity or finding of unfitness to plead).]

(4) An officer may only give an authorisation under subs.(3) above if he has reasonable grounds—

(a) for suspecting the involvement of the person from whom the sample is to be taken in a [recordable offence]; and

(b) for believing that the sample will tend to confirm or disprove his involvement.

(5) An officer may give an authorisation under subs.(3) above orally or in writing but, if he gives it orally, he shall confirm it in writing as soon as is practicable.

[(5A) An officer shall not give an authorisation under subs.(3) above for the taking from any person of a non-intimate sample consisting of a skin impression if—

---

[34] Subs.(12) substituted by Terrorism Act 2000, s.125(1), Sch. 15, para. 5(1), (8): in force, February 19, 2001 (except in relation to a person detained prior to that date).

[35] Word "superintendent" repealed and word "inspector" substituted by Criminal Justice and Police Act 2001, s.80(1): in force on a date to be appointed.

(a) the skin impression of the same part of the body has already been taken from that person in the course of the investigation of the offence; and

(b) the impression previously taken is not one that has proved insufficient.]³⁶

(6) Where—

(a) an authorisation has been given; and

(b) it is proposed that a non-intimate sample shall be taken in pursuance of the authorisation,

an officer shall inform the person from whom the sample is to be taken—

    (i) of the giving of the authorisation; and

    (ii) of the grounds for giving it.

(7) The duty imposed by subs.(6)(ii) above includes a duty to state the nature of the offence in which it is suspected that the person from whom the sample is to be taken has been involved.

(8) If a non-intimate sample is taken from a person by virtue of subsection (3) above—

(a) the authorisation by virtue of which it was taken; and

(b) the grounds for giving the authorisation,

shall be recorded as soon as is practicable after the sample is taken.

[(8A) In a case where by virtue of subs.(3A) [, (3B) or (3C) above] a sample is taken from a person without the appropriate consent—

(a) he shall be told the reason before the sample is taken; and

(b) the reason shall be recorded as soon as practicable after the sample is taken.]

[(8B) If a non-intimate sample is taken from a person at a police station, whether with or without the appropriate consent—

(a) before the sample is taken, an officer shall inform him that it may be the subject of a speculative search; and

(b) the fact that the person has been informed of this possibility shall be recorded as soon as practicable after the sample has been taken.]

(9) If a non-intimate sample is taken from a person detained at a police station, the matters required to be recorded by subs.(8) [or (8A) [or (8B)] above shall be recorded in his custody record.

[(9A) Subsection (3B) above shall not apply to any person convicted before April 10, 1995 unless he is a person to whom s.1 of the Criminal Evidence (Amendment) Act 1997 applies (persons imprisoned or detained by virtue of pre-existing conviction for sexual offence etc).]

---

³⁶ Subs.(5A) inserted by Criminal Justice and Police Act 2001, s.80(3): in force on a date to be appointed.

[(9A) Where a non-intimate sample consisting of a skin impression is taken electronically from a person, it must be taken only in such manner, and using such devices, as the Secretary of State has approved for the purpose of the electronic taking of such an impression.][37]

[(10) Nothing in this section applies to a person arrested or detained under the terrorism provisions.][38]

[Fingerprints and samples: supplementary provisions]

44–39A   **63A.**—[[(1) Where a person has been arrested on suspicion of being involved in a recordable offence or has been charged with such an offence or has been informed that he will be reported for such an offence, fingerprints or samples or the information derived from the samples taken under any power conferred by this Part of this Act from the person may be checked against—

(a) other fingerprints or samples to which the person seeking to check has access and which are held by or on behalf of [any one or more relevant law-enforcement authorities or which][39] are held in connection with or as a result of an investigation of an offence;

(b) information derived from other samples if the information is contained in records to which the person seeking to check has access and which are held as mentioned in paragraph (a) above.

[(1A)[40] In subs.(1) above "relevant law-enforcement authority" means—

(a) a police force;
(b) the National Criminal Intelligence Service;
(c) the National Crime Squad;
(d) a public authority (not falling within paragraphs (a) to (c) with functions in any part of the British Islands which consist of or include the investigation of crimes or the charging of offenders;
(e) any person with functions in any country or territory outside the United Kingdom which—
    (i) correspond to those of a police force; or
    (ii) otherwise consist of or include the investigation of conduct contrary to the law of that country or territory, or the apprehension of persons guilty of such conduct;
(f) any person with functions under any international agreement which consist of or include the investigation of conduct which is—
    (i) unlawful under the law of one or more places,
    (ii) prohibited by such an agreement, or
    (iii) contrary to international law,

---

[37] Second subs.(9A) inserted by Criminal Justice and Police Act 2001, s.80(4): in force on a date to be appointed.
[38] Subs.(10) substituted by Terrorism Act 2000, s.125(1), Sch. 15, para. 5(1), (9): in force, February 19, 2001 (except in relation to a person detained prior to that date).
[39] Words in square brackets substituted by Criminal Justice and Police Act 2001, s.81(1): in force, May 11, 2001 (in the absence of any specific commencement provision).
[40] Subss.(1A)–(1D) substituted, for subs.(1A), by Criminal Justice and Police Act 2001, s.81(2): in force, May 11, 2001 (in the absence of any specific commencement provision).

or the apprehension of persons guilty of such conduct.

(1B) The reference in subs.(1A) above to a police force is a reference to any of the following—

(a) any police force maintained under s.2 of the Police Act 1996 (c 16) (police forces in England and Wales outside London);
(b) the metropolitan police force;
(c) the City of London police force;
(d) any police force maintained under or by virtue of s.1 of the Police (Scotland) Act 1967 (c 77);
(e) the Police Service of Northern Ireland;
(f) the Police Service of Northern Ireland Reserve;
(g) the Ministry of Defence Police;
(h) the Royal Navy Regulating Branch;
(i) the Royal Military Police;
(j) the Royal Air Force Police;
(k) the Royal Marine Police;
(l) the British Transport Police;
(m) the States of Jersey Police Force;
(n) the salaried police force of the Island of Guernsey;
(o) the Isle of Man Constabulary.

(1C) Where—

(a) fingerprints or samples have been taken from any person in connection with the investigation of an offence but otherwise than in circumstances to which subs.(1) above applies, and
(b) that person has given his consent in writing to the use in a speculative search of the fingerprints or of the samples and of information derived from them,

the fingerprints or, as the case may be, those samples and that information may be checked against any of the fingerprints, samples or information mentioned in para. (a) or (b) of that subsection.

(1D) A consent given for the purposes of subs.(1C) above shall not be capable of being withdrawn.]]

(2) Where a sample of hair other than pubic hair is to be taken the sample may be taken either by cutting hairs or by plucking hairs with their roots so long as no more are plucked than the person taking the sample reasonably considers to be necessary for a sufficient sample.

(3) Where any power to take a sample is exercisable in relation to a person the sample may be taken in a prison or other institution to which the Prison Act 1952 applies.

[(3A) Where—

(a) the power to take a non-intimate sample under s.63(3B) above is exercisable in relation to any person who is detained under Pt III of the Mental Health Act 1983 in pursuance of—
(i) a hospital order or interim hospital order made following his conviction for the recordable offence in question, or
(ii) a transfer direction given at a time when he was detained in pursuance of any sentence or order imposed following that conviction, or

(b) the power to take a non-intimate sample under s.63(3C) above is exercisable in relation to any person,

the sample may be taken in the hospital in which he is detained under that Part of that Act.

Expressions used in this subsection and in the Mental Health Act 1983 have the same meaning as in that Act.

(3B) Where the power to take a non-intimate sample under s.63(3B) above is exercisable in relation to a person detained in pursuance of directions of the Secretary of State under [s.92 of the Powers of Criminal Courts (Sentencing) Act 2000][41] the sample may be taken at the place where he is so detained.]

(4) Any constable may, within the allowed period, require a person who is neither in police detention nor held in custody by the police on the authority of a court to attend a police station in order to have a sample taken where—

(a) the person has been charged with a recordable offence or informed that he will be reported for such an offence and either he has not had a sample taken from him in the course of the investigation of the offence by the police or he had had a sample so taken form him but either it was not suitable for the same means of analysis or, though so suitable, the sample proved insufficient; or
(b) the person has been convicted of a recordable offence and either he has not had a sample taken from him since the conviction or he has had a sample taken from him (before or after his conviction) but either it was not suitable for the same means of analysis or, though so suitable, the sample proved insufficient.

(5) The period allowed for requiring a person to attend a police station for the purpose specified in subs.(4) above is—

(a) in the case of a person falling within paragraph (a), one month beginning with the date of the charge [or of his being informed as mentioned in that paragraph] or one month beginning with the date on which the appropriate officer is informed of the fact that the sample is not suitable for the same means of analysis or has proved insufficient, as the case may be;
(b) in the case of a person falling within paragraph (b), one month beginning with the date of the conviction or one beginning with the date on which the appropriate officer is informed of the fact that the sample is not suitable for the same means of analysis or has proved insufficient, as the case may be.

(6) A requirement under subs.(4) above—

(a) shall give the person at least 7 days within which he must so attend; and
(b) may direct him to attend at a specified time of day or between specified times of day.

---

[41] Words "section 92" to "Act 2000" in square brackets substituted by Powers of Criminal Courts (Sentencing) Act 2000, s.165(1), Sch. 9, para. 97: in force, August 25, 2000.

(7) Any constable may arrest without a warrant a person who has failed to comply with a requirement under subs.(4) above.

(8) In this section "the appropriate officer" is—

(a) in the case of a person falling within subs.(4)(a), the officer investigating the offence with which that person has been charged or as to which he was informed that he would be reported;

(b) in the case of a person falling within subs.(4)(b), the officer in charge of the police station from which the investigation of the offence of which he was convicted was conducted.]

[Testing for presence of Class A drugs][42]

63B.—[(1) A sample of urine or a non-intimate sample may be taken from a **44–39B** person in police detention for the purpose of ascertaining whether he has any specified Class A drug in his body if the following conditions are met.

(2) The first condition is—

(a) that the person concerned has been charged with a trigger offence; or

(b) that the person concerned has been charged with an offence and a police officer of at least the rank of inspector, who has reasonable grounds for suspecting that the misuse by that person of any specified Class A drug caused or contributed to the offence, has authorised the sample to be taken.

(3) The second condition is that the person concerned has attained the age of 18.

(4) The third condition is that a police officer has requested the person concerned to give the sample.

(5) Before requesting the person concerned to give a sample, an officer must—

(a) warn him that if, when so requested, he fails without good cause to do so he may be liable to prosecution; and

(b) in a case within subs.(2)(b) above, inform him of the giving of the authorisation and of the grounds in question.

(6) A sample may be taken under this section only by a person prescribed by regulations made by the Secretary of State by statutory instrument.

No regulations shall be made under this subsection unless a draft has been laid before, and approved by resolution of, each House of Parliament.

(7) Information obtained from a sample taken under this section may be disclosed—

(a) for the purpose of informing any decision about granting bail in criminal proceedings (within the meaning of the Bail Act 1976) to the person concerned;

---

[42] Inserted by Criminal Justice and Courts Services Act 2000, s.57(1), (2): in force, June 20, 2001 (Nottinghamshire, Staffordshire and Metropolitan police districts for the purposes of exercising any order-making powers); July 2, 2001 (Nottinghamshire, Staffordshire and Metropolitan police districts for remaining purposes); May 20, 2002 (Bedfordshire, Devon & Cornwall, Lancashire, Merseyside, South Yorkshire and North Wales police districts); date to be appointed for remaining purposes.

    (b) where the person concerned is in police detention or is remanded in or committed to custody by an order of a court or has been granted such bail, for the purpose of informing any decision about his supervision;
    (c) where the person concerned is convicted of an offence, for the purpose of informing any decision about the appropriate sentence to be passed by a court and any decision about his supervision or release;
    (d) for the purpose of ensuring that appropriate advice and treatment is made available to the person concerned.

(8) A person who fails without good cause to give any sample which may be taken from him under this section shall be guilty of an offence.

[Testing of presence of Class drugs: supplementary][43]

44–39C   **63C.**—[(1) A person guilty of an offence under s.63B above shall be liable on summary conviction to imprisonment for a term not exceeding three months, or to a fine not exceeding level 4 on the standard scale, or to both.

(2) A police officer may give an authorisation under section 63B above orally or in writing but, if he gives it orally, he shall confirm it in writing as soon as is practicable.

(3) If a sample is taken under s.63B above by virtue of an authorisation, the authorisation and the grounds for the suspicion shall be recorded as soon as is practicable after the sample is taken.

(4) If the sample is taken from a person detained at a police station, the matters required to be recorded by subs.(3) above shall be recorded in his custody record.

(5) Subss.(11) and (12) of s.62 above apply for the purposes of s.63B above as they do for the purposes of that section; and s.63B above does to prejudice the generality of ss.62 and 63 above.

(6) In s.63B above—

"Class A drug" and "misuse" have the same meanings as in the Misuse of Drugs Act 1971;
"specified" (in relation to a Class A drug) and "trigger offence" have the same meanings as in Pt III of the Criminal Justice and Court Services Act 2000.]

Destruction of fingerprints and samples

44–40   **64.**—[(1A)[44] Where—

    (a) fingerprints or samples are taken from a person in connection with the investigation of an offence, and
    (b) subs.(3) below does not require them to be destroyed,

---

[43] Inserted by Criminal Justice and Courts Services Act 2000, s.57(1), (2): in force, July 2, 2001 (Notinghamshire, Staffordshire and Metropolitan police districts); May 20, 2002 (Bedfordshire, Devon & Cornwall, Lancashire, Merseyside, South Yorkshire and North Wales police districts); date to be appointed for remaining purposes.
[44] Subss.(1A), (1B) substituted, for subss.(1), (2) as originally enacted, by Criminal Justice and Police Act 2001, s.82(1), (2), (6): in force, May 11, 2001 (in the absence of any specific commencement provision).

the fingerprints or samples may be retained after they have fulfilled the purposes for which they were taken but shall not be used by any person except for purposes related to the prevention or detection of crime, the investigation of an offence or the conduct of a prosecution.

(1B) In subs.(1A) above—

(a) the reference to using fingerprints includes a reference to allowing any check to be made against it under s.63A(1) or (1C) above and disclosing it to any person;

(b) the reference to using a sample includes a reference to allowing any check to be made under s.63A(1) or (1C) above against it or against information derived form it and to disclosing it or any such information to any person;

(c) the reference to crime includes a reference to any conduct which—
   (i) constitutes one or more criminal offences (whether under the law of a part of the United Kingdom or of a country or territory outside the United Kingdom); or
   (ii) is, or corresponds to, any conduct which, if it all took place in any one part of the United Kingdom, could constitute one or more criminal offence;
   and

(d) the references to an investigation and to a prosecution include references, respectively, to any investigation outside the United Kingdom of any crime or suspected crime and to a prosecution brought in respect of any crime in a country or territory outside the United Kingdom.]

(3) If—

(a) fingerprints or samples are taken from a person in connection with the investigation of an offence; and

(b) that person is not suspected of having committed the offence,

they must [, except as provided in [the following provisions of this section][45],] be destroyed as soon as they have fulfilled the purposes for which they were taken.

[(3AA)[46] Samples and fingerprints are not required to be destroyed under subs.(3) above if—

(a) they were taken for the purposes of the investigation of an offence of which a person has been convicted; and

(b) a sample or, as the case may be, fingerprint was also taken from the convicted person for the purposes of that investigation.

(3AB) Subject to subs.(3AC) below, where a person is entitled under subs.(3) above to the destruction of any fingerprint or sample taken from him (or would

---

[45] Words "the following provisions of this section" substituted by Criminal Justice and Police Act 2001, s.82(1), (3): in force, May 11, 2001 (in the absence of any specific commencement provision).

[46] Subss.(3AA)–(3AD) substituted, for subss.(3A), (3B), by the Criminal Justice and Police Act 2001, s.82(1), (4), (6): in force, May 11, 2001(in the absence of any specific commencement provision).

be but for subs.(3AA) above), neither the fingerprint nor the sample, nor any information derived from the sample, shall be used—

(a) in evidence against the person who is or would be entitled to the destruction of that fingerprint or sample; or

(b) for the purposes of the investigation of any offence;

and subs.(1B) above applies for the purposes of this subsection as it applies for the purposes of subs.(1A) above.

(3AC) Where a person from whom a fingerprint or sample has been taken consents in writing to its retention—

(a) that sample need not be destroyed under subs.(3) above;

(b) subs.(3AB) above shall not restrict the use that may be made of the fingerprint or sample or, in the case of a sample, of any information derived from it; and

(c) that consent shall be treated as comprising a consent for the purposes of s.63A(1C) above;

and a consent given for the purpose of this subsection shall not be capable of being withdrawn.

(3AD) For the purposes of subs.(3AC) above it shall be immaterial whether the consent is given at, before or after the time when the entitlement to the destruction of the fingerprint or sample arises.]

(4) . . . [47]

[(5) If fingerprints are destroyed—

(a) any copies of the fingerprints shall also be destroyed; and

(b) any chief officer or police controlling access to computer data relating to the fingerprints shall make access to the data impossible, as soon as it is practicable to do so.]

(6) A person who asks to be allowed to witness the destruction of his fingerprints or copies of them shall have a right to witness it.

[(6A) If—

(a) subs.(5)(b) above falls to be complied with; and

(b) the person to whose fingerprints the data relates asks for a certificate that it has been complied with,

such a certificate shall be issued to him, not later than the end of the period of three months beginning with the day on which he asks for it, by the responsible chief officer of police or a person authorised by him or on his behalf for the purposes of this section.

(6B) In this section—

. . .

---

[47] Repealed by Criminal Justice and Police Act 2001, s.137, Sch. 7, Pt 2(1): in force, June 19, 2001.

"the responsible chief officer of police" means the chief officer of police in whose [police] area the computer data were put on to the computer.]

(7) Nothing in this section—

(a) affects any power conferred by para. 18(2) of Sch. 2 of the Immigration Act 1971 [or s.20 of the Immigration and Asylum Act 1999 (c 33) (disclosure of police information to the Secretary of State for use for immigration purposes)][48]; or
(b) applies to a person arrested or detained under the terrorism provisions.

[Photographing of suspects etc][49]

64A.—[(1) A person who is detained at a police station may be   **44–40A**
photographed—

(a) with the appropriate consent; or
(b) if the appropriate consent is withheld or it is not practicable to obtain it, without it.

(2) A person proposing to take a photograph of any person under this section—

(a) may, for the purposes of doing so, require the removal of any item or substance worn on or over the whole or any part of the head or face of the person to be photographed; and
(b) if the requirement is not complied with, may remove the item or substance himself.

(3) Where a photograph may be taken under this section, the only persons entitled to take the photograph are—

(a) constables; and
(b) persons who (without being constables) are designated for the purposes of this section by the chief officer of police for the police area in which the police station in question is situated;

and s.117 (use of force) applies to the exercise by a person falling within paragraph (b) of the powers conferred by the preceding provisions of this section as it applies to the exercise of those powers by a constable.
(4) A photograph taken under this section—

(a) may be used by, or disclosed to, any person for any purpose relating to the prevention or detention of crime, the investigation of an offence or the conduct of a prosecution; and
(b) after being so used or disclosed, may be retained but may not be used or disclosed except for a purpose so related.

---

[48] Words in square brackets inserted by Criminal Justice and Police Act 2001, s.82(1), (5): in force, May 11, 2001 (in the absence of any specific commencement provision).
[49] Inserted by Anti-terrorism, Crime and Security Act 2001, s.92: in force, December 14, 2001.

(5) In subs.(4)—

(a) the reference to crime includes a reference to any conduct which—
  (i) constitutes one or more criminal offences (whether under the law of a part of the United Kingdom or of a country or territory outside the United Kingdom); or
  (ii) is, or corresponds to, any conduct which, if it all took place in any one part of the United Kingdom, would constitute one or more criminal offences;
  and
(b) the reference to an investigation and to a prosecution include references, respectively, to any investigation outside the United Kingdom of any crime or suspected crime and to a prosecution brought in respect of any crime in a country or territory outside the United Kingdom.

(6) References in this section to taking a photograph include references to using any process by means of which a visual image may be produced; and references to photographing a person shall be construed accordingly.]

Part V—supplementary

44–41   **65.**—[(1)][50] In this Part of this Act—

["analysis", in relating to a skin impression, includes comparison and matching;][51]
"appropriate consent" means—

(a) In relation to a person who has attained the age of 17 years, the consent of that person;
(b) in relation to a person who has not attained the age but has attained the age of 14 years, the consent of that person and his parent or guardian; and
(c) in relation to a person who has not attained the age of 14 years, the consent of his parent or guardian;

["drug trafficking" and "drug trafficking offence" have the same meaning as in the [Drug Trafficking Act 1994]]
"Fingerprints" includes palm prints;
["fingerprints", in relation to any person, means a record (in any form and produced by any method) of the skin pattern and other physical characteristics or features of—

(a) any of that person's fingers; or
(b) either of his palms;][52]

["intimate sample" means—

---

[50] Numbered as such by Criminal Justice and Police Act 2001, s.80(5): in force on a date to be appointed.
[51] Definition of "analysis" inserted by Criminal Justice and Police Act 2001, s.80(5)(a): in force on a date to be appointed.
[52] Definition of "fingerprints" substituted by Criminal Justice and Police Act 2001, s.78(8): in force on a date to be appointed.

(a) a sample of blood, semen or any other tissue fluid, urine or pubic hair;
(b) a dental impression;
(c) a swab taken from a person's body orifice other than the mouth;]

["intimate search" means a search which consists of the physical examination of a person's body orifices other than the mouth;]
["non-intimate sample" means—

(a) a sample of hair other than pubic hair;
(b) A sample taken from a nail or from under a nail;
(c) a swab taken from any part of a person's body including the mouth but not any other body orifice;
(d) saliva;
(c) a footprint or a similar impression of any part of a person's body other than a part of his hand;
[(e) a skin impression;]][53]

["registered dentist" has the same meaning as in the Dentists Act 1984;
["skin impression", in relation to any person, means any record (other than a fingerprint) which is a record (in any form and produced by any method) of the skin pattern and other physical characteristics or features of the whole or any part of his foot or of any other part of his body;][54]
"speculative search", in relation to a person's fingerprints or samples, means such a check against other fingerprints or samples or against information derived from other samples as is referred to in s.63A(1) above;
"sufficient" and "insufficient", in relation to a sample, means [subject to sub.(2) below)][55] sufficient or insufficient (in point of quantity or quality) for the purpose of enabling information to be produced by the means of analysis used or to be used in relation to the sample;]
["the terrorism provisions" means s.41 of the Terrorism Act 2000, and any provision of Sch. 7 to that Act conferring a power of detention; and
"terrorism" has the meaning given in s.1 of that Act;][56]
    [. . . references in this Part to any person's proceeds of drug trafficking are to be construed in accordance with the [Drug Trafficking Act 1994]].
    [(2) References in this Part of this Act to a sample's proving insufficient include references to where, as a consequence of—

(a) the loss, destruction or contamination of the whole or any part of the sample;
(b) any damage to the whole or a part of the sample, or
(c) the use of the whole or a part of the sample for an analysis which produced no results or which produced results some or all of which must be regarded, in the circumstances, as unreliable.

---

[53] Subs.(1)(e) substituted by Criminal Justice and Police Act 2001, s.80(5)(b): in force on a date to be appointed.
[54] Definition of "skin impression" inserted by Criminal Justice and Police Act 2001, s.80(5)(c): in force on a date to be appointed.
[55] Words in square brackets inserted by Criminal Justice and Police Act 2001, s.80(5)(d): in force on a date to be appointed.
[56] Definitions of "the terrorism provisions" and "terrorism" substituted by Terrorism Act 2000, s.125(1), Sch. 15, para. 5(1), (10): in force, February 19, 2001 (except in relation to a person detained prior to that date).

The sample has become unavailable or insufficient for the purpose of enabling information, or information of a particular description, to be obtained by means of analysis of the sample.][57]

Codes of practice

44–42   **66.**—[(1)][58] The Secretary of State shall issue codes of practice in connection with—

   (a) the exercise by police officers of statutory powers—
     (i) to search a person without first arresting him; or
     (ii) to search a vehicle without making an arrest;
   (b) the detention, treatment, questioning and identification of persons by police officers;
   (c) searches of premises by police officers; and
   (d) the seizure of property found by police offices on persons or premises.

[(2) Codes shall (in particular) include provision in connection with the exercise by police officers of powers under s.63B above.][59]

Codes of practice—supplementary

44–43   **67.**—(2) This section applies to a code of practice under s.60[, 60A][60] or 66 above.

[(7A) Subject to subs.(7B) below, the Secretary of State may by order provide that a code of practice for the time being in force is to be treated as having effect with such modifications as may be set out in the order.

(7B) The effect of the modifications made by an order under subs.(7A) above must be confined to one or more of the following—

   (a) the effect of the code in relation to such area of England and Wales as may be specified in the order;
   (b) the effect of the code during such period, not exceeding two years, as may be so specified;
   (c) the effect of the order in relation to such offences or descriptions of offender as may be so specified.

(7C) An order under subs.(7A) above shall be made by statutory instrument and shall be subject to annulment in pursuance of a resolution of either House of Parliament.][61]
  (8) . . . [62]

---

[57] Subs.(2) inserted by Criminal Justice and Police Act 2001, s.80(6): in force on a date to be appointed.
[58] Numbered as such by Criminal Justice and Courts Services Act 2000, s.57(1), (4): in force, July 2, 2001 (for certain purposes); on a date to be appointed for remaining purposes.
[59] Inserted by Criminal Justice and Courts Services Act 2000, s.57(1), (4). In force, July 2, 2001 (for certain purposes); May 20, 2002 (Bedfordshire, Devon & Cornwall, Lancashire, Merseyside, South Yorkshire and North Wales police districts); on a date to be appointed for remaining purposes.
[60] "60A" inserted by Criminal Justice and Police Act 2001, s.76(2): in force, June 19, 2001.
[61] Subss.(7A)–(7C) inserted by Criminal Justice and Police Act, s.77: in force, June 19, 2001.
[62] Repealed by Police Act 1996, s.103, Sch. 9, Pt II: in force, April 1, 1999.

(12) In this section "criminal proceedings" include—

(a) proceedings in the United Kingdom or elsewhere before a court-martial constituted under the Army Act 1955, the Air Force Act 1955 or the Naval Discipline Act 1957 ... ;[63]

Convictions and acquittals

Proof of convictions and acquittals

73.—(2) For the purposes of this section a certificate of conviction or of   **44–44**
acquittal—

(a) shall, as regards a conviction or acquittal on indictment, consist of a certificate, signed by the [proper officer][64] of the court where the conviction or acquittal took place, giving the substance and effect (omitting the formal parts) of the indictment and of the conviction or acquittal; and

[(3) In subs.(2) above "proper officer" means—

(a) in relation to a magistrates' court in England and Wales, the justices' chief executive for the court; and
(b) in relation to any other court, the clerk of the court, his deputy or any other person having custody of the court record.][65]

Provisions supplementary to section 74

75.—(3) Nothing in any of the following—   **44–46**

(a) [s.14 of the Powers of Criminal Courts (Sentencing) Act 2000][66] (under which a conviction leading to probation or discharge is to be disregarded except as mentioned in that section);

... Compellability of accused's spouse[67]

80.—(1) ... [68]   **44–51**
[(2) In any proceedings the wife or husband of a person charged in the proceedings shall, subject to subs.(4) below, be compellable to give evidence on behalf of that person.

---

[63] Words omitted repealed by Armed Forces Act 2001, s.38, Sch. 7, Pt 1: in force, February 28, 2002.
[64] Words "proper officer" in subs.(2)(a) and (b) substituted by Access to Justice Act 1999, s.90(1), Sch. 13, paras 125, 128(1) and (2): in force, April 1, 2001.
[65] Subs.(3) substituted by Access to Justice Act 1999, s.90(1), Sch. 13, paras 125, 128(1) and (3): in force, April 1, 2001.
[66] Words in square brackets substituted by Powers of Criminal Courts (Sentencing) Act 2000, s.165(1), Sch. 9, para. 98: in force, August 25, 2000.
[67] Words omitted in provision heading repealed by Youth Justice and Criminal Evidence Act 1999, s.67(1), Sch. 4, paras 12, 13(1), (4): in force, July 24, 2002.
[68] Repealed by Youth Justice and Criminal Evidence Act 1999, s.67(1), (3), Sch. 4, paras 12, 13(1), (2), Sch. 6: in force, July 24, 2002.

(2A) In any proceedings the wife or husband of a person charged in the proceedings shall, subject to subs.(4) below, be compellable—

(a) to give evidence on behalf of any other person charged in the proceedings but only in respect of any specified offence with which that other person is charged; or
(b) to give evidence for the prosecution but only in respect of any specified offence with which any person is charged in the proceedings.

(3) In relation to the wife or husband of a person charged in any proceedings, an offence is a specified offence for the purposes of subs.(2A) above if—

(a) it involves an assault on, or injury or a threat of injury to, the wife or husband or a person who was at the material time under the age of 16;
(b) it is a sexual offence alleged to have been committed in respect of a person who was at the material time under that age; or
(c) it consists of attempting or conspiring to commit, or of aiding, abetting, counselling, procuring or inciting the commission of, an offence falling within paragraph (a) or (b) above.

(4) No person who is charged in any proceedings shall be compelled by virtue of subs.(2) or (A) above to give evidence in the proceedings.

(4A) References in this section to a person charged in any proceedings do not include a person who is not, or is no longer, liable to be convicted of any offence in the proceedings (whether as a result of pleading guilty or for any other reason).][69]

(5) In any proceedings a person who has been but is no longer married to the accused shall be ... compellable to give evidence as if that person and the accused had never been married.[70]

(6) Where in any proceedings the age of any person at any time is material for the purposes of subs.(3) above, his age at the material time shall for the purposes of that provision be deemed to be or to have been that which appears to the court to be or to have been his age at that time.

(7) In subs.(3)(b) above "sexual offence" means an offence under the Sexual Offences Act 1956, 4 & 5 Eliz.2, c 69; the Indecency with Children Act 1960, the Sexual Offences Act 1967, c 60, s.54 of the Criminal Law Act 1977 8 & 9 Eliz.2, c 33; or the Protection of Children Act 1978, c 37.[71]

[Rule where accused's spouse not compellable]

44–52   **80A.** [The failure of the wife or husband of a person charged in any proceedings to give evidence in the proceedings shall not be made the subject to any comment by the prosecution.][72]

---

[69] Subss.(2), (2A), (3), (4), (4A) substituted, for subss.(2)–(4) as originally enacted, by Youth Justice and Criminal Evidence Act 1999, s.67(1), Sch. 4, paras 12, 13(1), (3): in force, July 24, 2002.
[70] Words omitted repealed by Youth Justice and Criminal Evidence Act 1999, s.67(1), (3), Sch. 4, paras 12, 13(1), (4), Sch. 6: in force, July 24, 2002.
[71] Subs.(8) repealed by Youth Justice and Criminal Evidence Act 1999, s.67(1), (3), Sch. 4, paras 12, 13(1), (2), Sch. 6: in force, July 24, 2002.
[72] s.80A inserted by Youth Justice and Criminal Evidence Act 1999, s.67(1), Sch. 4, paras 12, 14: in force, July 24, 2002.

Part VIII—Interpretation

82.—(1) In this Part of this Act—   **44–54**

"court-martial" means a court-martial constituted under the Army Act 1955, the Air Force Act 1955 or the Naval Discipline Act 1957 . . . ;[73]
"proceedings" means criminal proceedings, including—

    (a) proceedings in the United Kingdom or elsewhere before a court-martial constituted under the Army Act 1955 [, the Air Force Act 1955 or the Naval Discipline Act 1957];[74]
    (b) proceedings in the United Kingdom or elsewhere before the Courts-Martial Appeal Court—
       (i) on an appeal from a court-martial so constituted[75] . . . ; or

SCHEDULE 1

SPECIAL PROCEDURE

Making of orders by circuit judge

5. Where the material consists of information contained in a computer [stored   **44–55** in any electronic form][76]

    (a) an order under para. 4(a) above shall have effect as an order to produce the material in a form in which it can be taken away and in which it is visible and legible [or from which it can readily be produced in a visible and legible form][77]; and

---

[73] Words omitted repealed by Armed Forces Act 2001, s.38, Sch. 7, Pt 1: in force, February 28, 2002.
[74] Words from "constituted" to "1957" repealed by Youth Justice and Criminal Evidence Act 1999, s.67(3), Sch. 6: in force on a date to be appointed.
[75] Words "so constituted" repealed by Youth Justice and Criminal Evidence Act 1999, s.67(3), Sch. 6: in force on a date to be appointed.
[76] Words "contained in a computer" repealed and subsequent words in square brackets substituted by Criminal Justice and Police Act 2001, s.70, Sch. 2, Pt 2, para. 14(a): in force on a date to be appointed.
[77] Words in square brackets inserted by Criminal Justice and Police Act 2001, s.70, Sch. 2, Pt 2, para. 14(b): in force on a date to be appointed.

CRIMINAL JUSTICE ACT 1988

First-hand hearsay

44–58   **23.**—(1) Subject—

(a) to subs.(4) below; [and][78]
(b) to para. 1A of Sch. 2 to the Criminal Appeal Act 1968 (evidence given
      orally at original trial to be given orally at retrial);
(c) . . . [79]

[(5) This section shall not apply to proceedings before a magistrates' court
inquiring into an offence as examining justices.][80]

Business etc. documents

44–59   **24.**—(1) Subject—

(a) to subss.(3) and (4) below; [and][81]
(b) to para. 1A of Sch. 2 to the Criminal Appeal Act 1968; . . .
(c) . . . [82]

[Video recordings of testimony from child witnesses][83]

44–67A   **32A.**

Abolition of requirement of corroboration for unsworn evidence of children

34.—(3) Unsworn evidence admitted by virtue of [s.56 of the Youth Justice
and Criminal Evidence Act 1999][84] may corroborate evidence (sworn or
unsworn) given by any other person.

---

[78] Word in square brackets inserted by Youth Justice and Criminal Evidence Act 1999, s.67(1), Sch.
4, paras 15, 16: in force, April 14, 2000.
[79] Omitted words in (b) and (c) repealed by Youth Justice and Criminal Evidence Act 1999, s.67(3),
Sch. 6: in force, April 14, 2000.
[80] Subs.(5) inserted, in relation to alleged offences into which no criminal procedure has begun before
April 1, 1997, by Criminal Procedure and Investigations Act 1996, s.47, Sch. 1, para. 28 (see SIs
1997/682 and 1997/683).
[81] "and" inserted by Youth Justice and Criminal Evidence Act 1999, s.67(1), Sch. 4, paras 15, 16: in
force, April 14, 2000.
[82] Omitted words repealed by Youth Justice and Criminal Evidence Act 1999, s.67(3), Sch. 6: in
force, April 14, 2000.
[83] s.32A repealed with savings by Youth Justice and Criminal Evidence Act 1999, s.67(3), (4), Sch.
6, Sch. 7, para. 3: in force, for certain purposes, July 24, 2002. In force, for remaining purposes, on
a date to be appointed.
[84] Words in square brackets substituted by Youth Justice and Criminal Evidence Act 1999, s.67(1),
Sch. 4, paras 15, 17: in force, April 14, 2000.

CRIMINAL JUSTICE AND PUBLIC ORDER ACT 1994

Effect of accused's failure to mention facts when questioned or charged

34.—[(2A) Where the accused was at an authorised place of detention at the **44–73** time of the failure, subss.(1) and (2) above do not apply if he had not been allowed an opportunity to consult a solicitor prior to being questioned, charged or informed as mentioned in subs.(1) above.][85]

Effect of accused's silence at trial

35.—(1) At the trial of any person . . . for an offence,[86] subss.(2) and (3) below **44–74** apply unless—
   (6) . . . [87]

Effect of accused's failure or refusal to account for objects, substances or marks

36.—[(4A) Where the accused was at an authorised place of detention at the **44–75** time of the failure or refusal, subss.(1) and (2) above do not apply if he had not been allowed an opportunity to consult a solicitor prior to the request being made.][88]

Effect of accused's failure or refusal to account for presence at a particular place

37.—[(3A) Where the accused was at an authorised place of detention at the **44–76** time of the failure or refusal, subss.(1) and (2) do not apply if he had not been allowed an opportunity to consult a solicitor prior to the request being made.][89]

CIVIL EVIDENCE ACT 1995

Short title, commencement and extent

16.—[(3) Subject to subs.(3A), the provisions of this Act shall not apply in **44–94** relation to proceedings begun before commencement.][90]

---

[85] Subs.(2A) inserted by Youth Justice and Criminal Evidence Act 1999, ss.58(1), (2), 67, Sch. 7, para. 8, in relation to proceedings instituted on or after the date for s.58 thereof, whether the relevant failure or refusal on the part of the accused took place before or after that date: in force on a date to be appointed.
[86] Words omitted repealed by Crime and Disorder Act 1998, ss.35(a), 120(2), Sch. 10: in force, September 30, 1998.
[87] Repealed by Crime and Disorder Act 1998, ss.35(b), 120(2), Sch. 10: in force, September 30, 1998.
[88] Inserted by Youth Justice and Criminal Evidence Act 1999, ss.58(1), (3), 67, Sch. 7, para. 8: in force on a date to be appointed.
[89] Inserted by Youth Justice and Criminal Evidence Act 1999, ss.58(1), (4), 67, Sch. 7, para. 8: in force on a date to be appointed.
[90] Substituted by SI 1999/1217, arts 2, 4(a): in force, April 26, 1999.

[(3A) Transitional provisions for the application of the provisions of this Act to proceedings begun before commencement may be made by rules of court or practice directions.][91]

CRIMINAL PROCEDURE AND INVESTIGATIONS ACT 1996

PART 1—DISCLOSURE

Introduction

Application of this Part

44–97   **1.**—(2) This Part also applies where—

[(cc) a person is charged with an offence for which he is sent to trial under s.51 (no committal proceedings for indictable-only offences) of the Crime and Disorder Act 1998,][92]

(f) a bill of indictable charging a person with an indictable offence is preferred under s.22B(3)(a) of the Prosecution of Offences Act 1985].[93]

Primary disclosure by prosecutor

44–99   **3.**—(7) Material must not be disclosed under this section to the extent that [it is material the disclosure of which is prohibited by s.17 of the Regulation of Investigatory Powers Act 2000].[94]

Compulsory disclosure by accused

44–101   **5.**—[(3A) Where this Part applies by virtue of s.1(2)(cc), this section does not apply unless—

(a) copies of the documents containing the evidence have been served on the accused under regulations made under para. 1 of Sch. 3 to the Crime and Disorder Act 1998; and

(b) a copy of the notice under subs.(7) of s.51 of that Act has been served on him under that subsection.][95]

---

[91] Inserted by SI 1999/1217, arts 2, 4(b): in force, April 26, 1999.

[92] Subs.(2): para. (cc) inserted by Crime and Disorder Act 1998, s.119, Sch. 8, para. 125(a): in force, for certain purposes, January 4, 1999; for remaining purposes, January 15, 2001.

[93] Subs.(2), para. (f) inserted by Crime and Disorder Act 1998, s.119, Sch. 8, para. 125(b): in force, June 1, 1999.

[94] Words in square brackets substituted by Regulation of Investigatory Powers Act 2000, s.82(1), Sch. 4, para. 7(1): in force, October 2, 2000.

[95] Subs.(3A) inserted by Crime and Disorder Act 1998, s.119, Sch. 8, para. 126. Date in force, for certain purposes, January 4, 1999; for remaining purposes, January 15, 2001.

Secondary disclosure by prosecutor

7.—(6) Material must not be disclosed under this section to the extent that [it   **44–103** is material the disclosure of which is prohibited by s.17 of the Regulation of Investigatory Powers Act 2000].[96]

Application by accused for disclosure

8.—(6) Material must not be disclosed under this section to the extent that [its   **44–104** material the disclosure of which is prohibited by s.17 of the Regulation of Investigatory Powers Act 2000].[97]

Continuing duty of prosecutor to disclose

9.—(9) Material must not be disclosed under this section to the extent that [it   **44–105** is material the disclosure of which is prohibited by s.17 of the Regulation of Investigatory Powers Act 2000].[98]

Code of practice

23.—(6) The code must so be framed that it does not apply to material   **44–111** intercepted in obedience to a warrant issued under s.2 of the Interception of Communications Act 1985 [or under the authority of an interception warrant under s.5 of the Regulation of Investigatory Powers Act 2000].[99]

CIVIL PROCEDURE RULES 1998

PART 22. STATEMENTS OF TRUTH

22.1—(1) The following documents must be verified by a statement of   **44–115** truth—

(a) a statement of case;
(b) a response complying with an order under r.18.1 to provide further information;
(c) a witness statement;
(d) an acknowledgement of service in a clam begun by way of the Part 8 procedure;

---

[96] Words in square brackets substituted by Regulation of Investigatory Powers Act 2000, s.82(1), Sch. 4, para. 7(1): in force, October 2, 2000.
[97] Words in square brackets substituted by Regulation of Investigatory Powers Act 2000, s.82(1), Sch. 4, para. 7(1): in force, October 2, 2000.
[98] Words in square brackets substituted by Regulation of Investigatory Powers Act 2000, s.82(1), Sch. 4, para. 7(1): in force, October 2, 2000.
[99] Inserted by Regulation of Investigatory Powers Act 2000, s.82(1), Sch. 4, para. 7(2): in force, October 2, 2000.

    (e) a certificate stating the reasons for bringing a possession claim or a landlord and tenant claim in the High Court in accordance with rr.55.3(2) and 56.2(2); and

    (f) any other document where a rule or practice direction requires.

(2) Where a statement of case is amended, the amendments must be verified by a statement of truth unless the court orders otherwise.

(Pt 17 provides for amendments to statements of case)

(3) If an applicant wishes to rely on matters set out in his application notice as evidence, the application notice must be verified by a statement of truth.

(4) Subject to para. (5), a statement of truth is a statement that—

    (a) the party putting forward the document; or

    (b) in the case of a witness statement, the maker of the witness statement,

believes the facts stated in the document are true.

(5) If a party is conducting proceedings with a litigation friend, the statement of truth in—

    (a) a statement of case;

    (b) a response; or

    (c) an application notice,

is a statement that the litigation friend believes the facts stated in the document being verified are true.

(6) The statement of truth must be signed by—

    (a) in the case of a statement of case, a response or an application—

        (i) the party of litigation friend; or

        (ii) the legal representative on behalf of the party or litigation friend; and

    (b) in the case of a witness statement, the maker of the statement.

(7) A statement of truth which is not contained in the document which it verifies, must clearly identify that document.

(8) A statement of truth in a statement of case may be made by—

    (a) a person who is not a party; or

    (b) by two parties jointly,

where this is permitted by a relevant practice direction.

44–116   **22.2**—(1) If a party fails to verify his statement of case by a statement of truth—

    (a) the statement of case shall remain effective unless struck out; but

    (b) the party may not rely on the statement of case as evidence of any of the matters set out in it.

(2) The court may strike out *(GL)* a statement of case which is not verified by a statement of truth.

(3) Any party may apply for an order under para. (2).

22.3 If the maker of a witness statement fails to verify the witness statement **44–117** by a statement of truth the Court may direct that it shall not be admissible as evidence.

22.4—(1) The Court may order a person who has failed to verify a document **44–118** in accordance with r.22.1 to verify the document.
(2) Any party may apply for an order under paragraph (1).

PRACTICE DIRECTION—STATEMENTS OF TRUTH

This Practice Direction supplements CPR Part 22

1.1 Rule 22.1(1) sets out the documents which must be verified by a statement **44–119** of truth. The documents include:

(1) a statement of case,
(2) a response complying with an order under r.18.1 to provide further information,
(3) a witness statement,
(4) an acknowledgement of service in a claim begun by the Pt 8 procedure,
(5) a certificate stating the reasons for bringing a possession claim or a landlord and tenant claim in the High Court in accordance with rr.55.3(2) and 56.2(2),
(6) an application notice for—

(a) a third party debt order (r.72.3),
(b) a hardship payment order (r.72.7), or
(c) a charging order (r.73.3).

1.2 If an applicant wishes to rely on matters set out in his application notice as evidence, the application notice must be verified by a statement of truth.
1.3 An expert's report should also be verified by a statement of truth. For the form of the statement of truth verifying an expert's report (which differs from that set out below) see the practice direction which supplements Pt 35.
1.4 In addition, a notice of objections to an account being taken by the court should be verified by a statement of truth unless verified by an affidavit or a witness statement.
1.5 The statement of truth may be contained in the document it verifies or it may be in a separate document served subsequently, in which case it must identify the document to which it relates.
1.6 Where the form to be used includes a jurat for the content to be verified by an affidavit then a statement of truth is not required in addition.

2.1 The form of the statement of truth verifying a statement of case, a **44–120** response, an application notice or a notice of objections should be as follows:

'[I believe][the (*claimant or as may be*) believes] that the facts stated in this [*name document being verified*] are true.'

2.2 The form of the statement of truth verifying a witness statement should be as follows:

'I believe that the facts stated in this witness statement are true.'

2.3 Where the statement of truth is contained in a separate document, the document containing the statement of truth must be headed with the title of the proceedings and the claim number. The document being verified should be identified in the statement of truth as follows:

    (1) claim form: 'the claim form issued on [*date*]',
    (2) particulars of claim: 'the particulars of claim issued on [*date*]',
    (3) statement of case: 'the [*defence or as may be*] served on the [*name of party*] on [*date*]',
    (4) application notice: 'the application notice issued on [*date*] for [*set out the remedy sought*]',
    (5) witness statement: [the witness statement filed on [*date*] or served on [*party*] on [*date*]'.

3.1 In a statement of case, a response or an application notice, the statement of truth must be signed by:

    (1) the party or his litigation friend, or
    (2) the legal representative of the party or litigation friend.

3.2 A statement of truth verifying a witness statement must be signed by the witness.

3.3 A statement of truth verifying a notice of objections to an account must be signed by the objecting party or his legal representative.

3.4 Where a document is to be verified on behalf of a company or other corporation, subject to para. 3.7 below, the statement of truth must be signed by a person holding a senior position in the company or corporation. That person must state the office or position he holds.

3.5 Each of the following persons is a person holding a senior position:

    (1) in respect of a registered company or corporation, a director, the treasurer, secretary, chief executive, manager or other officer of the company or corporation, and
    (2) in respect of a corporation which is not a registered company, in addition to those persons set out in (1), the mayor, chairman, president or town clerk or other similar officer of the corporation.

3.6 Where the document is to be verified on behalf of a partnership, those who may sign the statement of truth are:

    (1) any of he partners, or
    (2) a person having the control or management of the partnership business.

3.6A An insurer or the Motor Insurers' Bureau may sign a statement of truth in a statement of case on behalf of a party where the insurer or the Motor

Insurers' Bureau has a financial interest in the result of proceedings brought wholly or partially by or against that party.

3.6B If insurers are conducting proceedings on behalf of many claimants or defendants a statement of truth in a statement of case may be signed by a senior person responsible for the case at a lead insurer, but—

(1) the person signing must specify the capacity in which he signs;
(2) the statement of truth must be a statement that the lead insurer believes that the facts stated in the document are true; and
(3) the court may order that a statement of truth also be signed by one or more of the parties.

3.7 Where a party is legally represented, the legal representative may sign the statement of truth on his behalf. The statement signed by the legal representative will refer to the client's belief, not his own. In signing he must state the capacity in which he signs and the name of his firm where appropriate.

3.8 Where a legal representative has signed a statement of truth, his signature will be taken by the court as his statement:

(1) that the client on whose behalf he has signed had authorised him to do so;
(2) that before signing he had explained to the client that in signing the statement of truth he would be confirming the client's belief that the facts stated in the document were true, and
(3) that before signing he had informed the client of the possible consequences to the client if it should subsequently appear that the client did not have an honest belief in the truth of those facts (see r.32.14).

3.9 The individual who signs a statement of truth must print his full name clearly beneath his signature.

3.10 A legal representative who signs a statement of truth must sign in his own name and not that of his firm or employer.

3.11 The following are examples of the possible application of his practice direction describing who may sign a statement of truth verifying statements in documents other than a witness statement. These are only examples and not an indication of how a court might apply the practice direction to a specific situation.

Managing Agent	An agent who manages property or investments for the party cannot sign a statement of truth. I must be signed by the party or by the legal representative of the party.
Trusts	Where some or all of the trustees comprise a single party one, some or all of the trustees comprising the party may sign a statement of truth. The legal representative of the trustees may sign it.
Insurers and the Motor Insurers' Bureau	If an insurer has a financial interest in a claim involving its insured then, if the insured is the party, the insurer may sign a

	statement of truth in a statement of case for the insured party. Paras 3.4 and 3.5 apply to the insurer if it is a company. The claims manager employed by the insurer responsible for handling the insurance claim or managing the staff handling the claim may sign the statement of truth for the insurer (see next example). The position for the Motor Insurers' Bureau is similar.
Companies	Paras 3.4 and 3.5 apply. The word manager will be construed in the context of the phrase "a person holding a senior position" which it is used to define. The court will consider the size and nature of the claim. It would expect the manager signing the statement of truth to have personal knowledge of the content of the document or to be responsible for managing those who have that knowledge of the content. A small company may not have a manager, apart from the directors, who holds a senior position. A large company will have many such managers. In a larger company with specialist claims, insurance or legal departments the statement may be signed by the manager of such a department if he or she is responsible for handling the claim or managing the staff handling it.
In-house legal representatives	Legal representative is defined in r.2.3(1). A legal representative employed representatives by a party may sign a statement of truth. However a person who is not a solicitor, barrister or other authorised litigator, but who is employed by the company and is managed by such a person, is not employed by that person and so cannot sign a statement of truth. (This is unlike the employee of a solicitor in private practice who would come within the definition of legal representative.) However such a person may be a manager and able to sign the statement on behalf of the company in that capacity.

44–122 **4.1** If a statement of case is not verified by a statement of truth, the statement of case will remain effective unless it is struck out, but a party may not rely on the contents of a statement of case as evidence until it has been verified by a statement of truth.

4.2 Any party may apply to the court for an order that unless within such period as the court may specify the statement of case is verified by the service of a statement of truth, the statement of case will be struck out.

4.3 The usual order for the costs of an application referred to in para. 4.2 will be that the costs be paid by the party who had failed to verify in any event and forthwith.

5. Attention is drawn to r.31.14 which sets out the consequences of verifying **44–123** a statement of case containing a false statement without an honest belief in its truth, and to the procedures set out in para. 27 of the practice direction supplementing Pt 32.

Civil Procedure Rules Part 32

32.1—(1) The Court may control the evidence by giving directions as to— **44–124**

(a) the issues on which it requires evidence;
(b) the nature of the evidence which it requires to decide those issues; and
(c) the way in which the evidence is to be placed before the court.

(2) The court may use its power under this rule to exclude evidence that would otherwise be admissible.

(3) The court may limit cross-examination *(GL)*.

32.2—(1) The general rule is that any fact which needs to be proved by the **44–125** evidence of witnesses is to be proved—

(a) at trial, by their oral evidence given in public; and
(b) at any other hearing, by their evidence in writing.

(2) This is subject—

(a) to any provision to the contrary contained in these Rules or elsewhere; or
(b) to any order of the court.

32.3 The court may allow a witness to give evidence through a video link or **44–126** by other means.

32.4—(1) A witness statement is a written statement signed by a person which **44–127** contains the evidence which that person would be allowed to give orally.

(2) The court will order a party to serve on the other parties any witness statement of the oral evidence which the party serving the statement intends to rely on in relation to any issues of fact to be decided at the trial.

(3) The court may give directions as to—

(a) the order in which witness statements are to be served; and
(b) whether or not the witness statements are to be filed.

44–128　**32.5**—(1) If—

    (a) a party has served a witness statement; and

    (b) he wishes to rely at trial on the evidence of the witness who made the statement,

he must call the witness to give oral evidence unless the court orders otherwise or he puts the statement in as hearsay evidence.

(Pt 33 contains provisions about hearsay evidence)

(2) Where a witness is called to give oral evidence under paragraph (1), his witness statement shall stand as his evidence in chief *(GL)* unless the court orders otherwise.

(3) A witness statement giving oral evidence at trial may with the permission of the court—

    (a) amplify his witness statement; and

    (b) give evidence in relation to new matters which have arisen since the witness statement was served on the other parties.

(4) The court will give permission under para. (3) only if it considers that there is good reason not to confine the evidence of the witness to the contents of his witness statement.

(5) If a party who has served a witness statement does not—

    (a) call the witness to give evidence at trial; or

    (b) put the witness statement as hearsay evidence, any other party may put the witness statement in as hearsay evidence.

44–129　**32.6**—(1) Subject to para. (2), the general rule is that evidence at hearings other than the trial is to be by witness statement unless the court, a practice direction or any other enactment requires otherwise.

(2) At hearings other than the trial, a party may, rely on the matters set out in—

    (a) his statement of case; or

    (b) his application notice, if the statement of case or application notice is verified by a statement of truth.

44–130　**32.7**—(1) Where, at a hearing other than the trial, evidence is given in writing, any party may apply to the court for permission to cross-examine the person giving the evidence.

(2) If the court gives permission under para. (1) but the person in question does not attend as required by the order, his evidence may not be used unless the court gives permission.

44–131　**32.8** A witness statement must comply with the requirements set out in the relevant practice direction.

(Pt 22 requires a witness statement to be verified by a statement of truth)

44–132　**32.9**—(1) A party who—

    (a) is required to serve a witness statement for use at trial; but

(b) is unable to obtain one, may apply, without notice, for permission to serve a witness summary instead.

(2) A witness summary is a summary of—

(a) the evidence, if known, which would otherwise be included in witness statement; or
(b) if the evidence is not known, the matters about which the party serving the witness summary proposes to question the witness.

(3) Unless the court does otherwise, a witness summary must include the name and address of the intended witness.

(4) Unless the court orders otherwise, a witness summary must be served within the period in which a witness statement would have had to be served.

(5) Where a party serves a witness summary, so far as practicable rr.32.4 (requirement to serve witness statements for use at trial), 32.5(3) (amplifying witness statements), and 32.8 (form a witness statement) shall apply to the summary.

32.10 If a witness statement or a witness summary for use at trial is not served   **44–133**
in respect of an intended witness within the time specified by the court, then the witness may not be called to give oral evidence unless the court gives permission.

32.11 Where a witness is called to give evidence at trial, he may be cross-   **44–134**
examined on his witness statement whether or not the statement or any part of it was referred to during the witness's evidence in chief.

32.12—(1) Except as provided by this rule, a witness statement may be used   **44–135**
only for the purpose of the proceedings in which it is served.

(2) Paragraph (1) does not apply if and to the extent that—

(a) the witness gives consent in writing to some other use of it;
(b) the court gives permission for some other use; or
(c) the witness statement has been put in evidence at a hearing held in public.

32.13—(1) A witness statement which stands as evidence in chief is open to   **44–136**
inspection during the course of the trial unless the court otherwise directs.

(2) Any person may ask for a direction that a witness statement is not open to inspection.

(3) The court will not make a direction under para. (2) unless it is satisfied that a witness statement should not be open to inspection because of—

(a) the interests of justice;
(b) the public interest;
(c) the nature of any expert medical evidence in the statement;
(d) the nature of any confidential information (including information relating to personal financial matters) in the statement; or
(e) the need to protect the interests of any child or patient.

(4) The court may exclude from inspection words or passages in the statement.

44–137   **32.14**—(1) Proceedings for contempt of court may be brought against a person if he makes, or causes to be made, a false statement in a document verified by a statement of truth without an honest belief in its truth.
(Pt 22 makes provision for a statement of truth)
(2) Proceedings under this rule may be brought only—

(a) by the Attorney General; or
(b) with the permission of the court.

44–138   **32.15**—(1) Evidence must be given by affidavit instead of or in addition to witness statement if this is required by the court, a provision contained in any other rule, a practice direction or any other enactment.
(2) Nothing in these Rules prevents a witness giving evidence by affidavit at hearing other than the trial if he chooses to do so in a case where para. (1) does not apply, but the party putting forward the affidavit may not recover the additional cost of making it from any other party unless the court orders otherwise.

44–139   **32.16** An affidavit must comply with the requirements set out in the relevant practice direction.

44–140   **32.17** A person may make an affidavit outside the jurisdiction in accordance with—

(a) this Part; or
(b) the law of the place where he makes the affidavit.

44–141   **32.18**—(1) A party may serve notice on another party requiring him to admit the facts, or the part of the case of the serving party, specified in the notice.
(2) A notice to admit facts must be served no later than 21 days before the trial.
(3) Where the other party makes any admission in response to the notice, the admission may be used against him only—

(a) in the proceedings in which the notice to admit is served; and
(b) by the party who served the notice.

(4) The court may allow a party to amend or withdraw any admission made by him on such terms as it thinks just.

44–142   **32.19**—(1) A party shall be deemed to admit the authenticity of a document disclosed to him under Pt 31 (disclosure and inspection of documents) unless he serves notice that he wishes the document to be proved at trial.
(2) A notice to prove a document must be served—

(a) by the latest date for serving witness statements; or
(b) within 7 days of disclosure of the document, whichever is later.

PRACTICE DIRECTION—WRITTEN EVIDENCE

This Practice Direction supplements CPR Part 32

1.1 Rule 32.2 sets out how evidence is to be given and facts are to be **44–143** proved.

1.2 Evidence at a hearing other than the trial should normally be given by witness statement (see para. 17 onwards). However a witness may give evidence by affidavit if he wishes to do so (and see para. 1.4 below).

1.3 Statements of case (see para. 26 onwards) and application notices may also be used as evidence provided that their contents have been verified by a statement of truth.

(For information regarding evidence by deposition see Pt 34 and the practice direction which supplements it.)

1.4 Affidavits must be used as evidence in the following instances:

(1) where sworn evidence is required by an enactment, rule, order or practice direction,
(2) in any application for a search order, a freezing injunction, or an order requiring an occupier to permit another to enter his land, and
(3) in any application for an order against anyone for alleged contempt of court.

1.5 If a party believes that sworn evidence is required by a court in another jurisdiction for any purpose connected with the proceedings, he may apply to the court for a direction that evidence shall be given only by affidavit on any pre-trial applications.

1.6 The court may give a direction under r.32.15 that evidence shall be given by affidavit instead of or in addition to a witness statement or statement of case:

(1) on its own initiative, or
(2) after any party has applied to the court for such a direction.

1.7 An affidavit, where referred to in the Civil Procedure Rules or a practice direction, also means an affirmation unless the context requires otherwise.

2. A deponent is a person who gives evidence by affidavit or affirmation. **44–144**

3.1 The affidavit should be headed with the title of the proceedings (see para. **44–145** 4 of the practice direction supplementing Pt 7 and para. 7 of the practice direction supplementing Pt 20); where the proceedings are between several parties with the same status it is sufficient to identify the parties as follows:

	Number:
A.B. (and others)	Claimants/Applicants
C.D. (and others)	Defendants/Respondents
	(as appropriate)

3.2 At the top right hand corner of the first page (and on the backsheet) there should be clearly written:

(1) commence "I (*full name*) or (*address*) state on oath ... ... "
(2) if giving evidence in his professional, business or other occupational capacity, give the address at which he works in (1) above, the position he holds and the name of his firm or employer,
(3) give his occupation or, if he has none, his description, and
(4) state if he is a party to the proceedings or employed by a party to the proceedings, if it be the case.

44–146   **4.1** The affidavit must, if practicable, be in the deponent's own words, the affidavit should be expressed in the first person and the deponent should:

(1) commence "I (*full name*) of (*address*) state on oath . . . ",
(2) if giving evidence in his professional, business or other occupational capacity, give the address at which he works in (1) above, the position he holds and the name of his firm or employer,
(3) give his occupation or, if he has none, his description, and
(4) state if he is a party to the proceedings or employed by a party to the proceedings, if it be the case.

4.2 An affidavit must indicate:

(1) which of the statements in it are made from the deponent's own knowledge and which are matters of information or belief.
(2) the source for any matters of information or belief.

4.3 Where a deponent:

(1) refers to an exhibit or exhibits, he should state "there is now shown to me marked " . . . " the (*description of exhibit*)", and
(2) makes more than one affidavit (to which there are exhibits) in the same proceedings, the numbering of the exhibits should run consecutively throughout and not start again with each affidavit.

44–147   **5.1** The jurat of an affidavit is a statement set out at the end of the document whch authenticates the affidavit.
    5.2 It must:

(1) be signed by all deponents,
(2) be completed and signed by the person before whom the affidavit was sworn whose name and qualification must be printed beneath his signature,
(3) contain the full address of the person before whom the affidavit was sworn, and
(4) follow immediately on from the text and not be put on a separate page.

44–148   **6.1** An affidavit should:

(1) be produced on durable quality A4 paper with a 3.5cm margin,
(2) be fully legible and should normally be typed on one side of the paper only,
(3) where possible, be bound securely in a manner which would not hamper filing, or otherwise each page should be endorsed with the case number

and should bear the initials of the deponent and of the person before whom it was sworn,

(4) have the pages numbered consecutively as a separate document (or as one of several documents contained in a file),
(5) be divided into numbered paragraphs,
(6) have all numbers, including dates, expressed in figures, and
(7) give the reference to any document or documents mentioned either in the margin or in bond text in the body of the affidavit.

6.2 It is usually convenient for an affidavit to follow the chronological sequence of events or matters dealt with; each paragraph of an affidavit should as far as possible be confined to a distinct portion of the subject.

7.1 Where an affidavit is sworn by a person who is unable to read or sign it, the person before whom the affidavit is sworn must certify in the jurat that: **44–149**

(1) he read the affidavit to the deponent,
(2) the deponent appeared to understand it, and
(3) the deponent signed or made his mark, in his presence.

7.2 If that certificate is not included in the jurat, the affidavit may not be used in evidence unless the court is satisfied that it was read to the deponent and that he appeared to understand it. Two versions of the form of jurat with the certificate are set out at Annex 1 to this practice direction.

8.1 Any alteration to an affidavit must be initialled by both the deponent and   **44–150**
the person before whom the affidavit was sworn.
8.2 An affidavit which contains an alteration that has not been initialled may be filed or used in evidence only with the permission of the court.

9.1 Only the following may administered oaths and take affidavits: **44–151**

(1) Commissioners for oaths
(2) Practising solicitors
(3) other persons specified by statute
(4) certain officials of the Supreme Court
(5) a circuit judge or district judge
(6) any justice of the peace, and
(7) certain officials of any county court appointed by the judge of that court for the purpose.

9.2 An affidavit must be sworn before a person independent of the parties or their representatives.

10.1 If the court directs that an affidavit is to be filed, it must be filed in the   **44–152**
court or Division, or Office or Registry of the court or Division where the action in which it was or is to be used, is proceeding or will proceed.
10.2 Where an affidavit is in a foreign language:

(1) the party wishing to rely on it—
    (a) must have it translated, and
    (b) must file the foreign language affidavit with the court, and

(2) the translator must make and file with the court an affidavit verifying the translation and exhibiting both the translation and a copy of the foreign language affidavit.

44–153 **11.1** A document used in conjunction with an affidavit should be:

(1) produced to and verified by the deponent, and remain separate from the affidavit, and
(2) identified by a declaration of the person before whom the affidavit was sworn.

11.2 The declaration should be headed with the name of the proceedings in the same way as the affidavit.
11.3 The first page of each exhibit should be marked:

(1) as in para. 3.2 above, and
(2) with the exhibit mark referred to in the affidavit.

44–154 **12.1** Copies of individual letters should be collected together with exhibit in a bundle or bundles. They should be arranged in chronological order with the earliest at the top, and firmly secured.
12.2 When a bundle of correspondence is exhibited, the exhibit should have a front page attached stating that the bundle consists of original letters and copies.
They should be arranged and secured as above and numbered consecutively.

44–155 **13.1** Photographs instead of original documents may be exhibited provided the originals are made available for inspection by the other parties before the hearing and by the judge at the bearing.
13.2 Court documents must not be exhibited (official copies of such documents prove themselves).
13.3 Where an exhibit contains more than one document, a front page should be attached setting out a list of the documents contained in the exhibit; the list should contain the dates of the documents.

44–156 **14.1** Items other than documents should be clearly marked with an exhibit number or letter in such a manner that the mark cannot become detached from the exhibit.
14.2 Small items may be placed in a container and the container appropriate marked.

44–157 **15.1** Where an exhibit contains more than one document:

(1) the bundle should not be stapled but should be securely fastened in a way that does not hinder the reading of the documents, and
(2) the pages should be numbered consecutively at bottom centre.

15.2 Every page of an exhibit should be clearly legible; typed copies of illegible documents should be included, paginated with "a" numbers.
15.3 Where affidavits and exhibits have become numerous, they should be put into separate bundles and the pages numbered consecutively throughout.
15.4 Where on account of their bulk the service of exhibits or copies of exhibits on the other parties would be difficult or impracticable, the directions of

the court should be sought as to arrangements for bringing the exhibits to the attention of the other parties and as to their custody pending trial.

16 All provisions in this or any other practice direction relating to affidavits   **44–158** apply to affirmations with the following exceptions:

(1) the deponent should commence "I (*name*) of (*address*) do solemnly and sincerely affirm ... ", and
(2) in the jurat the word "sworn" is replaced by the word "affirmed".

17.1 The witness statement should be headed with the title of the proceedings   **44–159** (see para. 4 of the practice direction supplementing Pt 7 and para. 7 of the practice direction supplementing Pt 20); where the proceedings are between several parties with the same status it is sufficient to identify the parties as follows:

	Number:
A.B. (and others)	Claimants/Applicants
C.D. (and others)	Defendants/Respondents
	(as appropriate)

17.2 At the top right hand corner of the first page there should be clearly written:

(1) the party on whose behalf it is made,
(2) the initials and surname of the witness,
(3) the number of the statement in relation to that witness,
(4) the identifying initials and number of each exhibit referred to, and
(5) the date the statement was made.

18.1 The witness statement must, if practicable, be in the intended witness's   **44–160** own words, the statement should be expressed in the first person and should also state:

(1) the full name of the witness,
(2) his place of residence or, if he is making the statement in his professional, business or other occupational capacity, the address at which he works, the position he holds and the name of his firm or employer,
(3) his occupation, or if he has none, his description, and
(4) the fact that he is a party to the proceedings or is the employee of such a party if it be the case.

18.2 A witness statement must indicate:

(1) which of the statements in it are made from the witness's own knowledge and which are matters of information or belief, and
(2) the source for any matters of information or belief.

18.3 An exhibit used in conjunction with a witness statement should be verified and identified by the witness and remain separate from the witness statement.
18.4 Where a witness refers to an exhibit or exhibits, he should state "I refer to the (*description of exhibit*) marked ' ... ' ".

18.5 The provisions of paras 11.3 to 15.4 (exhibits) apply similarly to witness statements as they do to affidavits.

18.6 Where a witness makes more than one witness statement to which there are exhibits, in the same proceedings, the numbering of the exhibits should run consecutively throughout and not start again with each witness statement.

44–161 **19.1** A witness statement should:

(1) be produced on durable quality A4 paper with a 3.5cm margin,
(2) be fully legible and should normally be typed on one side of the paper only,
(3) where possible, be bound securely in a manner which would not hamper filing, or otherwise each page should be endorsed with the case number and should bear the initials of the witness,
(4) have the pages numbered consecutively as a separate statement (or as one of several statements contained in a file),
(5) be divided into numbered paragraphs,
(6) have all numbers, including dates, expressed in figures, and
(7) give the reference to any document or documents mentioned either in the margin or in bold text in the body of the statement.

19.2 It is usually convenient for a witness statement to follow the chronological sequence of the events or matters dealt with, each paragraph of a witness statement should as far as possible be confined to a distinct portion of the subject.

44–162 **20.1** A witness statement is the equivalent of the oral evidence which that that witness would, if called, give in evidence; it must include a statement by the intended witness that he believes the facts in it are true.

20.2 To verify a witness statement the statement of truth is as follows:

"I believe that the facts stated in this witness statement are true"

20.3 Attention is drawn to r.32.14 which sets out the consequences of verifying a witness statement containing a false statement without an honest belief in its truth.

44–163 **21.1** Where a witness statement is made by a person who is unable to red or sign the witness statement, it must contain a certificate made by an authorised person.

21.2 An authorised person is a person able to administer oaths and take affidavits but need not be independent of the parties or their representatives.

21.3 The authorised person must certify:

(1) that the witness statement has been read to the witness,
(2) that the witness appeared to understand it and approved its content as accurate,
(3) that the declaration of truth has been read to the witness,
(4) that the witness appeared to understand the declaration and the consequences of making a false witness statement, and
(5) that the witness signed or made his mark in the presence of the authorised person.

21.4 The form of the certificate is set out at Annex 2 to this practice direction.

22.1 Any alteration to a witness statement must be initialled by the person **44–164** making the statement or by the authorised person where appropriate (see para. 21).

22.2 A witness statement which contains an alteration that has not been initialled may be used in evidence only with the permission of the court.

23.1 If the court directs that a witness statement is to be filed, it must be filed **44–165** in the court or Division, or Office or Registry of the court or Division where the action in which it was or is to be used, is proceeding or will proceed.

23.2 Where the court has directed that a witness statement in a foreign language is to be filed:

(1) the party wishing to rely on it must—
  (a) have it translated, and
  (b) file the foreign language witness statement with the court, and
(2) the translator must make and file with the court an affidavit verifying the translation and exhibiting both the translation and a copy of the foreign language witness statement.

24.1 Where the court has ordered that a witness statement is not to be open to **44–166** inspection by the public or that words or passages in the statement are not to be open to inspection the court officer will so certify on the statement and make any deletions directed by the court under r.32.13(4).

25.1 Where: **44–167**

(1) an affidavit.
(2) a witness statement, or
(3) an exhibit to either an affidavit or a witness statement,

does not comply with Pt 32 or this practice direction in relation to its form, the court may refuse to admit it as evidence and may refuse to allow the costs arising from its preparation.

25.2 Permission to file a defective affidavit or witness statement or to use a defective exhibit may be obtained from a judge in the court where the case is proceeding.

26.1 A statement of case may be used as evidence in an interim application **44–168** provided it is verified by a statement of truth.

26.2 To verify a statement of case the statement of truth should be set out as follows:

"[I believe][the *party on whose behalf the statement of case is being signed*) believes] that the facts stated in the statement of case are true".

26.3 Attention is drawn to r.32.14 which sets out the consequences of verifying a witness statement containing a false statement without an honest belief in its truth.

(for information regarding statements of truth see Pt 22 and the practice direction which supplements it.)

44–168A **27.1** The court may give directions requiring the parties to use their best endeavours to agree a bundle or bundles of documents for use at any hearing.

27.2 All documents contained in bundles which have been agreed for use at a hearing shall be admissible at that hearing as evidence of their contents, unless—

(1) the court orders otherwise; or
(2) a party gives written notice of objection to the admissibility of particular documents.

44–168B **28.1**—(1) Where a party alleges that a statement of truth or a disclosure statement is false the party shall refer that allegation to the court dealing with the claim in which the statement of truth or disclosure statement has been made.

(2) The court may—

(a) exercise any of its powers under the rules;
(b) initiate steps to consider if there is a contempt of court and, where there is, to punish it;
     (The practice direction to RSC Ord. 52 (Sch. 1) and CCR Ord. 29 (Sch. 2) makes provision where committal to prison is a possibility if contempt is proved)
(c) direct the party making the allegation to refer the matter to the Attorney General with a request to him to consider whether he wishes to bring proceedings for contempt of court.

28.2—(1) An application to the Attorney General should be made to his chambers at: 9 Buckingham Gate, London SE1E 6JP in writing. The Attorney General will initially require a copy of the order recording the direction of the judge referring the matter to him and information which—

(a) identifies the statement said to be false; and
(b) explains—
     (i) why it is false, and
     (ii) why the maker knew it to be false at the time he made it; and
(c) explains why contempt proceedings would be appropriate in the light of the overriding objective in Pt 1 of the Civil Procedure Rules.

(2) The practice of the Attorney General is to prefer an application that comes from the court, and so has received preliminary consideration by a judge, to one made direct to him by a party to the claim in which the alleged contempt occurred without prior consideration by the court. An application to the Attorney General is not a way of appealing against, or reviewing, the decision of the judge.

28.3 Where a party makes an application to the court for permission for that party to commence proceedings for contempt of court, it must be supported by written evidence containing the information specified in para. 27.2(1) and the result of the application to the Attorney General made by the applicant.

28.4 The rules do not change the law of contempt or introduce new categories of contempt. A person applying to commence such proceedings should consider whether the incident complained of does amount to contempt of court and whether such proceedings would further the overriding objective in Pt 1 of the Civil Procedure Rules.

29.1 Guidance on the use of video conferencing in the civil courts is set out at   **44–168C**
Annex 3 to this practice direction.

ANNEX 1

Certificate to be used where a deponent to an affidavit is unable to read or sign it

Sworn at   this   day of   . Before me, I having first read   **44–169**
over the contents of this affidavit to the deponent [*if there are exhibits, add* 'and
explained the nature and effect of the exhibits referred to in it'] who appeared to
understand it and approved its content as accurate, and made his mark on the
affidavit in my presence.

Or; (after, *Before me*) the witness to the mark of the deponent having been first
sworn that he had been over etc. (*as above*) and that he saw him make his mark
on the affidavit. (*Witness must sign*).

Affirmed at   this   day of   . Before me, I have first read
over the contents of this affirmation to the deponent [*if there are exhibits, add*
'and explained the nature and effect of the exhibits referred to in it'] who
appeared to understand it and approved its content as accurate, and made his
mark on the affirmation in my presence.

Or, (after, *Before me*) the witness to the mark of the deponent having been first
sworn that he had read over etc. (as above) and that he saw him make his mark
of the affirmation. (*Witness must sign*).

ANNEX 2

Certificate to be used where a witness is unable to read or sign a witness statement

I certify that I [*name and address of authorised person*] have read over the   **44–170**
contents of this witness statement and the declaration of truth to the witness [*if
there are exhibits,* 'and explained the nature and effect of the exhibits referred to
in it'] who appeared to understand (a) the statement and approved its content as
accurate and (b) the declaration of truth and the consequences of making a false
witness statement, and made his mark in my presence.

ANNEX 3

Video conferencing guidance

   This guidance is for the use of video conferencing (VCF) in civil proceedings.   **44–171A**
It is in part based, with permission, upon the protocol of the Federal Court of

Australia. It is intended to provide a guide to all persons involve in the use of VCF, although it does not attempt to cover all the practical questions which might arise.

1. The guidance covers the use of VCF equipment both (a) in a courtroom, whether via equipment which is permanently placed there or via a mobile unit, and (d) in a separate studio or conference room. In either case, the location at which the judge sits is referred to as the "local site". The other site or sites to and from which transmission is made are referred to as 'the remote site' and in any particular case any such site may be another courtroom. The guidance applies to cases where FCF is used for the taking of evidence and also to its use for other parts of any legal proceedings (for example, interim applications, case management conferences, pre-trial reviews).

2. VCF may be a convenient way of dealing with any part of proceedings: it can involve considerable savings in time and cost. Its use for the taking of evidence from overseas witnesses will, I particular, be likely to achieve a material saving of costs, and such savings may also be achieved by its use for taking domestic evidence. It is, however, inevitably not as ideal as having the witness physically present in court. Its convenience should not therefore be allowed to dictate its use. A judgment must be made in every case in which the use of VCF is being considered not only as to whether it will achieve an overall cost saving but as to whether its use will be likely to be beneficial to the efficient, fair and economic disposal of the litigation. In particular, it needs to be recognised that the degree of control a court can exercise over a witness at the remote site is or may be more limited than it can exercise over a witness physically before it.

3. When used for the taking of evidence, the objective should be to make the VCF session as close as possible to the usual practice in a trial court where evidence is taken in open court. To gain the maximum benefit, several differences have to be taken into account. Some mattes, which are taken for granted when evidence is taken in the conventional way, take on a different dimension when it is taken by VCF: for example, the administration of the oath, ensuring that the witness understands who is at the local site and what their various roles are, the raising of any objections to the evidence and the use of documents.

4. It should not be presumed that all foreign governments are willing to allow their nationals or others within their jurisdiction to be examined before a court in England or Wales by means of VCF. If there is any doubt about this, enquiries should be directed to the Foreign and Commonwealth office (International Legal Matters Unit, Consular Division) with a view to ensuring that the country from which the evidence is to be taken raises no objection to it at diplomatic level. The party who is directed to be responsible for arranging the VCF (see para. 8 below) will be required to make all necessary inquiries about this well in advance of the VCF and must be able to inform the court what those inquiries were and of their outcome.

5. Time zone differences need to be considered when a witness abroad is to be examined in England or Wales by VCF. The convenience of the witness, the parties, their representatives and the court must all be taken into account. The cost of the use of a commercial studio is usually greater outside normal business hours.

6. Those involved with VCF need to be aware that, even with the most advanced systems currently available, there are the briefest of delays between the receipt of the picture and that of the accompanying sound. If due allowance is not made for this, there will be a tendency to 'speak over' the witness, whose voice

will continue to be heard for a millisecond or so after he or she appears on the screen to have finished speaking.

7. With current technology, picture quality is good, but not as good as a television picture. The quality of the picture is enhanced if those appearing on VCF monitors keep their movements to a minimum.

8. The court's permission is required for any part of any proceedings to be dealt with by means of VCF. Before seeking a direction, the applicant should notify the listing officer, diary manager or other appropriate court office of the intention to seek it, and should enquire as to the availability of court VCF equipment for the day or days of the proposed VCF. The application for a direction should be made to the Master, District Judge or Judge, as may be appropriate. If all parties consent to a direction, permission can be sought by letter, fax or email, although the court may still require an oral hearing. All parties are entitled to be heard on whether or not such a direction should be given and as to its terms. If a witness at a remote site is to give evidence by an interpreter, consideration should be given at this stage as to whether the interpreter should be at the local site or the remote site. If a VCF direction is given, arrangements for the transmission will then need to be made. The court will ordinarily direct that the party seeking permission to use VCF is to be responsible for this. That party is hereafter referred to as "the VCF arranging party".

9. Subject to any order to the contrary, all costs of the transmission, including the costs of hiring equipment and technical personnel to operate it, will initially be the responsibility of, and must be met by, the VCF arranging party. All reasonable efforts should be made to keep the transmission to a minimum and so keep the costs down. All such costs will be considered to be part of the costs of the proceedings and the court will determine at such subsequent time as is convenient or appropriate who, as between the parties, should be responsible for them and (if appropriate) in what proportions.

10. The local site will, if practicable, be a courtroom but it may instead be an appropriate studio or conference room. The VCF arranging party must contact the listing officer, diary manager or other appropriate officer of the court which made the VCF direction and make arrangements for the VCF transmission. Details of the remote site, and of the equipment to be used both at the local site (if not being supplied by the court) and the remote site (including the number of ISDN lines and connection speed), together with all necessary contact names and telephone numbers, will have to be provided to the listing officer, diary manager or other court officer. The court will need to be satisfied that any equipment provided by the parties for use at the local site and also that at the remote site is of sufficient quality for a satisfactory transmission. The VCF arranging party must ensure that an appropriate person will present at the local site to supervise the operation of the VCF throughout the transmission in order to deal with any technical problems. That party must also arrange for a technical assistant to be similarly present at the remote site for like purposes.

11. It is recommended that the judge, practitioners and witness should arrive at their respective VCF sites about 20 minutes prior to the scheduled commencement of the transmission.

12. If the local site is not a courtroom, but a conference room or studio, the judge will need to determine who is to sit where. The VCF arranging party must take care to ensure that the number of microphones is adequate for the speakers

and that the panning of the camera for the practitioners' table encompasses all legal representatives so that the viewer can see everyone seated there.

13. The proceedings, wherever they may take place, form part of a trial to which the public is entitled to have access (unless the court has determined that they should be heard in private). If the local site is to be a studio or conference room, the VCF arranging party must ensure that it provides sufficient accommodation to enable a reasonable number of members of the public to attend.

14. In cases where the local site is a studio or conference room, the VCF arranging party should make arrangements, if practicable, for the royal coat of arms to be placed above the judge's seat.

15. In cases in which the VCF is to be used for the taking of evidence, the VCF arranging party must arrange for recording equipment to be provided by the court which made the VCF direction so that the evidence can be recorded. An associate will normally be present to do likewise when it is a studio or conference room. The equipment should be set up and tested before the VCF transmission. It will often be a valuable safeguard for the VCF arranging party also to arrange for the provision of recording equipment at the remote site. This will provide a useful back-up if there is any reduction in sound quality during the transmission. A direction from the court for the making of such back-up recording must, however, be obtained first. This is because the proceedings are court proceedings and, save as directed by the court, no other recording of them must be made. The court will direct what is to happen to the back-up recording.

16. Some countries may require that any oath or affirmation to be taken by a witness accord with local custom rather than the usual form of oath or affirmation used in England and Wales. The VCF arranging party must make all appropriate prior inquiries and put in place all arrangements necessary to enable the oath or affirmation to be taken in accordance with any local custom. That party must be in a position to inform the court what those inquiries were, what their outcome was and what arrangements have been made. If the oath or affirmation can be administered in the manner normal in England and Wales, the VCF arranging party must arrange in advance to have the appropriate holy book at the remote site. The associate will normally administer the oath.

17. Consideration will need to be given in advance to the documents to which the witness is likely to be referred. The parties should endeavour to agree on this. It will usually be most convenient for a bundle of the copy documents to be prepared in advance, which the VCF arranging party should then send to the remote site.

18. Additional documents are sometimes quite properly introduced during the course of a witness's evidence. To cater for this, the VCF arranging party should ensure that equipment is available to enable documents to be transmitted between sites during the course of the VCF transmission. Consideration should be given to whether to use a document camera. If it is decided to use one, arrangements for its use will need to be established in advance. The panel operator will need to know the number and size of documents or objects if their images are to be sent by document camera. In many cases, a simpler and sufficient alternative will be to ensure that there are fax transmission and reception facilities at the participating sites.

19. The procedure for conducting the transmission will be determined by the judge. He will determine who is to control the cameras. In cases where VCF is being used for an application in the course of the proceedings, the judge will ordinarily not enter the local site until both sites are on line. Similarly, at the

conclusion of the hearing, he will ordinarily leave the local site while both sites are still on line. The following paragraphs apply primarily to cases where the VCF is being used for the taking of the evidence of a witness at a remote site. In all cases, the judge will need to decide whether court dress is appropriate when using VCF facilities. It might be appropriate when transmitting from courtroom. It might not be when a commercial facility is being used.

20. At the beginning of the transmission, the judge will probably wish to introduce himself and the advocates to the witness. He will probably want to know who is at the remote site and will invite the witness to introduce himself and anyone else who is with him. He may wish to give directions as to the seating arrangements at the remote site so that those present are visible at the local site during the taking of the evidence. He will probably wish to explain to the witness the method of taking the oath or of affirming, the manner in which the evidence will be taken, and who will be conducting the examination and cross-examination. He will probably also wish to inform the witness of the matters referred to in paras 6 and 7 above (co-ordination of picture with sound, and picture quality).

21. The examination of the witness at the remote site should follow as closely as possible the practice adopted when a witness is in the courtroom. During examination, cross-examination and re-examination, the witness must be able to see the legal representative asking the question and also any other person (whether another legal representative or the judge) making any statements in regard to the witness's evidence. It will in practice be most convenient if everyone remains seated throughout the transmission.

Part 33. Miscellaneous Rules About Evidence

33.1 In this Part—   **44–171**

   (a) "hearsay" means a statement made, otherwise than by a person while giving oral evidence in proceedings, which is tendered as evidence of the matters stated; and

   (b) references to hearsay include hearsay of whatever degree.

33.2—(1) Where a party intends to rely on hearsay evidence at trial and   **44–172**
either—

   (a) that evidence is to be given by a witness giving oral evidence; or

   (b) that evidence is contained in a witness statement of a person who is not being called to give oral evidence;

that party complies with s.2(1)(a) of the Civil Evidence Act 1995 serving a witness statement on the other parties in accordance with the court's order.

(2) Where para. (1)(b) applies, the party intending to rely on the hearsay evidence must, when he serves the witness statement—

   (a) inform the other parties that the witness is not being called to give oral evidence; and

   (b) give the reason why the witness will not be called.

(3) In all other cases where a party intends to rely on hearsay evidence at trial, that party complies with s.2(1)(a) of the Civil Evidence Act 1995 by serving a notice on the other parties which—

(a) identifies the hearsay evidence;
(b) states that the party serving the notice proposes to rely on the hearsay evidence at trial; and
(c) gives the reason why the witness will not be called.

(4) The party proposing to rely on the hearsay evidence must—

(a) serve the notice no later than the latest date for serving witness statements; and
(b) if the hearsay evidence is to be in a document, supply a copy to any party who requests him to do so.

44–173   **33.3** Section 2(1) of the Civil Evidence Act 1995 (duty to give notice of intention to rely on hearsay evidence) does not apply—

(a) to evidence at hearings other than trials;
   (aa) to an affidavit or witness statement which is to be used at trial but which does not contain hearsay evidence;
(b) to a statement which a party to a probate action wishes to put in evidence and which is alleged to have been made by the person whose estate is the subject of the proceedings; or
(c) where the requirement is excluded by a practice direction.

44–174   **33.4**—(1) Where a party—

(a) proposes to rely on hearsay evidence; and
(b) does not propose to call the person who made the original statement to give oral evidence,

the court may, on the application of any other party, permit that party to call the maker of the statement to be cross-examined on the contends to the statement.
(2) An application for permission to cross-examine under this rule must be made not more than 14 days after the day on which a notice of intention to rely on the hearsay evidence was served on the applicant.

44–175   **33.5**—(1) Where a party—

(a) proposes to rely on hearsay evidence; but
(b) does not propose to call the person who made the original statement to give oral evidence; and
(c) another party wishes to call evidence to attack the credibility of the person who made the statement,

the party who so wishes must give notice of his intention to the party who proposes to give the hearsay statement in evidence.
(2) A party must give notice under para. (1) not more than 14 days after the day on which a hearsay notice relating to the hearsay evidence was served on him.

33.6—(1) This rule applies to evidence (such as a plan, photograph or model)   **44–176**
which is not—

  (a) contained in a witness statement, affidavit or expert's report;
  (b) to be given orally at trial; or
  (c) evidence of which prior notice must be given under r.33.2.

(2) This rule includes documents which may be received in evidence without
further proof under s.9 of the Civil Evidence Act 1995.

(3) Unless the court orders otherwise the evidence shall not be receivable at a
trial unless the party intending to put it in evidence has given notice to the other
parties in accordance with this rule.

(4) Where the party intends to use the evidence as evidence of any fact then,
except where para.(6) applies, he must give notice not later than the latest date
for serving witness statements.

(5) He must give notice at least 21 days before the hearing at which he
proposes to put in the evidence, if—

  (a) there are not to be witness statements; or
  (b) he intends to put in the evidence solely in order to disprove an allegation
      made in a witness statement.

(6) Where the evidence forms part of expert evidence, he must give notice
when the expert's report is served on the other party.

(7) Where the evidence is being produced to the court for any reason other than
as part of factual or expert evidence, he must give notice at least 21 days before
the hearing at which he proposes to put in the evidence.

(8) Where a party has given notice that he intends to put in the evidence, he
must give every other party an opportunity to inspect it and to agree to its
admission without further proof.

33.7—(1) This rule sets out the procedure which must be followed by a party   **44–177**
who intends to put in evidence a finding on a question of foreign law by virtue
of s.4(2) of the Civil Evidence Act 1972.

(2) He must give any other party notice of his intention.

(3) He must give the notice—

  (a) if there are to be witness statements, not later than the latest date for
      serving them; or
  (b) otherwise, not less than 21 days before the hearing at which he proposes
      to put the finding in evidence.

(4) The notice must—

  (a) specify the question on which the finding was made; and
  (b) enclose a copy of a document where it is reported or recorded.

33.8 A document purporting to contain the written consent of a person to act   **44–178**
as trustee and to bear his signature verified by some other person is evidence of
such consent.

[213]

44–178A   **33.9**—(1) This rule applies where a claim is—

(a) for a remedy under s.7 of the Human Rights Act 1998 in respect of a judicial act which is alleged to have infringed the claimant's Article 5 Convention rights; and

(b) based on a finding by a court or tribunal that the claimant's Convention rights have been infringed.

(2) The court hearing the claim—

(a) may proceed on the basis of the finding of that other court or tribunal that there has been an infringement but it is not required to do so, and

(b) may reach its own conclusion in the light of that finding and of the evidence heard by that other court or tribunal.

PRACTICE DIRECTION—CIVIL EVIDENCE ACT 1995

44–179   **1.** Section 16(3A) of the Civil Evidence Act 1995 (c 38) (as amended) provides that transitional provisions for the application of the provisions of the Civil Evidence Act 1995 to proceedings begun before January 31, 1997 may be made by practice direction.

2. Except as provided for by para. 3, the provisions of the Civil Evidence Act 1995 apply to claims commenced before January 31, 1997.

3. Except as provided for by para. 3, the provisions of the Civil Evidence Act 1995 apply to claims commenced before January 31, 1997.

The provisions of the Civil Evidence Act 1995 do not apply to claims commenced before January 31, 1997 if, before April 26, 1999:

(a) directions were given, or orders were made, as to the evidence to be given at the trial or hearing; or

(b) the trial or hearing had begun.

PRACTICE DIRECTION—LAND REGISTRATION ACT 1925

44–179A   **1.** Attention is drawn to s.113 of the Land Registration Act 1925 which provides that office copies of the register and of documents filed in the Land Registry, including original charges, are admissible in evidence to the same extent as the originals.

2. This section applies in all proceedings, including proceedings for the possession of land.

PART 34. DEPOSITIONS AND COURT ATTENDANCE BY WITNESSES

44–180   **34.1**—(1) This Part provides—

(a) for the circumstances in which a person may be required to attend court to give evidence or to produce a document; and

(b) for a party to obtain evidence before a hearing to be used at the hearing.

34.2—(1) A witness summons is a document issued by the court requiring a   **44-181**
witness to—

(a) attend court to give evidence; or
(b) produce documents to the court.

(2) A witness summons must be in the relevant practice form.
(3) There must be a separate witness summons for each witness.
(4) A witness summons may require a witness to produce documents to the
court either—

(a) on the date fixed for a hearing; or
(b) on such date as the court may direct.

(5) The only documents that a summons under this rule can require a person
to produce before a hearing are documents which that person could be required
to produce at the hearing.

34.3—(1) A witness summons is issued on the date entered on the summons   **44-182**
by the court.
(2) A party must obtain permission from the court where he wishes to—

(a) have a summons issued less than 7 days before the date of the trial;
(b) have a summons issued for a witness to attend court to give evidence or
to produce documents on any date except the date fixed for the trial; or
(c) have a summons issued for a witness to attend court to give evidence or
to produce documents at any hearing except the trial.

(3) A witness summons must be issued by—

(a) the court where the case is proceeding; or
(b) the court where the hearing in question will be held.

(4) The court may set aside or vary a witness summons issued under this
rule.

34.4—(1) The court may issue a witness summons in aid of an inferior court   **44-183**
or of a tribunal.
(2) The court which issued the witness summons under this rule may set it
aside.
(3) In this rule, 'inferior court or tribunal' means any court or tribunal that does
not have power to issue a witness summons in relation to proceedings before
it.

34.5—(1) The general rule is that a witness summons is binding if it served at   **44-184**
least 7 days before the date on which the witness is required to attend before the
court or tribunal.
(2) The court may direct that a witness summons shall be binding although it
will be served less than 7 days before the date on which the witness is required
to attend before the court or tribunal.

(3) A witness summons which is—

(a) served in accordance with this rule; and
(b) requires the witness to attend court to give evidence,

is binding until the conclusion of the hearing at which the attendance of the witness is required.

44–185   **34.6**—(1) A witness summons is to be served by the court unless the party on whose behalf it is issued indicates in writing, when he asks the court to issue the summons, that he wishes to serve it himself.

(2) Where the court is to serve the witness summons, the party on whose behalf if it issued must deposit, in the court office, the money to be paid or offered to the witness under r.34.7.

44–186   **34.7** At the time of service of a witness summons the witness must be offered or paid—

(a) a sum reasonably sufficient to cover his expenses in travelling to and from the court; and
(b) such sum by way of compensation for loss of time as may be specified in the relevant practice direction.

44–187   **34.8**—(1) A Party may apply for an order for a person to be examined before the hearing takes place.

(2) A person from whom evidence is to be obtained following an order under this rule is referred to as a 'deponent' and the evidence is referred to as a 'deposition'.

(3) An order under this rule shall be for a deponent to be examined on oath before—

(a) a judge;
(b) an examiner of the court; or
(c) such other person as the court appoints.

(Rule 34.15 makes provision for the appointment of examiners of the court).

(4) The order may require the production of any document which the court considers is necessary for the purposes of the examination.

(5) The order must state the date, time and place of the examination.

(6) At the time of service of the order the deponent must be offered or paid—

(a) a sum reasonably sufficient to cover his expenses in travelling to and from the place of examination; and
(b) such sum by way of compensation for loss of time as may be specified in the relevant practice direction.

(7) Where the court makes an order for a deposition to be taken, it may also order the party who obtained the order to serve a witness statement or witness summary in relation to the evidence to be given by the person to be examined.

(Part 32 contains the general rules about witness statements and witness summaries).

34.9—(1) Subject to any directions contained in the order for examination, the **44–188** examination must be conducted in the same way as if the witness were giving evidence at a trial.

(2) If all the parties are present, the examiner may conduct the examination of a person not named in the order for examination if all the parties and the person to be examined consent.

(3) The examiner may conduct the examination in private if he considers it appropriate to do so.

(4) The examiner must ensure that the evidence given by the witness is recorded in full.

(5) The examiner must send a copy of the deposition—

(a) to the person who obtained the order for the examination of the witness; and
(b) to the court where the case is proceeding.

(6) The party who obtained the order must send each of the other parties a copy of the deposition which he receives from the examiner.

34.10—(1) If a person served with an order to attend before an examiner— **44–189**

(a) fails to attend; or
(b) refuses to be sworn for the purpose of the examination or to answer any lawful question or produce any document at the examination,

a certificate of his failure or refusal, signed by the examiner, must be filed by the party requiring the deposition.

(2) On the certificate being filed, the party requiring the deposition may apply to the court for an order requiring that person to attend or to be sworn or to answer any question or produce any document, as the case may be.

(3) An application for an order under this rule may be made without notice.

(4) The court may order the person against whom an order is made under this rule to pay any costs resulting from his failure or refusal.

34.11—(1) A deposition ordered under r.34.8 may be given in evidence at a **44–190** hearing unless the court orders otherwise.

(2) A party intending to put in evidence a deposition at a hearing must serve notice of his intention to do so on every other party.

(3) He must serve the notice at least 21 days before the day fixed for the hearing.

(4) The court may require a deponent to attend the hearing and give evidence orally.

(5) Where a deposition is given in evidence at trial, it shall be treated as if it were a witness statement for the purposes of r.31.23 (availability of witness statements for inspection).

34.12—(1) Where the court orders a party to be examined about his or any **44–191** other assets for the purpose of any hearing except the trial, the deposition may be used only for the purpose of the proceedings in which the order was made.

(2) However, it may be used for some other purpose—

(a) by the party who was examined;
(b) if the party who was examined agrees; or
(c) if the court gives permission.

44–192   **34.13**—(1) Where a party wishes to take a deposition from a person outside the jurisdiction, the High Court may order the issue of a letter of request to the judicial authorities of the country in which the proposed deponent is.
(2) A letter of requests is a request to a judicial authority to take the evidence of that person, or arrange for it to be taken.
(3) The High Court may make an order under this rule in relation to county court proceedings.
(4) If the government of a country allows a person appointed by the High Court to examine a person in that country, the High Court may make an order appointing a special examiner for that purpose.
(5) A person may be examined under this rule on oath or affirmation or in accordance with any procedure permitted in the country in which the examination is to take place.
(6) If the High Court makes an order for the issue of a letter of request, the party who sought the order must file—

(a) the following documents and, except where para. (7) applies, a translation of them—
   (i) a draft letter of request;
   (ii) a statement of the issues relevant to the proceedings;
   (iii) a list of questions or the subject matter of questions to be put to the person to be examined; and
(b) an undertaking to be responsible for the Secretary of State's expenses.

(7) There is no need to file a translation if—

(a) English is one of the official languages of the country where the examination is to take place; or
(b) a practice direction has specified that country as a country where no translation is necessary.

44–193   **34.14**—(1) An examiner of the court may charge a fee for the examination.
(2) He need not send the deposition to the court unless the fee is paid.
(3) The examiner's fees and expenses must be paid by the party who obtained the order for examination.
(4) If the fees and expenses due to an examiner are not paid within a reasonable time, he may report that fact to the court.
(5) The court may order the party who obtained the order for examination to deposit in the court office a specified sum in respect of the examiner's fees and, where it does so, the examiner will not be asked to act until the sum has been deposited.
(6) An order under this rule does not affect any decision as to the party who is ultimately to bear the costs of the examination.

44–194   **34.15**—(1) The Lord Chancellor shall appoint persons to be examiners of the court.

(2) The persons appointed shall be barristers or solicitor-advocates who have been practising for a period of not less than three years.

(3) The Lord Chancellor may revoke an appointment at any time.

(Other relevant rules can be found in Sch. 1, in the following RSC—O.70 (obtaining evidence for foreign court); O.79 (issue of witness summons in relation to criminal proceedings in the High Court)).

34.16 In this Part "the 1975 Act" means the Evidence (Proceedings in Other Jurisdictions) Act 1975. (1975 c 34).

34.17 An application for an order under the 1975 Act for evidence to be obtained—

    (a) must be—
        (i) made to the High Court;
        (ii) supported by written evidence; and
        (iii) accompanied by the request as a result of which the application is made, and where appropriate, a translation of the request into English; and
    (b) may be made without notice.

34.18—(1) The court may order an examination to be taken before—

    (a) any fit and proper person nominated by the person applying for the order;
    (b) an examiner of the court; or
    (c) any other person whom the court considers suitable.

(2) Unless the court orders otherwise—

    (a) the examination will be taken as provided by rule 34.9; and
    (b) rule 34.10 applies.

(3) The court may make an order under rule 34.14 for payment of the fees and expenses of the examination.

34.19—(1) The examiner must send the deposition of the witness to the Senior Master unless the court orders otherwise.

(2) The Senior Master will—

    (a) give a certificate sealed with the seal of the Supreme Court for use out of the jurisdiction identifying the following documents—
        (i) the request;
        (ii) the order of the court for examination; and
        (iii) the deposition of the witness; and
    (b) send the certificate and the documents referred to in paragraph (a) to—
        (i) the Secretary of State; or
        (ii) where the request was sent to the Senior Master by another person in accordance with a Civil Procedure Convention, to that other person, for transmission to the court or tribunal requesting the examination.

34.20—(1) This rule applies where—

    (a) a witness claims to be exempt from giving evidence on the ground specified in section 3(1)(b) of the 1975 Act; and

(b) that claim is not supported or conceded as referred to in section 3(2) of that Act.

(2) The examiner may require the witness to give the evidence which he claims to be exempt from giving.

(3) Where the examiner does not require the witness to give that evidence, the court may order the witness to do so.

(4) An application for an order under paragraph (3) may be made by the person who obtained the order under section 2 of the 1975 Act.

(5) Where such evidence is taken—

(a) it must be contained in a document separate from the remainder of the deposition;

(b) the examiner will send to the Senior Master—
   (i) the deposition; and
   (ii) a signed statement setting out the claim to be exempt and the ground on which it was made.

(6) On receipt of the statement referred to in paragraph (5)(b)(ii), the Senior Master will—

(a) retain the document containing the part of the witness's evidence to which the claim to be exempt relates; and

(b) send the statement and a request to determine that claim to the foreign court or tribunal together with the documents referred to in rule 34.17.

(7) The Senior Master will—

(a) if the claim to be exempt is rejected by the foreign court or tribunal, send the document referred to in paragraph (5)(a) to that court or tribunal;

(b) if the claim is upheld, send the document to the witness; and

(c) in either case, notify the witness and person who obtained the order under section 2 of the foreign court or tribunal's decision.

34.21 Where an order is made for the examination of witnesses under section 1 of the 1975 Act as applied by section 92 of the Patents Act 1977 (1975, c 37) the court may permit an officer of the European Patent Office to—

(a) attend the examination and examine the witnesses; or

(b) request the court or the examiner before whom the examination takes place to put specified questions to them.

PRACTICE DIRECTION—DEPOSITIONS AND COURT
ATTENDANCE BY WITNESSES

This Practice Direction supplements CPR Part 34

44–195   **1.1** A witness summons may require a witness to:

(1) attend court to give evidence,

(2) produce documents to the court, or

(3) both,

on either a date fixed for the hearing or such date as the court may direct.

1.2 Two copies of the witness summons should be filed with the court for sealing, one of which will be retained on the court file.

1.3 A mistake in the name or address of a person named in a witness summons may be corrected if the summons has not been served.

1.4 The corrected summons must be re-sealed by the court and marked 'Amended and Re-Sealed'.

2.1 A witness summons may be issued in the High Court or a county court in **44–196** aid of a court or tribunal which does not have the power to issue a witness summons in relation to the proceedings before it.

2.2 A witness summons referred to in para. 2.1 may be set aside by the court which issued it.

2.3 An application to set aside a witness summons referred to in para. 2.1 will be heard:

(1) in the High Court by a Master at the Royal Courts of Justice or by a district judge in a District Registry, and

(2) in a county court by a district judge.

2.4 Unless the court otherwise directs, the applicant must give at least 2 days' notice to the party who issued the witness summons of the application, which will normally be dealt with at a hearing.

3.1 When a witness is served with a witness summons he must be offered a **44–197** sum to cover his travelling expenses to and from the court and compensation for his loss of time.

3.2 If the witness summons is to be served by the court, the party issuing the summons must deposit with the court:

(1) a sum sufficient to pay for the witness's expenses in travelling to the court and in returning to his home or place of work, and

(2) a sum in respect of the period during which earnings or benefit are list, or such lesser sum as it may be proved that the witness will lose as a result of his attendance at court in answer to the witness summons.

3.3 The sum referred to in 3.2(2) is to be based on the sums payable to witnesses attending the Crown Court.

3.4 Where the party issuing the witness summons wishes to serve it himself, he must:

(1) notify the court in writing that he wishes to do so, and

(2) at the time of service offer the witness the sums mentioned in para. 3.2 above.

Depositions

4.1 A party may apply for an order for a person to be examined on oath **44–198** before:

(1) a judge,

(2) an examiner of the court, or

(3) such other person as the court may appoint.

4.2 The party who obtains an order for the examination of a deponent before an examiner of the court must:

(1) apply to the Foreign Process Section of the Masters' Secretary's Department at the Royal Courts of Justice for the allocation of an examiner,

(2) when allocated, provide the examiner with copies of all documents in the proceedings necessary to inform the examiner of the issues, and

(3) pay the deponent a sum to cover his travelling expenses to and from the examination and compensation for his loss of time.

4.3 In ensuring that the deponent's evidence is recorded in full, the court or the examiner may permit it be recorded on audiotape or videotape, but the deposition must always be recorded in writing by him or by a competent shorthand writer or stenographer.

4.4 If the deposition is not recorded word for word, it must contain, as nearly as may be, the statement of the deponent; the examiner may record word for word any particular questions and answers which appear to him to have special importance.

4.5 If a deponent objects to answering any question or where any objection is taken to any question, the examiner must:

(1) record in the deposition or a document attached to it—

   (a) the question,

   (b) the nature of and grounds for the objection, and

   (c) any answer given, and

(2) give his opinion as to the validity of the objection and must record it in the deposition or a document attached to it.

The court will decide as to the validity of the objection and any question of costs arising from it.

4.6 Documents and exhibits must:

(1) have an identifying number or letter marked on them by the examiner, and

(2) be preserved by the party or his legal representative who obtained the order for the examination, or as the court or the examiner may direct.

4.7 The examiner may put any question to the deponent as to:

(1) the meaning of any of his answers, or

(2) any matter arising in the course of the examination.

4.8 Where a deponent:

(1) fails to attend the examination, or

(2) refuses to:

   (a) be sworn, or

   (b) answer any lawful question, or

(c) produce any document,

the examiner will sign a certificate of such failure or refusal and may include in his certificate any comment as to the conduct of the deponent or of any person attending the examination.

4.9 The party who obtained the order for the examination must file the certificate with the court and may apply for an order that the deponent attend for examination or as may be. The application may be made without notice.

4.10 The court will make such order on the application as it thinks fit including an order for the deponent to pay any costs resulting from his failure or refusal.

4.11 A deponent who wilfully refuses to obey an order made against him under Pt 34 may be proceeded against for contempt of court.

4.12 A deposition must:

(1) be signed by the examiner,
(2) have any amendments to it initialled by the examiner and the deponent,
(3) be endorsed by the examiner with—
    (a) a statement of the time occupied by the examination, and
    (b) a record of any refusal by the deponent to sign the deposition and of his reasons for not doing so, and
(4) be sent by the examiner to the court where the proceedings are taking place for filing on the court file.

4.13 Rule 34.14 deals with the fees and expenses of an examiner.

5.1 Where a party wishes to take deposition from a person outside the jurisdiction, the High Court may order the issue of a letter of request to the judicial authorities of the country in which the proposed deponent is.   **44–199**

5.2 An application for an order referred to in para. 5.1 should be made by application notice in accordance with Pt 23.

5.3 The documents which a party applying for an order for the issue of a letter of request must file with his application notice are set out in r.34.13(6). They are as follows:

(1) a drafter letter of request in the form set out in Annex A to this practice direction,
(2) a statement of the issues relevant to the proceedings,
(3) a list of questions or the subject matter of questions to be put to the proposed deponent,
(4) a translation of the documents in (1), (2) and (3) above unless the proposed deponent is in a country—
    (a) of which English is one of the official languages, or
    (b) listed at Annex B to this practice direction, unless the particular circumstances of the case require a translation,
(5) an undertaking to be responsible for the expenses of the Secretary of State, and
(6) a draft order.

5.4 The above documents should be filed with the Masters' Secretary in Room E214, Royal Courts of Justice, Strand, London WC2A 2LL.

5.5 The application will be dealt with by the Senior Master of the Queen's Bench Division of the High Court who will, if appropriate, sign the letter of request.

5.6 Attention is drawn to the provisions of r.23.10 (application to vary or discharge an order made without notice).

5.7 If parties are in doubt as to whether a translation under para. 5.3(4) above is required, they should seek guidance from the Foreign Process Section of the Masters' Secretary's Department.

5.8 A special examiner appointed under r.34.13(4) may be the British Consul or the Consul-General or his deputy in the country where the evidence is to be taken if:

(1) there is in respect of that country a Civil Procedure Convention providing for the taking of evidence in that country for the assistance of proceedings in the High Court or other court in this country, or

(2) with the consent of the Secretary of State.

5.9 The provisions of paras 4.1 to 4.12 above apply to the depositions referred to in this paragraph.

44–200 **6.1** Section II of Pt 34 relating to obtaining evidence for foreign courts applies to letters of request and should be read in conjunction with this part of the practice direction.

6.2 The Evidence (Proceedings in Other Jurisdictions) Act 1975 applies to these depositions.

6.3 The written evidence supporting an application under r.34.17 (which should be made by application notice – see Pt 23) must include or exhibit:

(1) a statement of the issues relevant to the proceedings;

(2) a list of questions or the subject matter of questions to be put to the proposed deponent;

(3) a draft order; and

(4) a translation of the documents in (1) and (2) into English, if necessary.

6.4 (1) The Senior Master will send to the Treasury Solicitor any request—

(a) forwarded by the Secretary of State with a recommendation that effect should be given to the request without requiring an application to be made; or

(b) received by him in pursuance of a Civil Procedure Convention providing for the taking of evidence of any person in England and Wales to assist a court or tribunal in a foreign country where no person is named in the document as the applicant.

(2) in relation to such a request, the Treasury Solicitor may, with the consent of the Treasury—

(a) apply for an order under the 1975 Act; and

(b) take such other steps as are necessary to give effect to the request.

6.5 The order for the deponent to attend and be examined together with the evidence upon which the order was made must be served on the deponent.

6.6 Attention is drawn to the provisions of r.23.10 (application to vary or discharge an order made without notice).

6.7 Arrangements for the examination to take place at a specified time and place before an examiner of the court or such other person as the court may appoint shall be made by the applicant for the order (i.e. the agent referred to in para. 6.3 or the Treasury Solicitor) and approved by the Senior Master.

6.8 The provisions of para. 4.2 to 4.12 apply to the depositions referred to in this paragraph, except that the examiner must send the deposition to the Senior Master.

(For further information about evidence see Pt 32 and the practice direction which supplements it).

ANNEX A

Draft letter of request

The Competent Judicial Authority of   in **44–201**
the   of
I [*name*] Senior Master of the Queen's Bench Division of the Supreme Court of England and Wales respectfully request the assistance of your court with regard to the following matters.

1. A claim is now pending in the Division of the High Court of Justice in England and Wales entitled as follows [*set out full title and claim number*] in which [*name*] of [*address*] is the claimant and [*name*] of [*address*] is the defendant.

2. The names and addresses of the representatives or agents of [*set out names and addresses of representatives of the parties*].

3. The claim by the Claimant is for:

(a) [*set out nature of the claim*]
(b) [*the relief sought, and*]
(c) [*a summary of the facts.*]

4. It is necessary for the purposes of justice and for the due determination of the matters in dispute between the parties that you cause the following witnesses, who are resident within your jurisdiction, to be examined. The names and addresses of the witnesses are as follows:

5. The witnesses should be examined on oath or if that is not possible within your laws or is impossible of performance by reason of the internal practice and procedures of your court or by reason of practical difficulties, they should be examined in accordance with whatever procedure your laws provide for in these matters.

6. Either/
The witnesses should be examined in accordance with the list of questions annexed hereto.
Or/
The witnesses should be examined regarding [set out full details of evidence sought]

[225]

N.B. Where the witness is required to produce documents, these should be clearly identified.

7. I would ask that you cause me, or the agents of the parties (if appointed), to be informed of the date and place where the examination is to take place.

8. Finally, I request that you will cause the evidence of the said witnesses to be reduced into writing and all documents produced on such examinations to be duly marked for identification and that you will further be pleased to authenticate such examinations by the seal of your court or in such other way as is in accordance with your procedure and return the written evidence and documents produced to me as follows:

Senior Master of the Queen's Bench Division
Royal Courts of Justice
Strand
London
WC2A 2LL
England

ANNEX B

44–202   Countries where the translation referred to in para. 5.3(4) above should not be required:

Australia
Canada (other than Quebec)
Holland
New Zealand
The United States of America

PRACTICE DIRECTION—FEES FOR EXAMINERS OF THE COURT

44–202A   **1.1** This practice direction sets out:

(1) how to calculate the fees an examiner of the court ('an examiner') may charge; and
(2) the expenses he may recover.

(CPR r.34.8 (3) (b) provides that the court may make an order for evidence to be obtained by the examination of a witness before an examiner of the court).

1.2 The party who obtained the order for the examination must pay the fees and expenses of the examiner.

(CPR r.34.14 permits an examiner to charge a fee for the examination and contains other provisions about his fees and expenses, and r.34.15 provides who may be appointed as an examiner of the court).

2.1 An examiner may charge an hourly rate for each hour (or part of an hour) that he is engaged in examining the witnesses.

2.2 The hourly rate is to be calculated by reference to the formula set out in para. 3.

2.3 The examination fee will be the hourly rate multiplied by the number of hours the examination has taken. For example:

Examination fee = hourly rate × number of hours.

3.1 Divide the amount of the minimum annual salary of a post within Group 7 of the judicial salary structure as designated by the Review Body on Senior Salaries, by 220 to give '**x**'; and then divide '**x**' by **6** to give **the hourly rate**.

4.1 An examiner of court is also entitled to charge a single fee of twice the hourly rate (calculated in accordance with para. 3 above) as 'the appointment fee' when the appointment for the examination is made.

4.2 The examiner is entitled to retain the appointment fee where the witness fails to attend on the date and time arranged.

4.3 Where the examiner fails to attend on the date and time arranged he may not charge a further appointment fee for arranging a subsequent appointment.

(The examiner need not send the deposition to the court until his fees are paid—see CPR r.34.14 (2)).

5.1 The examiner of court is also entitled to recover the following expenses—

(1) all reasonable travelling expenses;
(2) any other expenses reasonably incurred; and
(3) subject to para. 5.2, any reasonable charge for the room where the examination takes place.

5.2 No expenses may be recovered under sub-paragraph (3) above if the examination takes place at the examiner's usual business address.

(If the examiner's fees and expenses are not paid within a reasonable time he may report the fact to the court, see CPR r.34.14 (4) and (5)).

PART 35. EXPERTS AND ASSESSORS

35.1 Expert evidence shall be restricted to that which is reasonably required to resolve the proceedings.   **44–208**

35.2 A reference to an 'expert' in this Part is a reference to an expert who has been instructed to give or prepare evidence for the purpose of court proceedings.   **44–209**

35.3—(1) It is the duty of an expert to help the court on the matters within his expertise.   **44–210**

(2) This duty overrides any obligation to the person from whom he has received instructions or by whom he is paid.

35.4—(1) No party may call an expert or put in evidence an expert's report without the court's permission.   **44–211**

(2) When a party applies for permission under this rule he must identify—

(a) the field in which he wishes to rely on expert evidence; and
(b) where practicable the expert in that field on whose evidence he wishes to rely.

(3) If permission is granted under this rule it shall be in relation only to the expert named or the field identified under para. (2).

(4) The court may limit the amount of the expert's fees and expenses that the party who wishes to rely on the expert may recover from any other party.

44–212   **35.5**—(1) Expert evidence is to be given in a written report unless the court directs otherwise.

(2) If a claim is on the fast track, the court will not direct an expert to attend a hearing unless it is necessary to do so in the interests of justice.

44–213   **35.6**—(1) A party may put to—

(a) an expert instructed by another party; or
(b) a single joint expert appointed under r.35.7, written questions about his report.

(2) Written questions under para. (1)—

(a) may be put once only;
(b) must be put within 28 days of service of the expert's report; and
(c) must be for the purpose only of clarification of the report, unless in any case—
   (i) the court gives permission; or
   (ii) the other party agrees.

(3) An expert's answers to questions put in accordance with para. (1) shall be treated as part of the expert's report.

(4) Where—

(a) a party has put a written question to an expert instructed by another party in accordance with this rule; and
(b) the expert does not answer that question, the court may make one or both of the following orders in relation to the party who instructed the expert—
   (i) that the party may not rely on the evidence of that expert; or
   (ii) that the party may not recover the fees and expenses of that expert from any other party.

44–214   **35.7**—(1) Where two or more parties wish to submit expert evidence on a particular issue, the court may direct that the evidence on that issue is to be given by one expert only.

(2) The parties wishing to submit the expert evidence are called 'the instructing parties'.

(3) Where the instructing parties cannot agree who should be the expert, the court may—

(a) select the expert from a list prepared or identified by the instructing parties; or

(b) direct that the expert be selected in such other manner as the court may direct.

35.8—(1) Where the court gives a direction under r.35.7 for a single joint   **44–215**
expert to be used, each instructing party may give instructions to the expert.
(2) When an instructing party gives instructions to the expert he must, at the
same time, send a copy of the instructions to the other instructing parties.
(3) The court may give directions about—

(a) the payment of the expert's fees and expenses; and
(b) any inspection, examination or experiments which the expert wishes to carry out.

(4) The court may, before an expert is instructed—

(a) limit the amount that can be paid by way of fees and expenses to the expert; and
(b) direct that the instructing parties pay that amount into court.

(5) Unless the court otherwise directs, the instructing parties are jointly and
severally liable for the payment of the expert's fees and expenses.

35.9 Where a party has access to information which is not reasonably available   **44–216**
to the other party, the court may direct the party who has access to the
information to—

(a) prepare and file a document recording the information; and
(b) serve a copy of that document on the other party.

35.10—(1) An expert's report must comply with the requirements set out in   **44–217**
the relevant practice direction.
(2) At the end of an expert's report there must be a statement that—

(a) the expert understands his duty to the court; and
(b) he has complied with that duty.

(3) The expert's report must state the substance of all material instructions,
whether written or oral, on the basis of which the report was written.
(4) The instructions referred to in para. (3) shall not be privileged against
disclosure but the court will not, in relation to those instructions—

(a) order disclosure of any specific document; or
(b) permit any questioning in court, other than by the party who instructed the
expert, unless it is satisfied that there are reasonable grounds to consider
the statement of instructions given under para. (3) to be inaccurate or
incomplete.

35.11 Where a party has disclosed an expert's report, any party may use that   **44–218**
expert's report as evidence at the trial.

35.12—(1) The court may, at any stage, direct a discussion between expert's   **44–219**
for the purpose of requiring the expert's to—

    (a) identify and discuss the expert issues in the proceedings; and

    (b) where possible, reach an agreed opinion on those issues.

(2) The court may specify the issues which the experts must discuss.

(3) The court may direct that following a discussion between the experts they must prepare a statement for the court showing—

    (a) those issues on which they agree; and

    (b) those issues on which they disagree and a summary of their reasons for disagreeing.

(4) The content of the discussion between the experts shall not be referred to at the trial unless the parties agree.

(5) Where experts reach agreement on an issue during their discussions, the agreement shall not bind the parties unless the parties expressly agree to be bound by the agreement.

44–220   **35.13** A party who fails to disclose an expert's report may not use the report at the trial or call the expert to give evidence orally unless the court gives permission.

44–221   **35.14**—(1) An expert may file a written request for directions to assist him in carrying out his function as an expert.

(2) An expert must, unless the court orders otherwise, provide a copy of any proposed request for directions under paragraph (1)—

    (a) to the party instructing him, at least 7 days before he files the request; and

    (b) to all other parties, at least 4 days before he files it.

(3) The court, when it gives directions, may also direct that a party be served with a copy of the directions.

44–222   **35.15**—(1) This rule applies where the court appoints one or more persons (an "assessor") under s.70 of the Supreme Court Act 1981 or s.63 of the County Courts Act 1984.

(2) The assessor shall assist the court in dealing with a matter in which the assessor has skill and experience.

(3) An assessor shall take such part in the proceedings as the court may direct and in particular the court may—

    (a) direct the assessor to prepare a report for the court on any matter at issue in the proceedings; and

    (b) direct the assessor to attend the whole or any part of the trial to advise the court on any such matter.

(4) If the assessor prepares a report for the court before the trial has begun—

    (a) the court will send a copy to each of the parties; and

    (b) the parties may use it at trial.

(5) The remuneration to be paid to the assessor for his services shall be determined by the court and shall form part of the costs of the proceedings.

(6) The court may order any party to deposit in the court office a specified sum in respect of the assessor's fees and, where it does so, the assessor will not be asked to act until the sum has been deposited.

(7) Paragraphs (5) and (6) do not apply where the remuneration of the assessor is to be paid out of money provided by Parliament.

PRACTICE DIRECTION—EXPERTS AND ASSESSORS

This Practice Direction supplements CPR Part 35

1.1 It is the duty of an expert to help the court on matters within his own **44–224** expertise: r.35.3 (1). This duty is paramount and overrides any obligation to the person from whom the expert has received instructions or by whom he is paid: r.35.3(2).

1.2 Expert evidence should be the independent product of the expert uninfluenced by the pressures of litigation.

1.3 An expert should assist the court by providing objective, unbiased opinion on matters within his expertise, and should not assume the role of an advocate.

1.4 An expert should consider all material facts, including those which might detract from his opinion.

1.5 An expert should make it clear:

(a) when a question or issue falls outside his expertise; and
(b) when he is not able to reach a definite opinion, for example because he has insufficient information.

1.6 If, after producing a report, an expert changes his view on any material matter, such change of view should be communicated to all the parties without delay, and when appropriate to the court.

2.1 An expert's report should be addressed to the court and not to the party **44–225** from whom the expert has received his instructions.

2.2 An expert's report must:

(1) give details of the expert's qualifications;
(2) give details of any literature or other material which the expert has relied on in making the report;
(3) contain a statement setting out the substance of all facts and instructions given to the expert which are material to the opinions expressed in the report or upon which those opinions are based;
(4) make clear which of the facts stated in the report are within the expert's own knowledge;
(5) say who carried out any examination, measurement, test or experiment which the expert has used for the report, give the qualifications of that person, and say whether or not the test or experiment has been carried out under the expert's supervision;

    (6) where there is a range of opinion on the matters dealt with in the
       report—
         (a) summarise the range of opinion, and
         (b) give reasons for his own opinion;
    (7) contain a summary of the conclusions reached;
    (8) if the expert is not able to give his opinion without qualification, state the
       qualification; and
    (9) contain a statement that the expert understands his duty to the court, and
       has complied and will continue to comply with that duty.

2.3 An expert's report must be verified by a statement of truth as well as containing the statements required in para. 2.2(8) and (9) above.

2.4 The form of the statement of truth is as follows:

"I confirm that insofar as the facts stated in my report are within my own knowledge I have made it clear which they are and I believe them to be true, and that the opinions I have expressed represent my true and complete professional opinion."

2.5 Attention is drawn to r.32.14 which sets out the consequences of verifying a document containing a false statement without an honest belief in its truth.

(For information about statements of truth see Pt 22 and the practice direction which accompanies it.)

44–226   **3.** Under r.35.9 the court may direct a party with access to information which is not reasonably available to an other party to serve on that other party a document which records the information. The document served must include sufficient details of all the facts, tests, experiments and assumptions which underlie any part of the information to enable the party on whom it is served to make, or to obtain, a proper interpretation of the information and an assessment of its significance.

44–227   **4.** The instructions referred to in para. 2.2(3) will not be protected by privilege (see r.35.10(4)). But cross-examination of the expert on the contents of his instructions will not be allowed unless the court permits it (or unless the party who gave the instructions consents to it). Before it gives permission the court must be satisfied that there are reasonable grounds to consider that the statement in the report of the substance of the instructions is inaccurate or incomplete. If the court is so satisfied, it will allow the cross-examination where it appears to be in the interests of justice to do so.

44–228   **5.1** Questions asked for the purpose of clarifying the expert's report (see r.35.6) should be put, in writing, to the expert not later than 28 days after receipt of the expert's report (see paras 1.2 to 1.5 above as to verification).

    5.2 Where a party sends a written question or questions direct to an expert, a copy of the questions should, at the same time, be sent to the other party or parties.

    5.3 The party or parties instructing the expert must pay any fees charged by that expert for answering questions put under r.35.6. This does not affect any decision of the court as to the party who is ultimately to bear the expert's costs.

6. Where the court has directed that the evidence on a particular issue is to be   **44–229**
given by one expert only (r.35.7) but there are a number of disciplines relevant
to that issue, a leading expert in the dominant discipline should be identified as
the single expert. He should prepare the general part of the report and be
responsible for annexing or incorporating the contents of any reports from
experts in other disciplines.

7.1 An assessor may be appointed to assist the court under r.35.15. Not less   **44–229A**
than 21 days before making any such appointment, the court will notify each
party in writing of the name of the proposed assessor, of the matter in respect of
which the assistance of the assessor will be sought and of the qualifications of the
assessor to give that assistance.
7.2 Where any person has been proposed for appointment as an assessor,
objection to him, either personally or in respect of his qualification, may be taken
by any party.
7.3 Any such objection must be made in writing and filed with the court within
7 days of receipt of the notification referred to in para. 6.1 and will be taken into
account by the court in deciding whether or not to make the appointment (s.63(5)
of the County Courts Act 1984).
7.4 Copies of any report prepared by the assessor will be sent to each of the
parties but the assessor will not give oral evidence or be open to cross-
examination or questioning.

Part 39. Miscellaneous Provisions Relating to Hearings

39.1 In this Part, reference to a hearing includes a reference to the trial.   **44–230**

39.2—(1) The general rule is that a hearing is to be in public.   **44–231**
(2) The requirement for a hearing to be in public does not require the court to
make special arrangements for accommodating members of the public.
(3) A hearing, or any part of it, may be in private if—

(a) publicity would defeat the object of the hearing;
(b) it involves matters relating to national security;
(c) it involves confidential information (including information relating to
    personal financial matters) and publicity would damage that confidenti-
    ality.
(d) a private hearing is necessary to protect the interests of any child or
    patient;
(e) it is a hearing of an application made without notice and it would be unjust
    to any respondent for there to be a public hearing;
(f) it involves uncontentious matters arising in the administration of trusts or
    in the administration of a deceased person's estate; or
(g) the court considers this to be necessary, in the interests of justice.

(4) The court may order that the identity of any party or witness must not be disclosed if it considers non-disclosure necessary in order to protect the interests of the party or witness.

(RSC Ord. 52, in Sch. 1, provides that a committal hearing may be in private)

44–232 **39.3**—(1) The court may proceed with a trial in the absence of a party but—

(a) if no party attends the trial, it may strike out the whole of the proceedings;

(b) if the claimant does not attend, it may strike out his claim and any defence to the counterclaim; and

(c) if a defendant does not attend, it may strike out his defence or counterclaim (or both).

(2) Where the court strikes out proceedings, or any part of them, under this rule, it may subsequently restore the proceedings, or that part.

(3) Where a party does not attend and the court gives judgment or makes an order against him, the party who failed to attend may apply for the judgment or order to be set aside.

(4) An application under para. (2) or para. (3) must be supported by evidence.

(5) Where an application is made under para. (2) or (3) by a party who failed to attend the trial, the court may grant the application only if the applicant—

(a) acted promptly when he found out that the court had exercised its power to strike out or to enter judgment or make an order against him;

(b) had a good reason for not attending the trial; and

(c) has a reasonable prospect of success at the trial.

44–233 **39.4** When the court sets a timetable for a trial in accordance with r.28.6 (fixing or confirming the trial date and giving directions—fast track) or r.29.8 (setting a trial timetable and fixing or confirming the trial date or week—multi-track) it will do so in consultation with the parties.

44–234 **39.5**—(1) Unless the court orders otherwise, the claimant must file a trial bundle containing the documents required by—

(a) a relevant practice direction; and

(b) any court order.

(2) The claimant must file the trial bundle not more than 7 days and not less than 3 days before the start of the trial.

44–235 **39.6** A company or other corporation may be represented at trial by an employee if—

(a) the employee has been authorised by the company or corporation to appear at trial on its behalf; and

(b) the court gives permission.

44–236 **39.7**—(1) Documents impounded by order of the court must not be released from the custody of the court except in compliance—

(a) with a court order; or

(b) with a written request made by a Law Officer or the Director of Public Prosecutions.

(2) A document released from the custody of the court under para. (1)(b) must be released into the custody of the person who requested it.

(3) Documents impounded by order of the court, while in the custody of the court, may not be inspected except by a person authorised to do so by a court order.

39.8 In a claim brought under s.57(1) of the Race Relations Act 1976, the court may, where it considers it expedient in the interests of national security—   **44–236A**

(a) exclude from all or part of the proceedings—
   (i) the claimant;
   (ii) the claimant's representatives; or
   (iii) any assessors appointed under s.67(4) or that Act.

(b) permit a claimant or representative to make a statement to the court before the start of the proceedings (or the part of the proceedings) from which he is excluded; or

(c) take steps to keep secret all or part of the reasons for its decision in the claim.

(Section 67(2) of the Race Relations Act 1976 provides that the Attorney General may appoint a person to represent the interests of a claimant in any proceedings from which he and his representatives are excluded).

PRACTICE DIRECTION—MISCELLANEOUS PROVISIONS
RELATING TO HEARINGS

This Practice Direction supplements CPR Part 39

1.1 In Pt 39, reference to a hearing includes reference to the trial.   **44–237**

1.2 The general rule is that a hearing is to be in public.

1.3 Rule 39.2(3) sets out the type of proceedings which may be dealt with in private.

1.4 The decision as to whether to hold a hearing in public or in private must be made by the judge conducting the hearing having regard to any representations which may have been made to him.

1.4A A The judge should also have regard to Article 6(1) of the European Convention on Human Rights. This requires that, in general, court hearings are to be held in public, but the press and public may be excluded in the circumstances specified in that Article. Article 6(1) will usually be relevant, for example, where a party applies for a hearing which would normally be held in public to be held in private as well where a hearing would normally be held in private. The Judge may need to consider whether the case is within any of the exceptions permitted by Article 6(1).

1.5 The hearings set out below shall in the first instance be listed by the court as hearings in private under r.39.2(3)(c), namely:

   (1) a claim by a mortgagee against one or more individuals for an order for possession of land,

   (2) a claim by a landlord against one or more tenants or former tenants for the repossession of a dwelling house based on the non payment of rent,

   (3) an application to suspend a warrant of execution or a warrant of possession or to stay execution where the court is being invited to consider the ability of a party to make payments to another party,

   (4) a redetermination under r.14.13 or an application to vary or suspend the payment of a judgment debt by instalments,

   (5) an application for a charging order (including an application to enforce a charging order), third party debt order, attachment of earnings order, administration order, or the appointment of a receiver,

   (6) an order to attend court for questioning,

   (7) the determination of the liability of an LSC funded client under regs 9 and 10 of the Community Legal Service (Costs) Regulations 2000, or of an assisted person's liability for costs under reg. 127 of the Civil Legal Aid (General) Regulations 1989,

   (8) an application for security for costs under s.726(1) of the Companies Act 1985, and

   (9) proceedings brought under the Consumer Credit Act 1974, the Inheritance (Provision for Family and Dependants) Act 1975 or the Protection from Harassment Act 1997,

  (10) an application by a trustee or personal representative for directions as to bringing or defending legal proceedings.

1.6 Rule 39.2(3)(d) states that a hearing may be in private where it involves the interests of a child or patient. This includes the approval of a compromise or settlement on behalf of a child or patient or an application for the payment of money out of court to such a person.

1.7 Attention is drawn to para. 5.1 of the practice direction which supplements Pt 27 (relating to the hearing of claims in the small claims track), which provides that the judge may decide to hold a small claim hearing in private if the parties agree or if a ground mentioned in r.39.2(3) applies. A hearing of a small claim in premises other than the court will not be a hearing in public.

1.8 Nothing in this practice direction prevents a judge ordering that a hearing taking place in public shall continue in private, or vice-versa.

1.9 If the court or judge's room in which the proceedings are taking place has a sign on the door indicating that the proceedings are private, members of the public who are not parties to the proceedings will not be admitted unless the court permits.

1.10 Where there is no such sign on the door of the court or judge's room, members of the public will be admitted where practicable. The judge may, if he thinks it appropriate, adjourn the proceedings to a larger room or court.

1.11 When a hearing takes place in public, members of the public may obtain a transcript of any judgment given or a copy of any order made, subject to payment of the appropriate fee.

1.12 When a judgment is given or an order is made in private, if any member of the public who is not a party to the proceedings seeks a transcript of the judgment or a copy of the order, he must seek the leave of the judge who gave the judgment or made the order.

1.13 A judgment or order given or made in private, when drawn up, must have clearly marked in the title:

"Before [*title and name of judge*] sitting in Private".

1.14 References to hearings being in public or private or in a judge's room contained in the Civil Procedure Rules (including the Rules of the Supreme Court and the County Court Rules scheduled to Pt 50) and the practice directions which supplement them do not restrict any existing rights of audience or confer any new rights of audience in respect of applications or proceedings which under the rules previously in force would have been heard in court or in chambers respectively.

1.15 Where the court lists a hearing of a claim by a mortgagee for an order for possession of land under para. 1.5(1) above to be in private, any fact which needs to be proved by the evidence of witnesses may be proved by evidence in writing.

(CPR r.32.2 sets out the general rule as to how evidence is to be given and facts are to be proved.)

2.1 Rule 39.3 sets out the consequences of a party's failure to attend the   **44-237A**
trial.

2.2 The court may proceed with a trial in the absence of a party. In the absence of:

    (1) the defendant, the claimant may—
        (a) prove his claim at trial and obtain judgment on his claim and for costs, and
        (b) seek the striking out of any counterclaim,
    (2) the claimant, the defendant may—
        (a) prove any counterclaim at trial and obtain judgment on his counterclaim and for costs, and
        (b) seek the striking out of the claim, or
    (3) both parties, the court may strike out the whole of the proceedings.

2.3 Where the court has struck out proceedings, or any part of them, on the failure of a party to attend, that party may apply in accordance with Pt 23 for the proceedings, or that part of them, to be restored and for any judgment given against that party to be set aside.

2.4 The application referred to in para. 2.3 above must be supported by evidence giving reasons for the failure to attend court and stating when the applicant found out about the order against him.

3.1 Unless the court orders otherwise, the claimant must file the trial bundle   **44-237B**
not more than 7 days and not less than 3 days before the start of the trial.

3.2 Unless the court orders otherwise, the trial bundle should include a copy of:

    (1) the claim form and all statements of case,

(2) a case summary and/or chronology where appropriate,

(3) requests for further information and responses to the requests,

(4) all witness statements to be relied on as evidence,

(5) any witness summaries,

(6) any notices of intention to rely on hearsay evidence under r.32.2,

(7) any notices of intention to rely on evidence (such as a plan, photograph etc.) under r.33.6 which is not—

    (a) contained in a witness statement, affidavit or experts report,

    (b) being given orally at trial,

    (c) hearsay evidence under r.33.2,

(8) any medical reports and responses to them,

(9) an experts' reports and responses to them,

(10) any order giving directions as to the conduct of the trial, and

(11) any other necessary documents.

3.3 The originals of the documents contained in the trial bundle, together with copies of any other court orders should be available at the trial.

3.4 The preparation and production of the trial bundle, even where it is delegated to another person, is the responsibility of the legal representative who has conduct of the claim on behalf of the claimant.

3.5 The trial bundle should be paginated (continuously) throughout, the indexed with a description of each documents and the page number. Where the total number of pages is more than 100, numbered dividers should be placed at intervals between groups of documents.

3.6 The bundle should normally be contained in a ring binder or lever arch file. Where more than one bundle is supplied, they should be clearly distinguishable, for example, by different colours or letters. If there are numerous bundles, a core bundle should be prepared containing the core documents essential to the proceedings, with references to the supplementary documents in the other bundles.

3.7 For convenience, experts' reports may be contained in a separate bundle and cross referenced in the main bundle.

3.8 If a document to be included in the trial bundle is illegible, a typed copy should be included in the bundle next to it, suitably cross-referenced.

3.9 The contents of the trial bundle should be agreed where possible. The parties should also agree where possible:

(1) that the documents contained in the bundle are authentic even if not disclosed under Pt 31, and

(2) that documents in the bundle may be treated as evidence of the facts stated in them even if a notice under the Civil Evidence Act 1995 has not been served.

Where it is not possible to agree the contents of the bundle, a summary of the points on which the parties are unable to agree should be included.

3.10 The party filing the trial bundle should supply identical bundles to all the parties to the proceedings and for the use of the witnesses.

44–237C   **4.1** Where:

(1) an offer to settle a claim is accepted,

(2) or a settlement is reached, or

(3) a claim is discontinued, which disposes of the whole of a claim for which a date or "window" has been fixed for the trial, the parties must ensure that the listing officer for the trial court is notified immediately.

4.2 If an order is drawn up giving effect to the settlement or discontinuance, a copy of the sealed order should be filed with the listing officer.

5.1 At any hearing, a written statement containing the following information **44–237D** should be provided for the court:

(1) the name and address of each advocate,
(2) his qualification or entitlement to act as an advocate, and
(3) the party for whom he so acts.

5.2 Where a party is a company or other corporation and is to be represented at a hearing by an employee the written statement should contain the following additional information:

(1) The full name of the company or corporation as stated in its certificate of registration.
(2) The registered number of the company or corporation.
(3) The position or office in the company or corporation held by the representative.
(4) The date on which and manner in which the representative was authorised to act for the company or corporation, e.g.   19   : written authority from managing director; or   19   : Board resolution dated   19   .

5.3 Rule 39.6 is intended to enable a company or other corporation to represent itself as a litigant in person. Permission under r.39.6(b) should therefore be given by the court unless there is some particular and sufficient reason why it should be withheld. In considering whether to grant permission the matters to be taken into account include the complexity of the issues and the experience and position in the company or corporation of the proposed representative.

5.4 Permission under r.39.6(b) should be obtained in advance of the hearing from, preferably, the judge who is to hear the case, but may, if it is for any reason impracticable or inconvenient to do so, be obtained from any judge by whom the case could be heard.

5.5 The permission may be obtained informally and without notice to the other parties. The judge who gives the permission should record in writing that he has done so and supply a copy to the company or corporation in question and to any other party who asks for one.

5.6 Permission should not normally be granted under r.39.6:

(a) in jury trials;
(b) in contempt proceedings.

6.1 At any hearing, whether in the High Court or a county court, the judgment **44–237E** (and any summing up given by the judge) will be recorded unless the judge directs otherwise. Oral evidence will normally be recorded also.

6.2 No party or member of the public may use unofficial recording equipment in any court or judge's room without the permission of the court. To do so without permission constitutes a contempt of court.

6.3 Any party or person may require a transcript or transcripts of the recording of any trial or hearing to be supplied to him, upon payment of the charges authorised by any scheme in force for the making of the recording or the transcript.

6.4 Where the person requiring the transcript or transcripts is not a party to the proceedings and the trial or hearing or any part of it was held in private under CPR r.39.2, para.6.3 does not apply unless the court so orders.

6.5 Attention is drawn to para. 7.9 of the Court of Appeal (Civil Division) Practice Direction which deals with the provisions of transcripts for use in the Court of Appeal at public expense.

44–237F   **7.** Exhibits which are handed in and proved during the course of the trial should be recorded on an exhibit list and kept in the custody of the court until the conclusion of the trial, unless the judge directs otherwise. At the conclusion of the trial it is the parties' responsibility to obtain the return of those exhibits which they handed in and to preserve them for the period in which any appeal may take place.

44–237G   **8.1** If it is necessary for a party to give evidence at a hearing of an authority referred to in s.2 of the Human Rights Act 1998—

(1) the authority to be cited should be an authoritative and complete report; and
(2) the party must give to the court and any other party a list of the authorities he intends to cite and copies of the reports not less than three days before the hearing.

(Section 2(1) of the Human Rights Act 1998 requires the court to take into account the authorities listed there)

(3) Copies of the complete original texts issued by the European Court and Commission either paper based or from the Court's judgment database (HUDOC), which is available on the Internet, may be used.

PRACTICE DIRECTION—COURT SITTINGS

44–237H   **1.1**—(1) The sittings of the Court of Appeal and of the High Court shall be four in every year, that is to say

(a) the Michaelmas sittings which shall begin on October 1 and end of December 21;
(b) the Hilary sittings which shall begin on January 11 and end on the Wednesday before Easter Sunday;
(c) the Easter sittings which shall begin on the second Tuesday after Easter Sunday and end on the Friday before the spring holiday; and
(d) the Trinity sittings which shall begin on the second Tuesday after the spring holiday and end on July 31.

(2) In the above paragraph 'spring holiday' means the bank holiday falling on the last Monday in May or any day appointed instead of that day under s.1(2) of the Banking and Financial Dealings Act 1971.

2.1—(1) One or more judges of each Division of the High Court shall sit in vacation on such days as the senior judge of that Division may from time to time direct, to hear such cases, claims, matters or applications as require to be immediately or promptly heard and to hear other cases, claims, matters or applications if the senior judge of that Division determines that sittings are necessary for that purpose.

(2) Any part to a claim or matter may at any time apply to the court for an order that such claim or matter be heard in vacation and, if the Court is satisfied that the claim or matter requires to be immediately or promptly heard, it may make an order accordingly and fix a date for the hearing.

(3) Any judge of the High Court may hear such other cases, claims, matters or applications in vacation as the court may direct.

2.2 The directions in paragraph 3.1 shall not apply in relation to the trial or hearing of cases, claims, matters or applications outside the Royal Courts of Justice but the senior Presiding Judge of each Circuit, with the concurrence of the Senior Presiding Judge, and the Vice-Chancellor of the County Palatine of Lancaster and the Chancery Supervising Judge for Birmingham, Bristol and Cardiff, with the concurrence of the Vice-Chancellor, may make such arrangements for vacation sittings in the courts for which they are respectively responsible as they think desirable.

2.3—(1) Subject to the discretion of the Judge, any appeal and any application normally made to a Judge may be made in the month of September.

(2) In the month of August, save with the permission of a Judge or under arrangements for vacation sittings in courts outside the Royal Courts of Justice, appeals to a Judge will be limited to the matters set out in para. 3.5 below, and only applications of real urgency will be dealt with, for example urgent applications in respect of injunctions or for possession under RSC Ord. 113 (Sch. 1 to the CPR).

(3) It is desirable, where this is practical, that applications or appeals are submitted to a Master, District Judge or Judge prior to the hearing of the application or appeal so that they can be marked "fit for August" or "fit for vacation". If they are so marked, then normally the Judge will be prepared to hear the application or appeal in August, if marked "fit for August" or in September if marked "fit for vacation". A request to have the papers so marked should normally be made in writing, shortly setting out the nature of the application or appeal and the reasons why it should be dealt with in August or in September, as the case may be.

2.4 There is no distinction between term time and vacation so far as business before the Chancery Masters is concerned. The Masters will deal with all types of business throughout the year, and when a Master is on holiday his list will normally be taken by a Deputy Master.

2.5—(1) An application notice may, without permission, be issued returnable before a Master in the month of August for any of the following purposes:

to set aside a claim for or particulars of claim, or service of a claim form or particulars of claim;
to set aside judgment; for stay of execution;
for any order by consent;
for judgment or permission to enter judgment;
for approval of settlements or for interim payment;
for relief from forfeiture; for charging order; for garnishee order;

for appointment or discharge of a receiver;
for relief by way of sheriff's interpleader;
for transfer to a county court or for trial by Master;
for time where time is running in the month of August;

(2) In any case of urgency any other type of application notice (that is other than those for the purposes in (1) above), may, with the permission of a Master be issued returnable before a Master during the month of August.

PRACTICE DIRECTION—COURT SITTINGS IN 2002

44–237I   In the year 2002 only, para. 1.1 of the Practice Direction—Court Sittings supplementing CPR Part 39 is modified so that:

(a) the Easter sittings of the Court of Appeal and the High Court will end on Friday May 31, 2002 (the Friday before the spring holiday which has been appointed to be on Tuesday June 4, 2002 in place of the last Monday in May);

(b) the Trinity sittings will begin on Tuesday June 11, 2002 (the first Tuesday after the spring holiday).

(These changes are made following the appointment of Monday June 3, 2002 to be a Bank Holiday to mark Her Majesty's Golden Jubilee, by Royal Proclamation pursuant to s.1(2) and 1(3) of the Banking and Financial Dealings Act 1971.)

PRACTICE DIRECTION—SUPPLEMENT TO RULE 39.8

44–237J   **1.1** Where a claimant and his representatives have been excluded from all or part of the proceedings under r.39.8(a), the court will inform the Attorney General of the proceedings.

1.2 The Attorney-General may appoint a person (a "special advocate") under s.67A(2) of the Race Relations Act 1976 to represent the claimant in respect of those parts of the proceedings from which he and his representative have been excluded.

1.3 In exercise of its powers under r.39.8(c), the court may order the special advocate not to communicate (directly or indirectly) with any persons (including the excluded claimant)—

(1) on any matter discussed or referred to, or
(2) with regard to any material disclosed,

during or with reference to any part of the proceedings from which the claimant and his representatives are excluded.

1.4 Where the court makes an order referred to in para. 1.3 (or any similar order), the special advocate may apply to the court for directions enabling him to seek instructions from, or otherwise to communicate with an excluded person.

Youth Justice and Criminal Evidence Act 1999

Short title, commencement and extent

68.—(7) . . . [1]   **44–296**

Schedule 4

Minor and Consequential Amendments

Criminal Appeal Act 1968 (c 19)

4.—(2) . . . [2]   **44–297**
5. . . . [3]

Magistrates' Court Act (c 43)

8. . . . [4]

---

[1] Subs.(7) repealed by Powers of Criminal Courts (Sentencing) Act 2000, s.165(4), Sch. 12, Pt I: in force, August 25, 2000.
[2] Repealed by Youth Justice and Criminal Evidence Act 1999, s.67(3), Sch. 6: in force, April 1, 2000.
[3] Paras 5, 20, 29, 30 repealed by Powers of Criminal Courts (Sentencing) Act 2000, s.165(4), Sch. 12, Pt I: in force, August 25, 2000.
[4] Repealed by Access to Justice Act 1999, s.106, Sch. 15, Pt V, Table (8): in force, February 19, 2001 (with transitional provisions).